D0204175

The Cinema of Robert Gardner

The Cinema of
Robert Gardner

Edited by
Ilisa Barbash and Lucien Taylor

Oxford • New York

All images are copyright Film Study Center, Harvard University.

First published in 2007 by
Berg
Editorial offices:
1st Floor, Angel Court, 81 St Clements Street, Oxford, OX4 1AW, UK
175 Fifth Avenue, New York, NY 10010, USA

Berg is the imprint of Oxford International Publishers Ltd.

Library of Congress Cataloging-in-Publication Data

The cinema of Robert Gardner /
edited by Ilisa Barbash and Lucien Taylor.
p. cm.
Includes bibliographical references and index.
ISBN-13: 978-1-84520-773-1 (cloth)
ISBN-10: 1-84520-773-4 (cloth)
ISBN-13: 978-1-84520-774-8 (pbk.)
ISBN-10: 1-84520-774-2 (pbk.)
1. Motion pictures in ethnology. 2. Ethnographic films.
3. Indigenous peoples in motion pictures. 4. Gardner, Robert, 1925–
I. Barbash, Ilisa, 1959– II. Taylor, Lucien.
GN347.C584 2007
305.8—dc22
2007037441

British Library Cataloguing-in-Publication Data

A catalogue record for this book is available from the British Library.

ISBN 978 1 84520 773 1 (Cloth)
ISBN 978 1 84520 774 8 (Paper)

Typeset by Apex Publishing, LLC, Madison, WI, USA
Printed in the United Kingdom by Biddles Ltd, King's Lynn

www.bergpublishers.com

CONTENTS

INTRODUCTION
RESOUNDING IMAGES

ILISA BARBASH AND LUCIEN TAYLOR

Nonfiction cinema has always been situated rather uneasily between science and art. In its avowed attachment to reality, its observation of human experience, and especially in its more expository and didactic moments, it often seems a close cousin to science. But in its aesthetic experimentation, its self-consciousness about form, and its endeavor to transfigure what it apprehends, it also displays affinities to art. Indeed, science and art coalesce with an uncommon intensity in the work of Robert Gardner, one of the most significant and original voices in the field over the past half century. For its ethnographic inflection and aesthetic assurance, his work bears comparison with that of Robert Flaherty, Basil Wright, Maya Deren, and Jean Rouch. Yet stylistically, his works are very much his own: in their cinematography and their editing they immediately and unmistakably announce themselves as Gardnerian. Among his major works are the three feature-length films for which he is best known: *Dead Birds* (1963), a lyric depiction of ritual warfare among the Dugum Dani, a people living in the highlands of Irian Jaya; *Rivers of Sand* (1974), a provocative portrayal of pained gender relations among the Hamar people of southwestern Ethiopia; and *Forest of Bliss* (1986), his controversial cinematic essay on the ancient city of Benares—now Varanasi—which explores with an unsparing and at times sublime acuity the ceremonies, rituals, and industries associated with death and regeneration on the banks of the Ganges.

Gardner's work is distinguished by its arresting cinematography, which conveys the sensation of living presence not only in a way unavailable to writing but also with a force rarely matched by other nonfiction filmmakers. At times the intensity is so overbearing and leaves so little interpretive freedom to the viewer that one is left reeling—its investment in beauty and stimulation flirts with spectacle and distraction. As Roland Barthes (1989) once remarked, "I crave, I long for Abstinence from Images, for every Image is bad" (356). Gardner is more interested in the agonistic and the ecstatic—in extremes of emotion and sentiment—than he is in the normal or the typical, and he lacks the patience of a Warhol, a Bill Viola, or indeed of many a contemporary video artist or ethnographic image maker in evoking the sense of duration of everyday experience—what Bazin used to call "objectivity in time," the world of living flux. One thinks of the assertiveness of his framing and composition, the prevalence of close-ups, the attention to expressive detail, the frequently radical juxtapositions of the editing, his desire to disclose a scene's meaning only gradually, the uncanny capacity in his later work to anticipate unscripted action, and his use of slow motion and occasional freeze frames at climactic moments. Gardner's refusal of a reductive realism as well as his penchant for allusion and ambiguity have also set him off from many ethnographic filmmakers. But his half century of filmmaking also shows a clear trajectory in its evolving configuration of film structure and in the tenuous balance of the verbal and the visual. In this introduction, we describe how that tension—between the discursive and the figural, one that is at the heart of visual anthropology—has played itself out in his work.

Early in his career, Gardner structured his films on a narrative or story, such as the reciprocal, ritualized warfare among the "feathered and fluttering" Dani in the highly scripted and directed *Dead Birds* (1963), or around an event, such as the unfolding of the Gerewol, the male beauty contest of the Bororo that he depicted in *Deep Hearts* (1981). In his later works, however, he has employed more poetic and even musical forms, such as his visually profuse city symphony of Benares, *Forest of Bliss* (1986), and his short "observation in four movements" of painter Sean Scully, in the video *Passenger* (1998). Gardner's films display an increasing distrust—or at any rate disinterest—in the word and especially the literal meaning of language. At the same time, he has consistently used metaphor and metonymy, although in his hands these modes of figuration are as visual as they are literary. Whereas Gardner's third-person voice-over is crucial to the narrative structure of *Dead Birds* and while *Rivers of Sand* (1975) hinges on the direct-address interview testimony of one main female subject, Omali Inda, there are few words of any kind in *Forest of Bliss,* and none of them, after the opening epigraph, are translated. This retreat from language seems to have gone hand in hand with a shift away from narrative, at least of the linear kind, and toward an exploration of the structural possibilities opened up by montage. Such image-based experimentation has brought with it a heightened visual sensibility.

This withdrawal from the verbal and the denotative in favor of the visual and the connotative has not in any way been accompanied by a disregard of sound. To the contrary, the sensory exploration (and even construction) of their subjects' aural environments, through heightened, polyvocal sound tracks, intricately orchestrated during postproduction—at times literally re-creating the sounds through Foley and effects—is one of the most striking qualities of Gardner's recent works and especially *Forest of Bliss* and *Passenger.* Ironically, this is almost diametrically opposed in spirit and effect to the increasing orientation to narrative and the discursive in recent written ethnography in which the preponderance of transcriptions of indigenous testimony seems frequently to be at the expense of descriptive and sensory attention to the whole kinesthetic and material context of what is spoken—the attenuated *langue* rather than the multidimensional *parole.*

Gardner's first film, made in 1951, was simply called *Blunden Harbour* and depicted the Kwakiutl at their seaside home on Vancouver Island in British Columbia. Although this is his one film where he was not himself behind the camera, *Blunden Harbour* bears his distinct aesthetic. There is a purposeful opacity to the film, with its mythopoetic sound track and fragmentary imagery. Yet it also contains a multitude of ethnographic details—in certain respects more so than if it had confined itself to linear sequences of real time—from the collection of fish and crabs and their preparation and consumption at the table to the various uses of wood in the construction of homes, boats, coffins, swings, toys, and, above all, masks. The narration starts with the telling of a local myth about founding of Blunden Harbour, and then outlines the central motif suggested by the images, the relationship the community maintains with both the forest and the sea. The rest deploys an aesthetic of repetition and allusion, developing the refrain "From the water, food. From the wood, a way of life."

Mythology was equally a part of the narration of *Dead Birds*, Gardner's first feature-length film, which opens with an allegory of the imbricated identities of birds and people and the etiology of human mortality. Of all his films, *Dead Birds*—the Dani term for weapons and other ornaments captured during warfare—is the one most obviously dominated by its verbal sound track. Indeed, it is his only film in which there is a direct and literal correlation between the words and images. When we see a field, we are told about that field, that watchtower, that action, those characters. Curiously, however, when the narration does attend to specific characters, particularly Weyak and Pua, it also works to universalize their predicament. Gardner has long articulated his conception of the relationship to the particular and the universal at an angle to the cultural relativism and orientation to cultural difference in mainstream anthropology. On the one hand, he said of *Dead Birds*, "My first responsibility, both to my own purposes and to the Dani, was to document with as much discernment as possible the most telling and important aspects of their life," but, on the other, "I seized the opportunity of speaking to *certain fundamental issues in human life*. The Dani were *less important* to me than those issues . . . I saw the Dani people, feathered and fluttering men and women, as enjoying the fate of all men and women. They dressed their lives with plumage, but faced as certain death as the rest of us drabber souls. The film attempts to say something about how we all, as humans, meet our animal fate" (Gardner 1972, 2, 34–35).

Despite the apparent dominance of the narration, it in no way eclipses the images of *Dead Birds*. The battle scenes, of course, were remarkable feats of daring, even if Gardner's long lenses allowed him to keep a safe distance between himself and the action. As with John Marshall's *The Hunters* (1958), on which Gardner collaborated, these scenes were subsequently controversial in view of their synthetic construction—composed as they were of shots taken from a multitude of battles occurring on different days—and displaying more regard for the film's diegesis than the profilmic reality they ostensibly depict. But the film also explores the performance of more mundane tasks with equally forceful cinematography and in tremendous detail, much as he might have in a narrative feature film. A two-and-a-half-minute scene of garden cultivation includes close-ups of faces, backs, legs, and hands and medium, long, and extreme long shots of men digging, weeding, and planting. Particularly notable are shots of a planter's reflections shimmering in a ditch and an over-the-shoulder shot with Pua in the foreground of the frame, languidly observing as men energetically toil in the background. The colors are lush and rich, the exposures right on, with a creative interplay between light and shadow. The compositions are artfully, if for the most part quite conventionally, framed, making much use of diagonals and the Z axis as well as playing with screen displacement and slow disclosure.

Gardner's aesthetic experimentation, in both picture and sound, has of course been influenced by the technology available at the time. The advent of portable sync sound in the 1960s, for instance, enabled nonfiction filmmakers to record sound in the field that was synchronous with action and so to record on-site interviews with their subjects. Unlike *Dead Birds,* both *The Nuer* (1971)—a lyrical evocation of pastoral life and male coming-of-age rituals in southern Sudan by Hilary Harris and George Breidenbach, for which Gardner contributed additional photography and voiced the narration—and *Rivers of Sand* employ such interviews to different ends. As with *Dead Birds,* Gardner's suggestive third-person narration interprets some of the activities we see on the screen (such as the symbolic significance of the frond of the Baraza tree to the Hamar). But in *Rivers of Sand,* his narration is both sparser and more laconic, granting more freedom to and so placing a greater exegetical burden on the images—and, at one remove, the spectators—themselves. Gardner's narration is accompanied in this film by the direct-address interview of a sole Hamar woman, Omali Inda—the only named individual in the whole film—who speaks, frequently in a tight close-up, in a generalized second-person mode of direct address to the camera and so to the spectators: "When your husband beats you, he will say…" Her commentary comes to constitute a kind of indigenous ethnographic present. As such, it suggests that she may not necessarily be speaking of her own firsthand experience. The later criticism by two anthropologists associated with the film—Jean Lydall and Ivo Strecker—that the film was indifferent to this disjuncture, misleadingly presenting Omali Inda's philosophical commentary as if it stemmed from her own experience (she had, they said, never been beaten herself), seems to have been made without any careful consideration of Omali Inda's actual rhetoric in the film. It is in fact Omali Inda's rather than Gardner's voice that does the most to set the mood of the film as a whole, both for its sheer poetry—rich and vivid metaphorical associations pile on top of each other, likening, for instance, the symbolic power of a woman's leg irons to a man's gun—and for its shockingly explicit testimony about sexual abuse and also for Omali Inda's astonishing poise and self-assurance.

Nonverbal aspects of the sound track are equally important to *Rivers of Sand*'s aesthetic. Gardner amplifies otherwise ordinary sync sounds so that they become extraordinary and defamiliarized. In so doing, he attaches to certain sounds particular symbolic significance: the clanking of a woman's bracelet as she walks, the swooshing of sand as it slides down a bank adjacent to a water hole, the slapping of dancing feet on the ground, the abrasions of grain on stone as women grind sorghum into flour, and the crack of a whip in an overtly ritualized performance of sexual desire and subjugation between Hamar men and women. Such embellishment of the sound track continues to be exceptional under prevailing ethnographic orthodoxies of nonfiction realism. At various moments in the film, having established such aural motifs, Gardner then separates images from their synchronous sounds and reblends sound and picture to symbolic ends. Toward the end, as we watch a girl walking resolutely by a field of sorghum, the visibly clanking metal chain links on her skirt are mute, and instead we hear the same (or perhaps another) girl lyrically chanting a song. The song continues as the film cuts to the again sync-soundless image of a women bent on grinding grain on a stone. Although the song is not translated, the film is clearly linking the girl to the woman, implying that the girl's imminent fate is to be put to the grindstone. Gardner cuts to a few sync shots of men conducting a ritualized benediction, punctuating their words by theatrically exhaling loud jets of coffee. He then cuts to Omali Inda, as she opines, "In the end you stay on, and when you are reconciled, your husband will leave you alone." The film closes with a shot that comes full circle, returning us to its opening: a Hamar man now walks down the "river of sand," away from the camera. The amplified sound of the loud padding of his feet gives way to a chorus of chanting women and the audible and rhythmic grinding of grain, thereby emphasizing Gardner's contention that Hamar culture binds women and men painfully yet inescapably together.

The picture track of *Rivers of Sand* marks an additional departure from *Dead Birds*. The film's structure depends less on narrative and the simulation of space–time continuity and more on montage and the creation of meaning through juxtaposition. In a sequence a little over two minutes long, we see the hammering on of bronze bracelets, men consulting an oracle, women grinding grain and hauling water, men hunting, and women dancing. At another point in the film, three men divide up the feathers of an ostrich they have just hunted. In a transition as metaphorical as it is visual, the film then cuts from the extended ostrich feathers to a raised frond in a pile of sorghum. At this point, Gardner's voice-over intones, "A frond of the Baraza tree at the top of the newly harvested sorghum is a sign that it is domesticated, stabilized, controlled." Given the solemnity of his tone, it is apparent that the reference is to something more than sorghum. The next cut is to a scene of a man hammering two metal neck rings onto a young girl and from there to the branding of a cow. In depicting the oppressive but, if not exactly consensual, nonetheless desirous accommodation of the sexes to one another, through images of women at work, men at rest, and spectacular rituals of sex and subjugation, Gardner asks his non-Hamar viewers to ponder larger themes from their own cultures: the women's movement of the 1970s, feminism, and sexual politics more generally.

The visual and aural sensuousness of *Rivers of Sand* is equaled in Gardner's next film. His 1981 *Deep Hearts* depicts a performance of the Gerewol, an annual social maturation ceremony of the seminomadic Nigerien Bororo and in particular its beauty contest between young, unmarried men. The droning of the chanting men precedes the picture and is mesmerizing in effect, as if style and substance, medium and message, and signifier and signified all coalesce. Likewise, the irrealism of some of the camera work, in conjunction with the fragmentariness of the editing, accentuates the spectacle of the performance itself, as if it is infused with its own aesthetic sensibility. Together with cinematographer Robert Fulton, Gardner employs extreme angles, both high and low, further elongating the naturally tall, statuesque bodies of the Bororo. Various of the long shots of the line of moving dancers use a fish-eye lens that distorts at the edges, causing the dancers to be gently arched around the edge of the frame. This provides a sense both of great number and of great immediacy: we are in the thick of things, encircled by the dancers. The slow-motion cinematography also draws our attention to both decorations and gestures that would otherwise be lost in the flurry of action. Equally striking are the still and moving close-ups, especially of wide, consuming eyes and mouths. As Gardner's narration asserts, "The Bororo...are particularly fearful of being 'devoured' by both the eyes and mouths of those around them with whom they compete as beautiful creatures..."

If Gardner's narration is most literal and specific in *Dead Birds*—and at times so omniscient of its subjects' thoughts and sentiments that it invites one to read it as fictional—it is most figurative and metaphysical in *Deep Hearts*. But it is in his most ambitious work that he gives freest reign to the images and sounds by relinquishing voice-over altogether. *Forest of Bliss* is the apogee of Gardner's efforts to recognize the polyvalency of the (aural and visual) images themselves, unmediated by any verbal exegesis circumscribing their meaning. Because of the absence of narration or even translated dialogue, the film virtually demands the viewer to respond nonverbally and, in certain respects, even viscerally. As such, it stimulates an interplay of the senses with an uncommon intensity: the camera's eye seems at once unusually tactile and unusually auditory. More than that, it is an olfactory eye and a haptic ear. We feel and smell the ghats and their pyres, the boats and their rowlocks, and the bamboo worker and his bidi as much as we see and hear them.

Even though *Forest of Bliss* contains three distinct main characters, there is little character development per se. Through interweaving different narrative threads, Gardner seems concerned more to situate them within the larger universe of Benares. This is a matrix of water, fire, marigolds, bamboo, and wood. It is an ecology of life and death, of dirt and cleanliness, of cows and corpses, of Siva linga and goddess mediums, of the sacred and the profane. The sheer number of rituals, both great and small, associated with death and with life—with keeping death at bay—is extraordinary. Yet at the same time, death is the local industry; Benares is the holiest place for Hindus to die. If *Forest of Bliss* is about the ecology of Benares, it is also about the economy—the *oiko-nomia*, the interconnected management and coordination—of death. There is a section toward the middle of the film where Gardner places a series of constantly moving scenes showing, among other things, the ways in which bodies are transported from one place to the next. There are two boat shots: one beautifully lit, almost picturesque; the next with oars parting flotsam-bearing waves; a body draped in orange cloth, carried on the top of a moving car; a bobbing body atop men's shoulders, supported on a laddered litter; a bundle of orange marigolds weighing down a bicycle; another body on shoulders; more flowers; another body; and so on. The effect of this is almost overwhelming—the viewer feels propelled, caught up in the interconnectedness of it all, transfixed by the propinquity of the sacred and the profane.

Despite the mesmerizing and at times transfiguring beauty of the images in the film, the sound is just as wrought as the picture track, a far cry from the usual insipid quality of location sound one has come to expect since Vérité. Almost all the nonverbal or ambient sounds are amplified, while the few verbal communications in the film appear—unlike the more guttural exclamations—to be muted somewhat, as if reflecting an intention on the part of the filmmaker to impart a *pre*linguistic, more corporeal sense of engagement and intersubjective participation with his subject. There are the respiratory and apparently arthritic sounds of the healer as he ascends the filthy stairways after his morning ablutions in the Ganges. There are the sounds of water throughout the film—as it is sprinkled or poured in rituals, as it slaps against boats gliding through the Ganges, as it is swept over concrete, as it is splashed by a bathing priest. As with the images, sound is used to explore and punctuate the relationship between the sacred and the profane. About a third of the way into the film, we see and hear a man cleaning the central courtyard of a hospice, adumbrating what is to come. Over the sounds of water being poured and swept around the square wafts the refrain of unseen men chanting what one imagines to be the last rites for a dying boarder. Later in the courtyard, the incantations are magnified as the men proceed clockwise around what we are surely to assume is the same person, now deceased, being laid out onto a funeral stretcher and adorned with bright pink cloth and orange marigolds. As the body is hoisted off through the streets and to the ghats, the courtyard's impurities are again swept away with water, and the dirge of the chorus recedes into the background.

The complex complementarity of picture and (nonverbal) sound is also explored in Gardner's 1998 *Passenger: An Observation in Four Movements,* which was shot on digital video and blown up to 35mm film. About the Irish painter Sean Scully, *Passenger* is one of a number of works, less well known in anthropological circles, that Gardner has made about what, in his interview with Ilisa Barbash (see chapter 5), he calls "the whole, coherent world" or "miniature culture" of a fellow Euro-American artist. (Others include the painter Mark Tobey, the sculptor Alexander Calder, and the filmmaker Miklós Jancsó.) The video follows Scully—with a deliberately if only slightly asynchronous time line—as he creates a single painting over the course of a few days. It is his painting called *Passenger.* There is no dialogue in Gardner's *Passenger,* only the various reverberating sounds (many of them, as Gardner also remarks in chapter 5, created using Foley effects) of Scully at work in a long, quiet, bare studio. Since Scully is the only person in the room other than the videographers, the video becomes an intense visual and aural observation of an individual, an abstract painter at work alone, or at least acting as if he were alone. *Passenger* reveals his relationship with his canvas, his paint, and his studio to be palpably, intensely physical, almost like that of a dancer and not only when he is actually painting. Scully spends much of his time ruminating on the canvas—from up close, a distance, standing still, hanging sideways, swaying from one foot to the other, on his hands and knees, pacing, seated, lying on the floor, even using the canvas as a background for martial arts practice. His actions are punctuated by sounds that he controls, whether or not he is conscious of them—his feet pacing on the wooden floor, the scraping of his spatula, the wallop of gobs of paint as he flings them into the garbage can, the hush of his brushstrokes, the silence of contemplation. In turn, his movements and, indirectly, his painting as well seem to respond to the respective musics of the studio. *Passenger* offers a rare, intimate, record–cum–re-creation of the interaction between an artist and his creation (and, at one remove, the videographer), one that refuses the persistent temptation of artistic or authorial hagiography.

In sum, over the course of a half century, Gardner has produced a body of work that experiments with both narrative and montage. His various juxtapositions of picture and sound have increasingly retreated from the verbal, toward a realm of greater aural and visual plenitude in which language, as in life, plays only a minor role. In so doing, he has conjured at a more phenomenal, prediscursive relationship between spectator and screen and between film and the world. But if his film style may then be described, in a word, as experiential, this is so only in a very particular sense. For Gardner's films are, paradoxically, at once experiential and not. In an earlier anthropological lexicon, they are simultaneously experience-near and experience-far. How is this so? Gardner plunges his audience into the cinematographically and acoustically enhanced ecological and sensory worlds of his subjects both visually and aurally. Such sensory engagement is achieved, above all, by his spectacular cinematography and especially his use of the close-up and corresponding aesthetic of the fragment, which is quite at odds with the prevailing fiction of holism, encapsulated in Karl Heider's (1978) dictum of "whole people, whole bodies and whole acts" (75), to which anthropology and ethnographic film, despite growing protestations and disclaimers, still typically tends. It is also achieved aurally—in his earlier work through artfully wrought mythopoetic, allegorical, and interpretive narration but increasingly through the layering and amplification of "natural," sync, or re-created sound, resulting in by turns hyper- and antirealist picture–sound juxtapositions. Because of this, we see and hear far more of (his renditions of) the lived environments and visual worlds of the Kwakiutl, the Dani, the Bororo, the Hamar, and the Benares ghats than would be revealed to us, not just by a written anthropological account but also by most filmmakers. And yet, because of Gardner's predilection for montage and allusion through juxtaposition, as well as his later disinterest in narrative and psychological character development, we are given far fewer opportunities for spectatorial identification with individual subjects than is the case with many observational and participatory films, whose narrative strategies are paradoxically modeled after neorealist *fiction* films. With the exception of the 1963 *Dead Birds,* whose mannerism is indebted far more to narrative cinema than to the emergent documentary trends of its day, Gardner's films eschew dominant norms and forms not only of realism but also of narrative styles suturing spectator to subject. Uniquely, his film work displays *at once* a radical commitment to depicting the world as he apprehends it, unfettered by any of the strains of moralism that lie behind the didactic dogmatism that mars much "educational" filmmaking, and also a commitment to experimenting with cinematic style that stems from an avant-garde tradition that typically has little time for "the real."

It would be easy enough to dismiss anthropological critics of Robert Gardner's cinema by taking his disavowal of anthropological intent at face value. Gardner considers narrative filmmakers fully as much his "totemic ancestors" as he does nonfiction documentarians. As he says in his interview in chapter 5, "If I could choose my genetic inheritance cinematically speaking, I would ask for equal parts of Andrei Tarkovsky and Basil Wright." Yet, as David MacDougall (1988, 72) has urged, one might interpret Gardner's declaration of his distance from academic anthropology in the same spirit as Robert Frost's disavowal of symbolic intent.

In fact, the phenomenological qualities of cinema and, in particular, the sensorial profligacy of Gardner's cinematography are in many ways in concert with current reappraisals of "culture" by anthropologists. Recent work by Michael Jackson (1989, 1995, 1998, 2005), Thomas Csordas (1994), and Maurice Bloch (1997), among others, represents an effort to elaborate a fundamentally *post*semiotic anthropology. This is an anthropology that foregrounds the phenomenological priority of embodiment in our apprehension of the world, as the existential condition of possibility of both self *and culture*. In short, it recontextualizes the intellectual work of semiosis—or, in Clifford Geertz's terms, of meaning making—in relation to perception more broadly and in turn recontextualizes perception in relation to sensation as a whole. As such, this emergent postsemiotic turn in anthropology opposes both an earlier conception of culture as a disembodied text and a conception of the body as a site exclusively of representation or surveillance. Both such conceptions turn on dualisms of mind and body, culture and biology, and subject(ivity) and object(ivity) that a postsemiotic anthropology calls into question.

This newfound anthropological interest in the role of embodied sensation in the constitution of selfhood and cultural praxis overlaps to a significant degree with recent developments in cognitive neuroscience that have concentrated on the relatively limited role that it appears language—especially in its sentential logical form—plays in cognition and social life. There is now a wealth of empirical evidence that shows that cultural cognition integrates sense experience, memory, and visual and aural imagery alongside and in many ways prior to language—that the brain, in the words of António Damasio, is first and foremost *body-minded*. In consequence, an unanticipated affinity is emerging between recent theoretical trends in academic anthropology and cognitive science—the former's emphasis on embodiment and the latter's on the role of multistranded networks of sensory signification in human cognition—and the medium of cinema, one that both anthropologists and nonfiction filmmakers might profitably exploit. In his essay "Metaphors of Vision," filmmaker Stan Brakhage (1985) contended that there may be a pursuit of knowledge that is alien to language and "founded upon visual communication, demanding a development of the optical mind, and dependent upon perception in the original and deepest sense of the world" (66). For all the romantic, essentialist sentiment conceivably undergirding such a contention, Brakhage raises intriguing questions not only of the part that optical perception plays in our lived experience but also of the role that visual perception may play in the production of knowledge itself. Anthropology's recent sensorial shift has loosened its almost biblical coupling of meaning and naming, of signification and language, and relativized the presumption of the hermeneutic turn that language is paradigmatic of meaning. This new climate invites us to reconsider the aesthetics of Robert Gardner's films.

The chapters in this volume address significant issues raised by Gardner's principal works. Grouped into three parts, the first contains general overviews of his work, the second detailed analyses of particular films and a photographic essay, and the third reminiscences of Gardner by fellow artists and academics.

In part I, Charles Warren takes as his subject Gardner's four "large" films, as he calls them, *Dead Birds, Rivers of Sand, Deep Hearts,* and *Forest of Bliss,* conceiving of them as a symphonic "tetralogy" that inquires into and reflects on the human condition. As a unique conjuncture of art and science, Warren notes that Gardner's cinema at once functions as a documentary record of the worlds it depicts but also offers up its own worlds and thereby forces "to a crisis" the tension between reality and imagination. Both Paul Henley and Marcus Banks move beyond the controversy about whether Gardner's work is properly anthropological—a controversy, in any event, that is finally fruitless and marred by the logical fallacy of petitio principii. Henley attends instead to what we can take from his cinema as examples of distinctive cinematographic methods and editing styles. He emphasizes Gardner's heavy reliance on montage, which is one of the ways in which his work differs from observational filmmakers, with whom he is often mistakenly identified. For all its documentary orientation, Henley suggests that Gardner's work should be recognized as signifying more transcendental realities, such as *Forest of Bliss's* evocation of Hindu eschatology. At the same time, he proposes that whereas observational filmmakers, especially those of a more participatory bent, attend principally to the significance of the lived experience of their subjects *to the subjects themselves,* Gardner by contrast is more concerned with what he himself makes of that experience—its significance *to him.* To Henley's mind, this relative disinterest in what he calls the "indigenous exegesis" of experience renders Gardner's sensibilities closer to those of an artist than of a mainstream anthropologist.

Henley's attention to the symbolic aspects of ethnographic film representation is maintained in Marcus Banks's chapter, which situates Gardner's Indian films within the larger history of colonial and postcolonial cinematic representations of religion and spirituality in the subcontinent. Banks notes that while anthropologists privilege the symbolic in their study of human action—for almost all human communication has symbolic as well as pragmatic dimensions—this is curiously also the source of an epistemological tension when it comes to cinematic representation. He suggests that the tension may be resolved, at least in part, by adopting a phenomenological perspective and an engagement with the poetics of documentary form. Tracing a trajectory from the analytical and naturalistic to the expressive and aesthetic in the evolution both of Gardner's work and of visual ethnographic representations of Indian spirituality more broadly, Banks contends that just as the "aesthetic turn" has become more established in writing, so ethnographic filmmakers should be bolder in their aesthetic experimentation.

In the next chapter, Karl Heider takes as his subject the significance of the opening shots in Gardner's films and the ways in which they may be freighted with resonances that disclose their significance only later. Whereas *Dead Birds,* for instance, begins apparently quite literally with "the very didactic narration...seemingly [leaving] nothing to the imagination" and *Forest of Bliss* altogether more opaquely, both open by setting the scene, by displaying a geography—and one that in both cases is suffused with mythological significance. Heider describes various ways in which the geographies that are so established are made directional in the films, or are what he and Gardner call "vectored." Finally, in an interview, Ilisa Barbash and Robert Gardner range over much of his work and reflect on how it has evolved stylistically, his cinematic influences, the relationship of film to language, and the ethics and aesthetics of documentary film form. Gardner also discusses his desire to make a narrative film so that he might direct rather than simply divine the action that unfolds in front of his camera—to be in a position to ask for things to happen rather than being obliged only and always to anticipate them.

Part II contains chapters that probe more deeply into particular works, in reverse chronological order. Anna Grimshaw and William Rothman each discuss two of Gardner's videos about artists, *Passenger* and *Dancing with Miklós,* while David MacDougall focuses on *Forest of Bliss,* Elizabeth Edwards on the photo-essay *Gardens of War,* and Roderick Coover on *Dead Birds.*

In "The Camera in the Studio," Anna Grimshaw addresses art-making in both painting and cinema, situating *Passenger* within the history of films about art and artists and also within the history of visual anthropology. Adopting a feminist critique of the heroic male artist and portraiture thereof, with its frequently romantic and modernist underpinnings, Grimshaw explores Gardner's commitment to aesthetic experimentation as something inseparable from epistemological inquiry. She also considers ways in which *Passenger* offers a model for a more expansive and aesthetically adventurous visual anthropology than has existed to date. William Rothman then focuses his jeweler's-eye hermeneutic vision—as open ended in its exegesis as it is close to the body of the work—on one of Gardner's "making of" videos, his 1993 *Dancing with Miklós.* He argues that even Gardner's ostensibly most "ethnographic" films are also deeply personal poems and that all his work reveals an essentially tragic conception of human existence and an almost dialectical drive to depict at once the cruelty and tenderness of our lives. Following Stanley Cavell, Rothman suggests that Gardner's films succeed in effect in bursting their form through their profound expression of the alterity or difference of their subject—their respect for their subject's mystery that paradoxically goes hand in hand with their trust in its capacity to communicate about, to reveal, itself. In this respect he proposes that the creation of "art" is also internal to the very subjects of Gardner's films.

In "Gardner's Bliss," David MacDougall notes that while both "textual" analyses and reception studies of particular works are now established genres within the scholarship on film, there is relatively little written or known about the actual making of films and all the aesthetic and intellectual decisions and processes they involve. With few exceptions, the filmmakers' perspective on the creative process is lost to history, for they typically have more pressing agendas than committing to print their own understandings of how and why they made their work. One notable exception is Gardner and his co-producer and anthropologist Ákos Östör's conversation about *Forest of Bliss,* published in 2001, which, although at times it may sound like "highly polished shoptalk," betraying a post hoc ratio-nalization of the film's meanings and metaphors, is also revealing of Gardner and Östör's respective relationships to the film and to each other. MacDougall uses this as a spring-board for a meticulous reflection on the multitude of choices and constraints involved in the making of this film. In the next chapter, Elizabeth Edwards takes as her subject Gardner and Karl Heider's 1968 photographic essay *Gardens of War* and considers both the nature of photographic narrative and the role of the photographic book in the production and transmission of anthropological knowledge. A rare attempt—sadly as rare today as it was then—to conjoin photography and anthropology in book form, Edwards argues that the way in which *Gardens of War* deploys narrative to engage the aesthetic and the subjec-tive prefigures later calls for a more expressive use of the visual in anthropology. Adding a phenomenological dimension to the more usual semiotic approach to photographic nar-rative, she emphasizes how the book is not just a series of images (and words) but also an actual material performance of them. Finally, Roderick Coover looks at the exegetical layering of material in another of Gardner's works, the reissue in 2004 on digital video disc of *Dead Birds* (1963). He attends both to digital reconstructions (of the film, its outtakes, still photographs, and field and production notes) and to Gardner's own reevaluation of his work and argues that this layering reveals an evolution in how nonfiction images may be imagined, constructed, and presented and also points to ways anthropological image makers may speak to larger issues of our times.

The final section of the book, part III, contains various reflections by fellow artists and academics on their relationships to Gardner—in his role as artist, teacher, and adminis-trator—and on what that has meant for their own work. The philosopher Stanley Cavell reflects back on the vision he and Gardner had for the program in film study at Harvard University, with its particular interlacing of practice and theory. The anthropologist Ákos Östör ponders the complementarity between audiovisual and discursive forms of anthro-pological knowledge as he describes his and Gardner's various collaborations in India. The Yugoslav filmmaker Dušan Makavejev humorously retraces all the crossed signals and paths that prefigured his and Gardner's eventual meeting. Sean Scully also returns to his and Gardner's initial encounter and the cinematic record Gardner has left him of his fam-ily. And whereas Cavell considers the particular forms of "anticipation" that Gardner sees as indispensable to the nonfiction filmmaker, the poet Susan Howe considers Gardner's melancholic attachment to the unrecoverable past—to portraying final chapters of worlds on the wane, redeeming cultural formations that are no more—and compares his hunting and gathering of images and sounds to her own for words and lines.

In reflecting on what anticipation might mean to Gardner and how he might practice it, Cavell quotes the final lines of Wallace Stevens's poem "Not Ideas about the Thing but the Thing Itself":

> It was like
> A new knowledge of reality.

This volume is a collective effort to grapple with the new knowledge of reality that Gardner's work provides us—its innovations, to be sure, but also its influences and effects in the larger fields of art, cinema, and anthropology in which it has carved out its niche.

REFERENCES

BARTHES, Roland. 1989. The image. In *The rustle of language,* trans. Richard Howard, 350–59. Berkeley: University of California Press.

BLOCH, Maurice. 1997. *How we think they think.* Boulder, CO: Westview Press.

BRAKHAGE, Stan. 1985. "Metaphors on vision." In *Film theory and criticism,* ed. Gerald Mass and Marshall Cohen, 66–75. Oxford: Oxford University Press.

CSORDAS, Thomas, ed. 1994. *Embodiment and experience.* Cambridge: Cambridge University Press.

GARDNER, Robert. 1972. "On the making of *Dead Birds.*" In *The Dani of West Irian,* ed. Karl Heider and Robert Gardner, 2-31–2-36. Berkeley, CA: MSS Modular Publications.

HEIDER, Karl. 1978. *Ethnographic film.* Austin: University of Texas Press.

JACKSON, Michael. 1989. *Paths towards a clearing.* Bloomington: Indiana University Press.

_____. 1995. *At home in the world.* Durham, NC: Duke University Press.

_____. 1998. *Minima ethnographica.* Chicago: University of Chicago Press.

_____. 2005. *Existential anthropology.* New York: Berghahn Books.

MACDOUGALL, David. 1998. *Transcultural cinema.* Princeton, NJ: Princeton University Press.

PART ONE: OVERVIEWS

1   THE MUSIC OF ROBERT GARDNER

CHARLES WARREN

> … we can regard the phenomenal world, or nature, and music as two different expressions
> of the same thing…
>
> —Schopenhauer, *The World as Will and Idea*

Jean-Luc Godard, appearing as himself in his recent film *Notre musique,* calls film "our music." He notes that words are reputed to divide the world up, implying that film images can be better attuned to the world's wholeness, though *Notre musique* itself has made the point by the time Godard speaks—as indeed all Godard films make the point—that film is a matter of fragments, of selections, and that images are not reality. Godard here simply invokes the power of shooting and editing and projecting to make revelations, to bring before us something needed and invaluable. He says film will shine a light into the darkness, and he calls the phenomenon "our music," attesting with the term to his love of film, acknowledging film's artfulness, pointing to the ineffability of what it is film does.

In an interview with Ilisa Barbash (chapter 5 in this volume), Robert Gardner says he would choose a large measure of Tarkovsky in making up an ideal cinematic genetic inheritance for himself—Tarkovsky, whose films with their intense moods, subjectivity, and thoroughgoing created quality, are easy to connect to music. Yet we should remember that Tarkovsky (1986) argues very strenuously in his manifesto *Sculpting in Time* for film as a means to knowledge.[1] All the art and technique of film is to be brought to bear for the sake of understanding the world, as only film can understand it, and in order to convey understanding to audiences.

Gardner's remarkable body of work represents a conjuncture unlike any other (Godard's, Tarkovsky's, Flaherty's, Jean Rouch's …) of science and art. There are numerous short films and the four large ones: *Dead Birds* (1964), shot in New Guinea; *Rivers of Sand* (1974) and *Deep Hearts* (1981), both shot in Africa; and *Forest of Bliss* (1986), shot in Benares, India; with *Ika Hands* (1988), shot in the mountains of Columbia, serving, as I see it, as a self-reflective coda to these four. Gardner's films are documentary, observing people and ways of life and places that the filmmaker has brought himself to and taken an interest in. Watching these films, we know we are meeting the world, here or there, and that it will stick with us as a fact of experience. Yet the films have their own world or worlds, their own look and colors and rhythm and sensibility and emphases. Gardner's films are most distinctive, and they force to a crisis in their own way the question of reality versus imagination.

Perhaps Gardner's music also speaks to Schopenhauer's question whether "the phenomenal world, or nature" (are these the same?) only (should one say?) expresses a deeper reality which music also expresses.

At the beginning of Gardner's first film, *Blunden Harbour* (1951), the camera moves on a boat across a forested bay on the coast of Vancouver Island as a voice-over relates the story of how the Kwakiutl's original godlike chief came here to establish a home, "become a real man," and begin the way of life of these people we observe throughout the 20-minute film. The film approaches its subject; the first few shots take us, we might say naturally, from the water to the dwellings and workplaces of the people who live along the water's edge and draw food from it. But in the movement of the camera and in our awareness of its uncanny power, to find out and to create, we sense something like the coming of the god. And in the beautiful black-and-white images of the water surface reflecting various light and the surrounding forest, we have a figure for the realm of imagination and the numinous, so important to these people's life and way of understanding themselves. In the water surface we have even a figure for the film screen and the power of the medium of film. Film converges with the larger imagination here.

Was there a god-man who began this life? One could only with prejudice say no. This film just by being film acknowledges, embodies, registers, and performs a creative act that is at the center of the humanity of these people, their sense of their past and present life. Just by being film, the camera naturally films the bay and comes to shore. But there is decision in the movement across the water, the editing together of certain images of the water, the not simply starting with activities on shore. Decision, a human spark, is endemic to film. What is human is crucial to letting this film converge with the world it films.

The bay of water, with the many resonances of this image, is a gift to the filmmaker. But the gift requires a human gesture to recognize it, to take it, to offer it up again—or a more-than-human gesture. Film has always seemed to find out water as an image for itself, for its own nature and powers especially as they link to the mental world of those living life. The always rippling sea and the mists invading the land in Eisenstein's *Potemkin* reflect the stirring of soul in the revolutionaries and their imagination and activity, to which film, *this* kind of film, belongs, or wants to belong. The ice fields and sea of *Nanook,* the sea of *Man of Aran* (there with *sound*), the bayou of *Louisiana Story,* surround and threaten and nourish human life, just as Flaherty's filmmaking both consumes and enables the life of those he meets and half creates. Renoir finds in the water of *Boudu* or *Une partie de campagne* a quickening for the stifled and starved, like the spirit of his own filmmaking. Bergman returns again and again to the shore, in *Summer with Monika, The Seventh Seal, Persona* ... Tarkovsky's inspiration is aquatic first to last—he opens the door to all the rest, with his vast reflecting surfaces, puddles and swamps, showers, dripping, a sea that is a living brain. Film offers to the world filmed and to viewers a baptism: die and be transfigured and be brought forth into a new life. Robert Gardner's films, along with all else that they are doing, move from the central self-aware image of the bay of Blunden Harbour on to many other pivotal water images, including the reverse image of dry riverbeds in southern

Ethiopia, rivers of sand, and on eventually to the Ganges, mirror of a city, grave for the dead, nourisher of a culture.

Blunden Harbour goes on from its opening to give many images of people at work, making mats, digging clams, cooking, fishing, working with wood. Characteristically of Gardner there is a focus on hands and their activity, as if the hand needs discovery and attention, or matters more, or means more, than the face. Film lives on the face, and Gardner's films do to a remarkable extent—think of the faces in pain in *Dead Birds* or *Rivers of Sand,* or the latter film's men's faces full of self-importance, or the interviewed woman's face with her determination and bitterness, or the faces in ecstasy in *Deep Hearts* or *Forest of Bliss.* But painting and sculpture and other forms of representation/imagination also live on the face. Film seems specially called on to attend to the activity of hands, letting it go on and evolve as it will, in time. Even brief shots of such activity remind us of the passage of time (activity on a face, filmed, can seem to stop time, drawing us into the soul, taking us out of the world—conversely, a face in painting, deepening as we look at it, virtually comes into activity). Hands may be a personal disposition of Gardner's. But in his many images of them fact seems to connect with film most purely. Something there in the world, interactive with it, ongoing in time, connects with the medium specially called on to meet it. We feel the weight of documentary, of a means to knowledge, most acutely here.

Midway through *Blunden Harbour,* the voice-over reminds us that a way of life is a way of death, as we view a stack of handcrafted coffins. (The voice we hear speaking Gardner's words, as the credits attribute them, is not Gardner's own, though perhaps it could just as well have been at a certain time. It is a cultivated mid-century American voice, a poet's voice like that of Richard Wilbur or Robert Lowell, open, elegiac, not denying its own identity—very much a factor in the overall music of the film.) Gardner's films acknowledge death quite explicitly, in various ways. The many ways of coming at it help give the sense of a fact, there in the world, to be found, or finding us, something more than film can encompass, the great counterforce to all the life and activity and use of imagination that we see in *Blunden Harbour* and the other films. This film draws to a close accumulating images and sounds of mask making and then ceremonial dancing, as if, on the part of the filmmaker as well as the Kwakiutl themselves, to fight off oblivion. "Poetry is born of insecurity," says the voice-over in Chris Marker's *Sans soleil,* thinking of Japanese culture from Sei Shonagon to the later poets and artists and the neon and the youth rites of modern Tokyo, all made in consciousness of the precariousness of existence—Japan's history of earthquakes, volcano eruptions, tidal waves, wars, now Hiroshima. The art and song of the people Gardner films, on which he likes to dwell, help us to see the people's whole way of life and use of imagination as poetry, as making, in face of death. And this poetry links to Gardner's own, the poetry of his filmmaking. Here the phenomenal world and filmmaking do seem to point to a something else deeper down that gives rise to them both, that they have in common, that makes them one in a sense.

Making in face of death—making of myths and masks and song, living life in a creative mode, filmmaking, poetry—is not to be taken as avoidance. Death makes life possible—the two are bound in a circle and in a way are interchangeable. Moreover, death is not to be taken as the fact, up against which human beings spin illusion. Life leaves our view, disappears so it seems, and we think about death, we conceive it. Perhaps it is no more real than the imagination of our art or the imagination we live out. It is better to think: both are real, death and life, both made in part of imagination.

Stanley Cavell (1979) argues in *The World Viewed* that film was born in a crisis of skepticism, in fear of loss of contact with the world, and as a way of meditating on the loss and seeking out contact, reconnection, letting the world, even a newly imagined or utopian world, assert that it is there.[2] Godard remarks in *Histoire(s) du cinéma* that film—meaning valid film art—was born in black and white, in mourning, during World War I. Film can acknowledge the world, meet the world, a real world, if we will forgo the kind of knowing a skeptic demands and that will never be satisfied. Film, with intelligence, with art, can face what is to be mourned and can project life.

The four large films, *Dead Birds, Rivers of Sand, Deep Hearts,* and *Forest of Bliss,* function as a tetralogy of investigation and meditation on the human condition. Or think of it as a large-scale four-movement symphony, each film with its own material and mood—four parts of the world—and yet each with links to the others, links in the nature of the material and also in the way material is treated. A symphony will have connections between the musical material from movement to movement, despite all the contrast, and connections, of course, in the composer's way of handling and developing musical ideas. The handling of material is partly a function of the composer's temperament and partly a function of the basic material itself, what its qualities are, what it asks for and allows. The composer for the most part invents the basic material, but this material can have the feel of something found, a folk tune, an interval hovering at the back of many people's consciousness. The purpose of a symphony is to go on a journey, to investigate, to question, to deepen and redeepen consideration, to subject listeners to a mood or series of moods—as does all music—but moods that take their place in an overall rational structure—sonata form, theme and variations, and so on—a structure of scientific inquiry we might even say, inquiring into what the material will yield, but where rationality, science, the spirit of inquiry, is reconceived or reformed on each occasion. Gardner's films show a similarity in material as he moves from culture to culture—people are seen to care about the same things and to live their lives and practice their crafts and make their art out of a similar consciousness of danger and profound encounter with the idea of death, for all the contrasts and variety we see in people's spirits, and for all that some are likable and sympathetic, and some quite dislikable. The similarity in material in Gardner's films raises the question of whether to a certain discerning eye human life is really to be found much the same in important respects from place to place or whether this is all more a matter of Gardner's temperament. This is not to be answered. Reality and the artistic, scientific temperament blur after a certain point. Open critical engagement with Gardner's films will give the sense of how far to trust—will give the sense, I believe, that we indeed do trust—his finding of material, just as we get the sense of trust in his handling and structuring of material, trust in his work as composer.

I press the musical analogy because we need a new way to conceive of documentary film beyond the two alternatives of transparent window onto reality, in accord with certifiable knowledge outside of film, or on the other hand illusion, seduction, cheat. Thinking in terms of this either/or can demolish any film, missing the new kind of knowledge a film may offer. I do not say that the musical analogy gives the key exactly to what the artistic nonfiction film is doing. There is no name for it, no set procedure. I mean the musical analogy just to point attention to something that cannot be spelled out.

Dead Birds is a film of grandeur, presenting warring tribes of the Dani in their vast lush valley setting in the highlands of central New Guinea. Seeing this film, one knows one has been brought into contact with a world of new and incontrovertible fact. It seems amazing that film can have found out this place and this life and can have brought it to the screen, as it seems amazing that Flaherty can have filmed the hostile far north or the heavy seas and the effort of hunting giant shark off the Aran Islands or that Buñuel can have found and mingled with the people of Las Hurdes. Gardner almost seems to have wanted to take film farther than it had ever gone, letting it luxuriate in what is to be found. The images of *Dead Birds*—the hills, the great valley and plain, the watchtowers, the battle scenes with masses of men, village life, wanderings in the bush at night—all seem to wash over one, the world seeking to assert itself, the images and the cutting from one image to the next seeming to emanate from a source other than the human, as Gardner's plainspoken commentary seems to try just to keep up, giving us explanations and bits of narrative we must have. The film knows that it cannot encompass everything, and its fragmentariness makes all the stronger the impression that film, this film, has come up against something that is there.

Gardner has a disposition, a willingness, in *Dead Birds* and elsewhere, to film death and the flowing of blood—here corpses, postbattle surgery, the bow-and-arrow slaughter of pigs held aloft, who scream. The hard fact of this footage, deeper than any particular cultural formations, lends a reality to all that we see, material that otherwise might seem airier or that we might think we know how to look at and comprehend, just as, on a more mental plane, the *idea* of death, announced at the beginning of *Dead Birds* in the story of the mortal bird and the immortal snake, lends possibility, reality, to life. The idea of death—surely derived from fact?—gives current to the activity, the making, the poetry, of those living life. The flying bird, whom we watch from above, is marked as mortal but goes on and on. The impossibility to disentangle fact and idea, fact and fancy—their relation as being a circle—is a situation, a condition of life, that film seems especially well suited to relay, to come to consciousness of. It is the very condition of the medium of film. From where do we look down on that flying bird and the changing earth beneath it? That first shot of Gardner's film signals a general point of view of film, out of this world, yet by virtue of its impossible position able to meet actuality.

The first movement of a symphony is traditionally the weightiest, the largest and most complex. The adagio may be more somber, but it is also more of one mood. And traditionally, the first movement is a presentation and a development, a probing, a bringing

together, of two distinct themes, two extended musical ideas, which is to say two entities that are at once emotional and intellectual, emotionally and intellectually workable. With *Dead Birds* there is the individual and the broader life. We are introduced right away to the man Weyak and the boy Pua, and throughout the film we are brought into their personal

concerns and reactions, even as we go again and again to the more general picture of a whole people's life committed to immemorial war, dominated by ghosts, lived under constant threat. And there are the two themes of death and life, death enabling life, and the two themes of the real and the idea, what film always faces, here taking form in a particular way at the ends of the earth, which of course is the center of the earth to others.

Water must show itself decisively. Near the beginning, a reflection in a puddle may be Weyak whom we have just first met, but it turns out to be Pua in his own first appearance. We will know these people and this world in a reflection on a surface. And there is the dangerous borderland river Aikhé, where those on both sides of the war invade and sneak up on each other, a place dangerous to walk. Gardner's camera returns here again and again, eventually finding a corpse at night whose face the camera contemplates and registers with use of a filmmaker's light—an encounter of film and death that could belong only to film. With the many images of the river, Gardner aligns the flowing, reflecting power of film with death, as I read it—just as surely as he aligns film with life in the activity of the village and its environs, with all the obsessively and lovingly observed work of hands, and where there is a safe stream along which women walk on their way to find salt and a safe spring from which Pua drinks.

The second half of the film enters a more subjective realm, with a religious festival and then news that a child has been killed and the ensuing funeral. The shots are much darker, with hut interiors and close views of skin and partial action that blots out the light. We get away from the broad setting to the space of people's feeling—absorption in ritual, excitement, worry, grief. Film, in the way it appears and in the sound it chooses and relays, wants to take in people's feeling and put this feeling into us. Film becomes the feeling, just as so often with Gardner film becomes the poetry of people's work and song. Like *Blunden Harbour, Dead Birds* ends with ongoing chant and dance, a lyrical outpouring that seems to transcend its cause and definition, a grief ceremony for the dead child, that turns into celebration on news of the death of an enemy.

Rivers of Sand, about the Hamar of southwestern Ethiopia, is Gardner's darkest film and is the adagio of the sequence. With its various means—a sparse voice-over commentary, a critical Hamar woman's recurrent address to the camera, shots of diverse and sometimes baffling activities of the Hamar, symbolism such as the dry riverbeds these people live among and look to with hope, or the perpetual grinding of sorghum that mirrors the grinding of women's spirits—the film has the feel of making one kind of attempt after another to look into a life that cannot be comprehended, in part because it is a forbidding horror. These beautifully formed and beautifully dressed people live a life of male oppression, male vanity and ineffectiveness, and female hard labor, whippings, decorative scarring where we see the blood flow, and cutting out of teeth to please the male eye. It is a world of hunger and thirst, hunger above all on the part of men and women to be liberated and not daring to think of taking the first step. Through everything, people maintain a perverse merriment.

Gardner's handheld camera moves restlessly over distances with people and domestic animals, seeking meaning, as if seeking escape. The camera's quieter attention is drawn, as always, to the work of hands, of women at work at home or men casting the "sandal oracle" to see how things will go with their needless ostrich hunt. The vistas are of dust and sand, the desolate background to these people's lives, or of an evening thunderstorm that seems to threaten destruction. With the film's editing, animals and their sounds, mostly cattle and

goats, are made very present, as if a chaotic animal nature is the energy feeding human life or as if the animal world cries out at its mistreatment by humans (there is marked contrast with *The Nuer,* made collaboratively by Gardner a few years earlier with Hilary Harris and George Breidenbach, where the cattle seem both loved and loving, and there is an ecstatic blurring of a gentle human nature with a gentle animal nature). *Rivers of Sand*'s mood of social critique, focused in the conscious and explicit feminism of the woman who talks to the camera, resonates with much thinking worldwide in the later 1960s and the 1970s. But the sense of a disturbing mystery that cannot be fathomed is more like a Faulkner novel than a confident political analysis. A protracted burial sequence in the middle of the film puts us in the grave, and this film as a whole may be said to bury us or lead us on a journey into the underworld and leave us there, needing another film, or the perspective of all Gardner's work, to get us farther or beyond this.

Gardner worked with experimental filmmaker Robert Fulton to make *Deep Hearts,* his most lighthearted film, the scherzo of the sequence one might say. The subject is the annual male beauty contest of the nomadic Bororo Fulani of central Niger in the southern Sahara. The words "deep hearts" suggest an Iago-like concealment of feeling, and we learn that the Bororo in fact value a deep heart and the hiding of desire and envy behind a sunny exterior. Further, Gardner's spoken commentary, sparser here than in *Rivers of Sand,* refers to the hard life of the Bororo outside these few days of festival in the brief rainy season, while the

images and sounds of the film give us a world of joy and good humor—a facade, it might seem. The power of film seeks out and yields to the varied scene of this special occasion: the preparation of makeup and coiffure and costumes, the lines of men dancing and singing on and on for days, the spectators, the everyday chores of maintaining a camp. Slow motion, freeze frames, swish pans, and altered sound help register and create the spirit of this prolonged lyrical outpouring that sublimates who knows what harsh experience or compromised feeling. The film brings us right into a particular event, without much distance or perspective. And yet the film works virtually on an abstract level, making the point of what a great gulf lies between, on the one hand, festival and art and, on the other, the matter of life we know must be resting there but that festival and art transmogrify or obscure. In this film we live for a time in the pure ecstatic world.

Deep Hearts is about men who dress and behave as women, with the aim that one of the men be chosen as exemplar by a woman, who may be acting at the behest of still other men. Central to the festival is a freeing of gender identity. And the camera itself enters a zone of gender ambiguity, just as it lets go of the perspectives of psychological and sociological analysis. Midway through the film Gardner's voice-over tells us the Bororo are worried about consumption by others' eyes, and this reference makes us think of the camera since nothing else in the film evokes such worry; we do not see it in the interpersonal relations of the people. The issue of the camera is raised, as it were out of the blue, and a few minutes later, still in the same sequence alternating views of performers and spectators, the camera

identifies itself with a woman, in a striking prolonged shot where we see a watching woman in sharp focus in the foreground and the performing men an out-of-focus blur in the background, their visibility, their existence, as if subject to the watching woman's whim. The camera in *Deep Hearts* lets go in many ways, transforming the film's subject matter overall into a dreamlike experience, perhaps a woman's experience, for the sake of getting close to, of getting to know, that initial subject matter, a certain reality.

With a complete withdrawal of voice-over commentary and subtitled translation of people's words, *Forest of Bliss* becomes a pure encounter of film's aural and visual sensitivities with a complex world, Benares, India, and its business of care for the dying and disposal of the dead. Old and specifically Indian customs come into play in dealing with death. But the film opens itself to something larger, the involvement of human activity in the general metamorphoses and cycles of water and earth, feeding and excrement, wood and fire and wind, light and dark, noise and silence. The film is specific and at the same time general, more profound than the specific, perhaps pointing to that realm that generates the world in its specificity and generates art in its own specificity.

Forest of Bliss yields itself up to what is to be seen and heard in Benares and also yields to the suggestions everything seems to make of analogy to something else, human beings to scavenging dogs, marigolds, or the spirit vaguely sensed in kites, boats, sails, and air. The

film yields itself up, but at the same time it makes metaphors, and even in observing, the camera is probing and active and the editing very deliberate, every cut seeming to start a new sentence. Some sounds are heightened, just as the camera finds visual close-ups in a larger perspective. One lives in the hospices and temples of Benares, in the lanes, along the ghats, and out on the broad Ganges. At times hu man faces and feeling, or the amazing funeral pyres, take over all consciousness. Yet one is aware throughout of an artist fashioning a film. On the large scale Gardner takes all the details and forms them into a dawn-to-dawn pattern, a day in the life of a city, like the old films of Vertov or Ruttmann, a genre sometimes called city symphony but more like the rondo or dance or theme and variations that commonly ends a symphony. (With *Forest of Bliss* in consideration, so intense, so complex in its suggestiveness, one wants to recall that Beethoven and subsequent composers began to put more relative weight on a symphony's final movement.)

Eliot Weinberger (1996, 165) has written that after spending considerable time in Benares over the years, he found *Forest of Bliss* amazingly true to the experience of being there—the film notices so much; it is so receptive, so extensive, in sound as well as image. I have myself spent time in Benares, and in one respect I found it very different from the film. For me, being in Benares was a fluid, seamless, gentle experience, for all the stimulation, even the occasional flaring of anger or a threat of crime. It was as if, on arrival, something induced a mood that would not waver. There was nothing like Gardner's hard cuts and surprising editing. And yet I accept *Forest of Bliss* as true. This work of an artist remarking, assembling, and creating a rhythm plays into my own memory, confirming me and showing me more. Benares exists somewhere among memory, reality, and creative presentation. Benares is film—as much as it is anything—and in its sacred river provides one of the most compelling of all images of film, accepting corpses and ashes and excrement and giving life to a city and a philosophy.

With *Ika Hands,* Gardner seems to look back on his way of doing things, taking the occasion of a race of people and way of life so strange and elusive as almost to defy filming—it is the filmmaker's ultimate interesting, mattering, difficult subject. The film begins with Gardner talking with anthropologist Gerardo Reichel-Dolmatoff, whose writings have led Gardner to want to film the Ika. Thus, these people begin as an idea for Gardner, something on paper and imagined. Reichel-Dolmatoff's voice comes back and back in the film, juxtaposed with what we see of the Ika and their high mountain world. In addition, brief intertitles occur to name or explain actions. All this comes to seem only a partial help to comprehend what is larger than our faculties. The camera follows these aristocratic, long-haired, essentially pre-Columbian beings as they walk ridges, sing, meditate, and see visions, and we seem to be in another time dimension or not on this earth. The many images of hands at work seem to want to ground the film, but there is a humanity or spirituality here widely distant from the hands, constantly seeming to take off and fly out of reach. The film takes us somewhere remarkable and makes us aware that we can never fully reach it.

Kierkegaard (1959) says that the essential quality of music is seduction, drawing one in toward what can never be attained and held, giving one an intimation, taking one partly along the way and leaving one deeply stirred in acknowledgment of what is before one. Perhaps seduction in this sense should be noted as the essential quality of film—a quality filmmakers inflect in their own ways, Gardner in his, with his particular curiosity about the world, his desire to know and make known, his making of solidarity with people's creative response to a sense of their vulnerability, his "impulse to preserve," as he calls it, taking the phrase from Philip Larkin.[3] The world comes to us in a creative guise. Something generates the world, perhaps love in embrace with death, asking of us a creative response as the way of knowledge, of acknowledgment—our music.

NOTES

1. Film as a means to knowledge is a persistent theme in Tarkovsky (1986).
2. The placing of film in relation to the crisis of skepticism is the point toward which everything works in Cavell (1971).
3. See Gardner (1996). Gardner (2006) elaborates on this idea.

REFERENCES

Cavell, Stanley. [1971] 1979. *The world viewed: Reflections on the ontology of film.* Enlarged ed. Cambridge, MA: Harvard University Press.

GARDNER, Robert. 1996. "The impulse to preserve." In *Beyond document: Essays on nonfiction film,* ed. Charles Warren, 169–80. Hanover, NH: Wesleyan University Press/University Press of New England.

———. 2006. *The impulse to preserve: Reflections of a filmmaker.* New York: Other Press.

KIERKEGAARD, Søren. [1843] 1959. "The immediate stages of the erotic or the musical erotic." In *Either/Or,* trans. David F. Swenson and Lillian Marvin Swenson, rev. Howard A. Johnson, 43–134. Reprint, Princeton, NJ: Princeton University Press.

TARKOVSKY, Andrey. 1986. *Sculpting in time: Reflections on the cinema,* trans. Kitty Hunter-Blair. Austin: University of Texas Press.

WEINBERGER, Eliot. 1996. "The camera people." In *Beyond document: Essays on nonfiction film,* ed. Charles Warren, 137–68. Hanover, NH: Wesleyan University Press/University Press of New England.

2   BEYOND THE BURDEN OF THE REAL

AN ANTHROPOLOGIST'S REFLECTIONS ON THE TECHNIQUE OF "A MASTERFUL CUTTER"

PAUL HENLEY

The films of Robert Gardner represent a challenge to all anthropologists interested in using visual media to represent human experience. But while some anthropologists have found his work inspiring, others have sought to deny it the label of "anthropology" entirely. Professors guarding the sacred flame of anthropological rectitude may declare their excommunication, but in my experience his films continue to enchant successive generations of students. Gardner himself seems somewhat ambiguous about the matter: sometimes he declares an interest in "a higher anthropology," while at others he denies that his work has any anthropological import or intention, though, as David MacDougall (1998a, 72) has commented, we should perhaps take this with a pinch of salt.

Of course, whether Gardner's work can be considered "anthropological" very much depends on how one defines this notoriously protean domain of intellectual activity. However, what unites Gardner's greatest admirers and perhaps the majority of even his most severe critics is the recognition that he is a master of the craft of nonfiction filmmaking. Most commentators, positive or negative, would recognize that he has both a distinctive method and a readily identifiable authorial signature. It is certainly the case that some aspects of his way of working in the field or the particular interpretations that he chooses to put on the cultural realities that he has explored through his films set him at odds with certain norms of contemporary social and cultural anthropology. But surely few would deny that purely in terms of craftsmanship, he has set an example that it would behoove all those interested in film as a medium of anthropological endeavor to examine in depth.

Some authors have argued, on theoretical grounds, that in order to serve anthropological purposes, it is necessary for anthropologists to invent some entirely new and distinctive mode of filmmaking. But so far, despite much exhortation over many years, there is not even the glimmer of such a thing on the horizon, suggesting that the idea is a chimera, analogous to the notion that in order for there to be a truly anthropological literature, it is necessary to invent some entirely new and distinctive mode of writing. In the circumstances, it seems more realistic to consider in what ways extant methods of filmmaking could serve anthropological purposes. Certainly, this would be much more in tune with the historical development of the discipline as a form of intellectual bricolage. These imported methods may have to be accommodated to anthropological requirements, though, clearly, the form and extent of these accommodations will depend critically on the nature of the anthropology that the filmmaking is supposed to serve.

This, it seems to me, is the most potentially rewarding angle from which anthropologists might approach the films of Robert Gardner. Let us simply acknowledge that he does what he does—and magnificently so. But what can us "drabber souls"—to use one of Gardner's own expressions—who plow our various furrows within the broad acres of anthropology, take from his films as examples of a distinctive cinematographic method?

Before we can even begin to answer this question, we must first seek to identify the nature of this method. This will be the principal objective of this chapter. Much has already been written on this subject over the years, with varying degrees of comprehensiveness and acuity. Of those with which I am familiar, I consider the writings of Peter Loizos (1993, 1995) to be particularly insightful.[1] However, there are a number of reasons why it may be valuable to return to the subject again now. The most important of these is the recent rerelease of both *Forest of Bliss* (2001) and *Dead Birds* (2004) on DVD accompanied by commentaries by Gardner himself on the process of making these films. Delivered in informal conversation with colleagues, these afford a new and privileged insight into his method of working. These commentaries are supplemented by the more general remarks that Gardner has offered in his interview with Ilisa Barbash (chapter 5 in this volume).

In this chapter, my focus is technical, but in the broadest sense, that is, including not just the practical aspects of his method but also the general principles and ideas by which it is informed.[2] However, for reasons of space, I restrict my attention almost exclusively to his technique in the edit suite. I begin by examining the way in which he combines the different components of particular sequences—material objects, space, sounds, subjects—through a variety of different types of editorial transition before passing on to consider how these sequences are ordered within larger, overarching narrative structures. Although I refer to other films, I explore these matters primarily with reference to *Forest of Bliss* (1986), which, purely from the point of view of editorial technique, surely represents Gardner's most complex work to date.

For most of his career, Gardner has acted as his own picture editor, though he has usually worked closely with highly skilled sound editors. Clearly, a comprehensive account of Gardner's technique would also examine the way in which he works in the field since this obviously determines the nature of the material that he has to work with in the edit suite in the first place. However, as this lies beyond the scope of this chapter, I confine myself to brief comments on two aspects of his location technique that are of particular relevance to the present discussion.

First, Gardner shoots his own material, and in terms of sheer skill as a cinematographer, he is surely a match for anyone working in the field of nonfiction filmmaking, be it for anthropological or any other purposes. Having learned to shoot in the days before portable synchronous sound technology was widely available, he continues to shoot without synchronous sound "most of the time" (see chapter 5 in this volume). Perhaps for this reason, he often works with a sound recordist who is not a professional but rather a collaborator involved in the project on other grounds. His camera style is predominantly realist, but within this stylistic register, he mixes a wide variety of shots, from handheld wide shots to tripod-based shots on the end of a long lens. He seems to shoot mostly in long, stable takes from a single but well-chosen position, though he is clearly not averse to cutting into these in the edit suite and using a clip of no more than a few seconds. With a few notable exceptions, he eschews dramatic angles, exaggerated movements of the zoom, or other such self-conscious demonstrations of virtuosity.[3] He does, however, have a predilection for the tight close-up shot of human body parts and for slow-motion and still frames, all of which contribute to his distinctive authorial repertoire. His camera is typically very engaged with the subjects, but while he often appears to be merely following the action, he is clearly prepared to intervene and direct his principal subjects as required. This is particularly evident in his earlier films, notably in *Dead Birds*.

A second aspect of Gardner's way of working in the field that it is particularly important to mention here is that although he has worked mostly in culturally exotic locations, he generally does not remain long enough to learn the language of his subjects. One consequence of this has been his dependence on collaborators of various ilks, often anthropologists, who have acted as his interpreters and who have provided him with the ethnographic context of his work. As is well documented, some of these collaborations appear to have been mutually richly rewarding, others less so (see Strecker 1988; Loizos 1993, 141–42). But the consequence of greatest significance to the present discussion is that his subjects' speech—probably as a result of his own limited communicative competence—usually plays only the most minor role in his films. Although his subjects are certainly not mute, it is normally the paralinguistic features of their speech, such as the tone and style of delivery, that carry significance, not the substantive content of what they are saying. With only one or two minor exceptions that prove the rule, there are no instances in Gardner's films of subjects directly addressing the camera verbally.[4]

Instead, Gardner's method is built on the intense observation and recording of the visual, which is then presented in conjunction with or in juxtaposition to nonverbal sound. It is perhaps because of the striking visual properties of his films that they have sometimes been referred to as examples of "observational cinema." It is true that there are some elements of similarity in the camerawork—the realist style, the often nondirectional strategy, and the occasional use of the long take—while some sequences in Gardner's films could be said to be conventionally chronologically progressive in a manner that is typical of observational films. But, as we will see, the fundamental principles underlying the two approaches could hardly be more different.

BEYOND THE BURDEN OF THE REAL

An interesting insight into Gardner's thinking about visual images is to be found in the supplementary material accompanying the *Dead Birds* DVD. In conversation with Lucien Taylor, Gardner explains that when the film first came out in 1964, he made a black-and-white copy that he confesses he much preferred to the color version, even though, for commercial reasons, it was the latter that was actually distributed. Over the opening shot of the black-and-white version, which shows a hawk gliding gracefully over a Dani village in the New Guinea Highlands, Gardner observes,

> Seeing the bird in black and white does summon up, for me, all the virtues of black and white. Because, for me, that bird is much more a bird in black and white than it was in color. It's that flight was much more flight. To see it in some more life-like way in color did not enliven the bird, it burdened the bird with data that was irrelevant to its birdness. And so, taking away, which is a wonderful thing to do, I think, in art, was the answer to arriving at this quintessential view of flight.[5]

In stating this preference for black-and-white images, I suggest that Gardner is providing us with an important key as to how we should read his work more generally. For, as Taylor comments, one of the effects of rendering an image in black and white is to encourage the spectator to consider its status as a symbolic statement. In the same spirit, rather than take Gardner's images at face value as descriptive registrations of the world as it is, I suggest that we should be constantly reading them as signifiers of some more transcendent meaning, even while bearing in mind that the phenomenal surface meaning of these images may be an obstacle to grasping this ulterior significance.

In order to help his spectators get past these surface meanings, Gardner makes abundant use of a very particular form of montage. This is not "montage" in the most common contemporary sense of the term, that is, a rapid sequence of images intended merely to truncate time or to summarize an event or some other body of visual information. It is more akin to the classical "Russian" montage, in which the aim is to generate, from the juxtaposition of two or more shots, a meaning that goes beyond the sum of the parts (see Barbash and Taylor 1997, 371–74; Reisz and Millar 1999, 112 ff.). But whereas classical Russian montage was typically based on a sequence of brief shots, often self-consciously nonrealist in character, in Gardner's films these montages are typically composed of stylistically realist shots, often of relatively long duration. Nor is this montage technique confined to the succession of shots within a sequence since, in the manner of "parallel editing," whole sequences based on a progressive, normal chronology may be intercut in order to generate not just the impression of temporal simultaneity but, in addition, significance. However, precisely because of the cinematographic realism and the often normal chronology, a viewer who is not alert to Gardner's semiotic purposes may be lulled into interpreting these juxtapositionings as being merely descriptive. This is one of the main reasons, I suspect, why some anthropologist colleagues have seemingly been unable to "read" the carefully wrought analyses that are embedded in Gardner's films and that are readily available to those who have the eyes to see and, equally important, the ears to hear them.

We will encounter many such juxtapositions later in this chapter, so here some simple examples will suffice. In a sequence close to the beginning of *Dead Birds,* Gardner intercuts between Weyak, the principal male subject, looking out for enemies from a watchtower silhouetted against the sky, and Lakha, his wife working in the gardens nearby, apparently in the same late afternoon. But as is clear from Gardner's discussion with fellow filmmaker Ross McElwee on the DVD, the intercutting of the activities of these two subjects is intended to indicate more than mere simultaneity. What Gardner wants us to understand from this juxtaposition is not merely the contrast between men's work (seemingly light) and women's work (seemingly heavy) but also that between men's symbolic identification with the sky (and hence with birds) and women's identification with the earth.

In *Dead Birds*, Gardner makes such semiotic intentions very clear right from the beginning, as the gliding hawk of the opening shot is immediately followed by a shot of the positioning on a funeral pyre of a Dani man killed in battle. Over the shot of the hawk, a portentous voice-over relates a Dani legend to the effect that the Bird, on winning a race with the Snake in mythological times, became destined thereafter to die. By following this comment with the shot of the dead man, Gardner establishes a clear association between birds and humans as sharing the common condition of mortality. This association is then heavily reinforced by the title graphics. These come up in two stages, in reverse order, with "BIRDS" over the end of the outgoing shot of the hawk and "DEAD" coming in only with the cut to the human corpse.

Throughout the remainder of *Dead Birds*, there are recurrent juxtapositions of images of men with images of birds and/or sounds of birds. Sometimes there are even images of men dressed as birds, with feathers in their hair. This symbolic interplay between birds and humans is intertwined at certain points in the narrative both with the contrast between men and women and with the contrast between Weyak and Pua, a young boy who anxiously anticipates his own manhood. Toward the end of the film, these various contrasts are elided as the women too become symbolic birds when they dance to celebrate the revenge killing of an enemy, while Pua kills and eats a bird and, as sign of his developing maturity, puts the feathers in his hair.

THINGS

But if the burden of symbolic meaning in particular images and their juxtapositions is relatively easy to read in *Dead Birds*, this is not the case with *Forest of Bliss*, released some 20 years later. In this film, not only are the symbolic elements more numerous, but their juxtapositions are more complex and varied as well. Nor does Gardner provide any convenient keys to interpretation through voice-over narration.

The text accompanying the rerelease of *Forest of Bliss* on DVD reproduces a conversation with the anthropologist with whom Gardner collaborated on the film, Ákos Östör. Here Gardner describes how he sought to impose some order on the "endless possibilities for confusion" that Benares represented for him.[6] He did so by approaching the reality of the city through a number of particular elements that, although very simple and very material, he saw as being laden with potentially illuminating symbolic meanings:

> Here was a city of institutionalized chaos—and what can you do with chaos? . . . It's hard
> to take it apart and see what is going on or what is meaningful about it. Photographed,

it just becomes visual noise, and the only way I could see to get away from the visual noise of Benares was to find refuge, almost literally, in the marigolds or the wood or something extremely simple yet somehow charged. The fact these so-called simple things exist and take their meaning from this world, this chaotic world, meant that world would be drawn in by implication. (Gardner and Östör 2001, 46)

Gardner explains that although he refined his understanding of the significance of these material elements in the edit suite, he formed the intention of using them in this way even while still on location. In fact, this was a technique that he had also used in his earlier films—in relation to men's weaving in *Dead Birds* and to women's grindstones in *Rivers of Sand*—but in *Forest of Bliss* it is used in a much more developed form, without any verbal assists:

[F]ilm seems to work best with simple motifs, with commonplaces. To escape the difficulty awaiting anyone who tries to film complexity as complexity and then maybe tries to explain their way out of these complexities in subtitles or voice-over, the idea in this film was to look for some ordinary realities, such as dogs, woods, kites, marigolds etc., and to plunge into them, trusting that they will provide an evocative journey into their meaning. (Gardner and Östör 2001, 45)

These comments confirm the interpretations of the most insightful reviewers at the time the film was first released (notably Oppitz 1988; Chopra 1989). Rather than opt for either doctrinal exposition by local ritual specialists or ethnographic exegesis by anthropologists, Gardner attempts the ambitious project of communicating the principles of Hindu eschatology through images of these particular concrete features of the material world within which the disposal of the dead takes place.

Central to this eschatology, as expounded by the Indian sociologist Radihka Chopra, who reviewed the film, is the idea that life is to death as creation is to destruction but that, even while being opposed, these binary oppositions are connected to one another cyclically. Far from being kept apart in everyday life, they exist side by side in a state of constant interpenetration with one another (cf. Chopra 1989, 2). In *Forest of Bliss,* this highly philosophical dialectic is played out by the recurrent juxtaposition of material symbolic opposites. Thus, the snarling dogs, scavengers of filth in the urban gutters, gnawers of human corpses, and, as such, symbols of extreme pollution as well as of the boundaries between human and animal and, beyond that, between life and death, are opposed to the beautiful and bright marigolds, gathered in the peaceful countryside and used as ritual markers of transition, adorning images of deities at the threshold of the human and the divine, a newly blessed boat about to be launched, as well as newly dead corpses, newly born babies, and even the neck of a young puppy.

Similarly, heavy piles of wood destined for the funeral pyres are associated with dead bodies, while both are juxtaposed and contrasted on the one hand with the healthy bodies of those who load the wood onto barges and row it downstream to the cremation grounds and on the other with the kites that are children's playthings and whose progress across the sky, dancing on the uplifting thermals from the cremation fires, evokes lightness, vitality, and vulnerability all at the same time. In the striking montage of shots with which the film begins, it is suggested, by editorial juxtaposition, that a young boy, in seeking to launch his kite, is also somehow pulling up the sun. Much later in the film, shortly before dusk, two of these kites happen to fall down into the river in the background of a shot just at the moment that a child's corpse is being committed to the river. At this moment, the dialectical connection between the symbolically opposed values of sky and river, of spirit and body, and of life and death is rendered in a form that is, as Gardner puts it, "powerfully actual" (Gardner and Östör 2001, 110).

SPACE

This last shot is but one example of the way in which the spatial relationship between the sky and the river is exploited symbolically in the film. There are frequent cuts from dogs or corpses, archetypal denizens of the river and its banks, to shots of birds tumultuously flocking in the azure sky. Sometimes the two come together, as when we hear the sound of carrion birds cawing in the background as dogs gnaw on something, perhaps a corpse, or as the birds flock around the boat bearing wood for the funeral pyres upstream. Some of these birds are kites, others vultures, others sparrows, but all of them, although symbolic of the vitality of life in the moment, are also, for Gardner, harbingers of mortality, just as birds of yet other species had been for him in New Guinea.[7]

Nor is this vertical symbolic interchange between sky and river the only form of movement through space that is used to symbolic effect in the film. Equally important is the horizontal relationship between upstream and downstream, as manifest in the movement of boats through the frame of the film: at the very beginning, they move from left to right, while at the very end, they move in the opposite direction. This was noted by Michael Oppitz in an early review, but this was not all: he also observed that the boats that we see at the beginning of the film come out of a haze and gradually take shape, while the boat in the final scene gets wrapped up again in this haze before it disappears into the void. Oppitz (1988) concludes that "the former may be taken as movements into life and the later ones as movements out of life" (211). Gardner's comments, although not published until some 15 years later, confirm that this change of direction was certainly intended, and although he does not quite confirm the interpretation offered by Oppitz, it seems very likely that this is what he had in mind, given the general thrust of his symbolic manipulations (Gardner and Östör 2001, 17–18, 20, 116).

On the other hand, Gardner is completely explicit in identifying the symbolic significance for him of the diagonal movements in space from one side of the river to the other, that is, from the populated western bank, site of the city and the cremation ghats, to the sandy and apparently unsettled eastern bank. Even before he began filming, Gardner formed an analogy in his mind between the Ganges and the Styx, with the eastern bank being that "far shore" from which no traveler returns, while the feral dogs that ranged there were none other than symbolic doppelgängers of Cerberus, the hellhound who guarded the entrance to the Underworld of Greek mythology. While the people of Benares themselves might consider it no more than a place of recreation and while even Östör thought of it as a peaceful refuge from the confusion of the city, for Gardner it was a place of "quite forbidding mystery," representing the world of death as opposed to the world of life on the more populated shore (Gardner and Östör 2001, 16–17, 38).

In this spatial distinction, Gardner saw yet another way to organize the "chaos" of Benares for the purposes of his film. Accordingly, the film opens with a series of shots from the "far shore," with "spectral galleons" passing through the mist and Cerberus-like dogs on patrol, before crossing to the inhabited shore with all its confusion and vitality, for the main body of the film. There the action remains, apart from one or two interpolated shots that act as a sort of memento mori, before seemingly returning to the "far shore" in the final prolonged shot of the film, in which a rowing boat disappears slowly and inexorably into the mist once again.

SOUNDS

This manipulation of the symbolic "charge" of material objects and spatial movement is complemented in *Forest of Bliss* by a similar manipulation of sounds. Even in his first film, *Blunden Harbour* (1951), Gardner used nonsynchronous drumming and shamanic chanting to suggest transcendent significance, but in his later ethnographic films, the sound editing becomes progressively more sophisticated. In *Dead Birds* (1964), the sound track is greatly enriched but for the most part in a straightforward realist manner. In *Rivers of Sand* (1974), it begins to take on a more metaphorical function, notably in the sounds of grinding stones and the jingling metal rings on women's skirts that are used asynchronously throughout the film to suggest female servitude. The principal sound editor of this film was Michel Chalufour, who later worked on *Forest of Bliss,* in which the manipulation of sounds for metaphorical purposes is even more substantially developed. This manipulation takes a variety of forms, but the primary metaphorical purpose is almost always to provide an aural complement to the many visual memento mori. The combined effect is to suggest that even in life, one is surrounded, if not by death itself, then at least by potentially fatal suffering or menace.

In some instances, this manipulation of sound consists merely of enhancing the diegetic synchronous sound. A simple example is the moment when a carpenter constructing a bamboo bier takes a break, lights up a cigarette, and then exhales. This exhalation has been much augmented, Gardner explains, in order to suggest the final expiration of a dying person. Although we do not quite know at this stage of the film what the purpose of these ladderlike artifacts might be, it is possible that we have an inkling, in which case the exhalation might mean something to us. If so, we might also be disposed to discern another memento mori in the immediately following shot of a man asleep on a pile of the bamboo poles from which the biers are made (cf. Gardner and Östör 2001, 57).

There are many such examples in the film. In some cases, the augmentation is so extreme that one suspects that they might be completely extradiegetic. This seems likely, for example, in the case of the footsteps of the dog in opening shot of the film. This was clearly executed on the end of a long lens since the foreshortening is considerable and since, in the circumstances, it seems unlikely that the sound recordist could have got such clear sound. But whether the sound was merely enhanced or represents a Foley effect recorded in a studio, the crisp, almost percussive sound of the footsteps gives a pronounced sense of menace to the image, presaging the violence of the snarling dogfight that follows shortly afterward. The same could be said of the similarly enhanced sound that features in the sequence in which the marigolds are shown being harvested in the countryside. Visually, the picking of the flowers is shown in close-up, and as each head is picked, there is an exaggerated rasping snap. Although marigolds have generally positive associations in the film, this particular sound implies, as with so many other symbols in *Forest of Bliss,* that there is an element of ambiguity about them since the rasping snap also suggests a certain menace, connotative perhaps not just of flower heads being culled but of human heads being metaphorically snapped off as well.[8]

But these mere augmentations of synchronous sounds can be distinguished from the more elaborate use of aural metaphors based on wild-track or on "intradiegetic" sound, that is, sound that features synchronously at some points but asynchronously elsewhere (cf. Hayward 2000, 85). One example of this technique involves the sound of the chopping or the splitting of wood, which throughout the film functions as a memento mori because of its association with the preparation of wood for the funeral pyres.[9] Often we see this in sync, but at other points the sound is featured in scenes in which the wood chopping itself is not visible. The first and most dramatic example occurs under the main title of the film, where one hears the sounds of trees being felled. Gardner and Östör discuss how they went to a great deal of trouble to film the felling of these trees at some distance from the city. However, in the end, they decided that the visual image of the woodsmen actually doing the felling would be "too puny" to carry such a heavy metaphorical charge.

Another acoustic effect used in this way is the sound of bells tolling. Although tolling bells do occur in sync in the sequences set in temples and shrines, they are also used in an intradiegetic way, with ambiguous effects since, as Östör suggests with regard to a usage very early in the film, one is not quite sure whether they are tolling to announce a death or are simply liturgical bells marking the time of day. Gardner confirms that this ambiguous effect was exactly what he wanted in order to encourage the spectators to ask questions:

> ...the bells are both merry and not so merry. They are meant to be full of the possibility of delight and, equally, the possibility of sorrow...Ambiguity plays such a prominent part in creating an atmosphere. It is this mood that I hope continues through the whole film until there is real clarity and the mysteries get solved. (Gardner and Östör 2001, 21–22)

Funeral chanting ("ram, nam, satya hai"—"God's name is truth"; Oppitz 1988, 211), the swishing of water, the barking of dogs, and the squawking of birds are all also used throughout the film in a highly metaphorical sense to emphasize and reinforce the juxtaposition of the symbolic opposites of life and death, of sky and water, of purity and pollution. But of all the aural metaphors used in *Forest of Bliss,* undoubtedly the most striking is the one that we hear for the first time about seven minutes into the film. Here it features over a shot of the prow of a boat that, together with a brief and difficult-to-discern shot of a dog gnawing at a half-submerged corpse, is inserted nonsequentially into the middle of an otherwise largely observational sequence of one of the main characters taking an early morning bath in the river. It is a strange, creaking, and somehow ominous sound that, like the sound of the tolling bells, is clearly intended to provoke a question in the mind of the viewer as to what it could be and, even more important, what it could mean.

This sound occurs on two further occasions over shots of a boatload of wood for the funeral pyres being rowed upstream, but it is not until some 30 minutes into the film that we finally discover what it is. It turns out to be the sound produced by the grating of bamboo oars in the small rope lassos that serve as rowlocks on these boats. Oppitz (1988) calls this acoustic device a "*coup de maître*" and suggests that it acts as "the musical *leitmotiv* of the entire film, a sound metaphor for terrestrial suffering, pain, labour, and disharmony." The most dramatic use of all is saved for the long final shot of the film, in which the rowing boat slowly disappears into the mist on its way to "the far side," both actually and metaphorically. With this use, Oppitz rightly remarks, "Gardner strikes his best transcendental string" (212).

SUBJECTS

One of the most striking features of Gardner's ethnographic films is that they are not populated by subjects of rounded, idiosyncratic character. Not coincidentally, his subjects rarely speak. In the early films, Gardner often speaks for them, describing what they are thinking or feeling. At the time of making *Blunden Harbour* and *Dead Birds,* there would have been limited alternative methods of presenting the subjects' thoughts or sentiments about the world simply because of technical constraints.[10] But Gardner continued to employ the strategy in his later work, as in *Deep Hearts* (1979), for example, when the development of synchronous sound technology would have allowed the subjects to speak for themselves if he had so wished. In other later films, his subjects do speak, but they speak either in an idealized form, as in the case of Omali Inda in *Rivers of Sand,* or in a form that is unintelligible (except for speakers of the local language), as with the three main subjects of *Forest of Bliss.*[11]

This lack of attention to the idiosyncrasy of his subjects and the substance of their speech may have caused adverse comment on the part of some anthropological reviewers over the years, but it is entirely consistent with Gardner's approach to phenomena generally. The subjects themselves are not of interest to him as actual, embodied individuals; what is of interest is what they signify in some more transcendent way. Nor has he been afraid to say so. As he put it succinctly with regard to the subjects of *Dead Birds,* "I seized the opportunity of speaking to certain fundamental issues in human life. The Dani were less important to me than those issues" (Gardner 1972, 34). Some 15 years later, in his conversation with Östör about *Forest of Bliss,* he suggests that the idea that one could capture the sense of an individual human being on film is anyway an illusion:

> Documenting a person, or personality, seems even more problematic to me than documenting a ritual or some other activity. It seems to me that all of our private views of another person are total fictions, yet somehow functional when it comes to knowing that other person. The very idea of finding a way to reproduce some reality that can be called another person is, on its face, a total absurdity. (Gardner and Östör 2001, 99)

David MacDougall has suggested that Gardner's apparent detachment from the subjects of his films should not be mistaken for coolness toward them but rather that it should be understood as restraint, derived from a respect for their dignity as human beings. As MacDougall (2001, 79) acknowledges, however, other filmmakers may find it hard to follow Gardner in this matter, particularly since it is filming people in all their complex individuality that is, for many, a source of endless fascination.

However one might choose to interpret this particular aspect of Gardner's way of working, the fact is that the subjects of Gardner's films are not characters of the kind that one

might expect to discover in the observational film canon, full of ideas and opinions and a range of moods and humors, often mutually contradictory, as in human experience generally. The closest that Gardner comes to such characters are Weyak and Pua in *Dead Birds,* but even they are mute and come across as archetypes rather than rounded individuals. With these partial exceptions, Gardner's characters are primarily vehicles through which he can explore particular "issues" or aspects of the human condition that he perceives as being played out within the cultural arena in which those subjects happen to live. By taking away the particularizing detail of their lives as revealed through the substance of their speech or, as he might put it, by freeing them of the burden of irrelevant data, Gardner seems to be encouraging us, rather in the manner of the hagiographers of Christian saints, to attend more directly to what his subjects' lives might signify transcendentally.

In *Forest of Bliss,* each of the three principal subjects represents different aspects of life in and around the funeral ghats, like so many characters in a morality play. There is no sustained attempt to establish the idiosyncratic person behind or beyond the role that each plays in the film. Even the device of personalizing the subjects through naming them, which Gardner himself notes he used in *Dead Birds* some 20 years previously, is not employed here. This gives rise to some concern on Gardner's part that the audience will not realize that the various appearances of certain subjects are of one and the same person. But in the end, he and Östör conclude that this does not really matter since it is the significance of what the character is doing in that moment, not who he is, that is important to the film (Gardner and Östör 2001, 49–50).

As with the manipulation of material symbols described previously, the three subjects are used to present a series of fundamental symbolic contrasts between which there can nevertheless be some degree of interplay. One pole of these contrasts is represented by Ragul Pandit, whom Östör describes as a "ritualist." He represents a series of positive values: wisdom, serenity, and purity. His ritual incantations at dawn, reminiscent to Gardner of Gregorian chant, are intended to provide some redemption for the audience at the end of the film after they have been taken through the valley of the shadow of death (Gardner and Östör 2001, 115). At the other pole stands the Untouchable, the Dom Raja, a character of "utter balefulness," as Gardner describes him. His ugly and sick body, his broken voice, and his manner of arrogant contempt concord perfectly with his very worldly business as supervisor of the funeral pyres, an enterprise that he seemingly pursues with greedy efficaciousness and a ruthless indifference to the bereavement of this clients.

If the Pandit represents the spiritual life and the possibility of renewal, the Dom Raja represents the utter ineluctability and meaninglessness of the material world. Between these two poles, as a sort of trickster, lies the "healer" Mithai Lal, who, like the Pandit, engages in ritual activity but who, like the Dom, is also vulgar and materialistic. Whereas the other two characters represent the rationality of their station in life unambiguously and with utter seriousness, the healer seems to be a joker, an ambiguous character, capable of both good and evil, banality and religious inspiration, whose mental state verges at some points on insanity (Gardner and Östör 2001, 102–4).

TRANSITIONS

As Michael Oppitz (1988, 211) pointed out with an astuteness that was unusual at the time of his review, Gardner effects these juxtapositions in *Forest of Bliss* through the deployment of a range of different types of editorial transition. Sometimes the sequence of shots is straightforwardly "serial" in the sense of being reiterative of the same point. Perhaps the most striking example of this is the one noted by Oppitz in which a number of different animals are shown being dragged down the steps of a ghat without ceremony in order to be disposed of in the river: first a donkey, then a cat, and finally a dog are hauled down, their bodies twisting awkwardly and their skulls resounding hollowly, probably with the aid of some acoustic enhancement. However, this serial montage is preceded and indeed made meaningful by a shot (also acoustically enhanced) of an elderly blind man also making his way, carefully and elegantly, down the steps of a ghat.

The clear implication here is that for all their dignity, human beings share what, many years before, Gardner had called "our animal fate" with other creatures; that is, we too will one day die and, actually or metaphorically, will be taken down the steps of a ghat and disposed of in a river somewhere.[12] In this sense, this juxtaposition of the human being with the animals going down the steps is not only serial but also contrastive in that it generates meaning, as in the example cited previously from the opening of *Dead Birds,* as much from the contrast as from the similarity between the subject matters of the shots conjoined.

Sometimes, semiotically significant juxtapositions in *Forest of Bliss* are disguised within a sequence that is ostensibly a real-time event but that has actually been constructed in the edit suite. Such is the case with a relatively early sequence in the film that begins with a lengthy series of shots of large trunks of wood being loaded onto a boat that then sets off upstream. As the boat progresses, there are two shots presented as if from the point of view of someone in the boat, first of vultures whirling in the sky, then of a corpse floating face-down in the shallows, anus toward the camera. In commenting on this sequence, Gardner is quite candid in admitting that these two shots were "connected by editing, not at all by actuality." His intention, he explains, was to intimate that this consignment of wood, the purpose of which has not yet been made clear, has "some death-related meaning, that it is not just for keeping people warm at night" (Gardner and Östör 2001, 48). Only later will we discover that this is the wood for the funeral pyres.

In other cases, it is extended real-time events that are associated by being intercut with one another. This is true of one of the most important scenes in the film in which a sequence of a new boat being launched into the river garlanded with marigolds is intercut with a sequence in which a corpse, similarly decorated with marigold garlands, is shown being brought down on a bier and immersed in the river. The meaning of the conjunction was abundantly clear to at least one of the early reviewers, Radhika Chopra (1989), without any need for explanatory narration:

> We see body and boat launched into the River Ganga in what are almost physically simi-
> lar movements. In the absence of a commentary, the visuals leave it to us to realize that
> the "inaugural" and the "end" partake of a shared meaning where death is clearly not an
> end but an inaugural into another journey. Such juxtapositioning brings us closer to an
> understanding of the river itself which provides both the physical and the metaphorical
> passage for the journey into another "state" of being. (3)[13]

Gardner reports that these events were not brought together in the edit suite but happened simultaneously and at the same ghat. While surely all documentarists live in the hope of being blessed with such epiphanies, Gardner is only too aware of how such simultaneities can be editorially manufactured. It was, after all, a technique that he had used very extensively in *Dead Birds,* frequently intercutting the daily routines of the principal characters, Weyak and Pua, or the activities of men engaged in warfare and women engaged in subsistence activities. Later, he also used intercutting to suggest simultaneity in *Rivers of Sand* though, as usual, with an additional metaphorical meaning, namely, underscoring the hard labor of women while men engaged in onanistic self-decoration.

He therefore now worries that despite "this sanction of reality," the conjunction of the two events in *Forest of Bliss* might be considered just too contrived. He also worries that the two events might be considered not only metaphorically linked but also metonymically; that is, the audience might presume that the deceased once owned the boat or that the boat is being launched for the purposes of carrying the corpse. "But," he concludes, "that may be part of the price you pay in order to get the effect you want" (Gardner and Östör 2001, 87).

Some sequences in *Forest of Bliss* are cut in a seemingly straightforward progressive manner, truncating the chronology of a particular event with a view simply to advancing the action in a time-efficient way. However, even within these more informational sequences, Gardner usually inserts one or more shots charged with metaphorical meanings that he wants the viewer to explore. Such is the case with the lengthy opening sequence in which the "healer" Mithai Lal makes his way down the steps of a ghat to bathe. On the way, he passes weighing scales and piles of wood, both of which Gardner has positioned in the frame in such a way as to encourage the viewer to inquire about their significance.

But once the healer has immersed himself in the water, the observational quality of the sequence is suddenly interrupted by an abrupt cut to a memento mori telephoto shot from the "far shore" framed tightly on a sail going by with a funeral pyre burning in the background. Then, after returning for another couple of shots of the healer frolicking in the water, there is a cut to two people launching an offering of marigolds set on a large leaf. This seems almost to be a functional "cutaway," and we might imagine that the event could be happening nearby. But this does not seem likely in the case of a third, more startling interruption in the healer's bath-time routine that follows shortly afterward. This consists of two shots, one of a dog gnawing at what could be a corpse and the other the prow of a boat featuring the grating sound of the unseen rope rowlocks. The exact import of these is not at all clear at this stage, but Gardner wants viewers at least to become aware that the river has many meanings beyond that of simply being a good place to bathe (for an extended discussion of this sequence, see Gardner and Östör 2001, 27–35).

If these irruptions in the realism of an observational sequence refer to contexts of metaphorical meaning that pertain to Benares in particular, there are other instances in *Forest of Bliss* in which they appear to be reaching out to meanings of more general significance. For Gardner's ultimate objective is to treat not just the subject of death in Benares but also, as he glosses it, poetically if euphemistically, "journeys to any far shore." This, he suggests, is not easy, given the very literal and specific nature of film as a medium (Gardner and Östör 2001, 89; on this point, see also Loizos 1993, 162). An example of the way in which Gardner seeks to achieve this generalization occurs in a key scene almost halfway through the film. This draws a number of previously disparate elements together into a single quasi-observational sequence, giving it a particular structural importance in the film as a whole. It takes place in a hospice for the dying, which we have been introduced to before in the film and now return to for a second time. On this occasion, we observe the corpse of a recently deceased person from a respectful distance as it is carried down from an upstairs room, wrapped in a white shroud, to the sound of chanting by the attendants. On the ground floor, it is placed on a simple bamboo bier and decorated with a single garland of marigolds before being carried out to the cremation ghats.

Although we have encountered all the elements of this scene before—the location, the chanting attendants, the marigolds, the bamboo bier, even, one supposes, the deceased since in the previous scene in the hospice we saw some old ladies in extremis—this is the first time that all the elements are presented to us in a single, coherent consecutive strand. However, what distinguishes this particular example of chronologically progressive editing from one that one might find, say, in an observational film is that toward the beginning of the sequence, just before the corpse is brought down by the attendants, there is a measured, perhaps even slightly slow-motion, subjective point-of-view shot descending the empty staircase. In that it is strikingly out of character stylistically with the detached observationalism of the rest of the sequence, this is clearly intended to remind the viewer that death is not just something that happens to other people in "other cultures." It is also the fate of Everyman, including, of course, both the viewer and the filmmaker.

STRUCTURES

All these symbolic elements and the transitions between them are usually located in Gardner's films within larger overarching narrative structures of a classical kind. These typically commence with the posing of some initial issue, problem, or mystery and then progressively carry the audience forward to some final culmination before returning actually or metaphorically to the beginning. In *Dead Birds,* after initially proposing the common mortality of men and birds, the narrative is thereafter both framed and advanced by the weaving of a band by one of the principal characters, Weyak. This functions as a sort of "clock," as Gardner himself has put it.[14] Weyak starts to weave the band at the beginning of the film, is shown working on it at various points during the film, and finally completes it at the end. As such, the progression of the band parallels the temporal progression of the film through a series of days and a series of events related to the ongoing ritual warfare between Weyak's group and their enemies. These culminate, in the classical manner, in a revenge killing and a celebratory dance. However, the band also represents the progression of time in a more sinister metaphorical sense since, as we discover about 10 minutes into the film, it is a funeral band. As Weyak completes his task after the celebratory dance, the film returns to the theme of the common mortality of men and birds.

In *Dead Birds,* the progression of the narrative is substantially assisted by voice-over narration, written and spoken in a very literary style. In addition to telling the viewer the significance of much of what is happening, the narration is also used for retailing a great deal of ethnographic information. Looking back at the film 40 years later, Gardner regrets this, saying that it resulted from a "weird" sense of the need to be a responsible witness. Thereafter, voice-over narration progressively disappears from his work, being much reduced in *Rivers of Sand* and no more than vestigial in *Deep Hearts.* By the time of *Forest of Bliss,* it has disappeared entirely, leaving both the progression of the narrative and the retailing of ethnographic information to visual and nonverbal sound means alone.

In the absence of an orientating voice-over, the narrative in *Forest of Bliss* is advanced primarily through a structure based on a conventional 24-hour cycle, running from one sunrise to the next. In effect, a wholesale rearrangement of chronology has taken place, with material that was shot over a 10-week period being construed as if it occurred in a single day. We may confidently assume, then, that certain sequences shot in the afternoon are presented as if they occurred in the morning and vice versa. The same may be assumed with sequences shot at dawn and at dusk. We are thus clearly far from the realm of ethnographic reportage here.

In addition to fulfilling the basic function of all narrative structures, that is, carrying the audience forward with the aid of subliminal signpostings of the progression of the day, the use of this particular structure also provides yet another echo of the principle of cyclical reiteration underlying Hindu eschatology. Intriguingly, Gardner reveals that he was initially considering using the reconstruction of the boat launched from the cremation ghat as the overall structuring device of the film. To this end, he shot a great deal of material of the boat being prepared for the launch, most of which he later discarded when he decided to opt for the diurnal structure instead. However, what is interesting is that this pilot structure also had a certain metaphorical value, namely, the symbolic parallel discussed previously between the launch of a "newborn" boat and a "newdead" person. What is even more interesting from a film practitioner's point of view is that Gardner apparently conceived these narrative-structuring devices for the film while still in the field and began shooting material specifically for them in an entirely purposive manner (Gardner and Östör 2001, 85–86).

However, the sunrise-to-sunrise structure provides more than an inert formal pattern for ordering the material. Using another classical strategy, Gardner animates this structure by posing a series of questions or enigmas that he hopes the viewers will be intrigued by and will therefore actively participate in allowing themselves to be carried forward to the next stage of the film. In narrative terms, *Forest of Bliss* develops by a process of slow disclosure, with each material component of the funeral procedures being introduced independently with, as it were, a question mark attached. Most of these are finally brought together in the scene in the hospice described previously, which occurs shortly before the midpoint of the film. Only one major component is missing, namely, the wood, but there is immediately a cut back to the lithe boatman, whom we have already seen a number of times before working his way upstream with a large load of logs destined for the funeral pyres.

Thereafter, the pace of proceedings picks up, and corpses on stretchers appear to converge on the Manikarnika cremation ground from all directions to the recurrent chant of "ram, nam, satya hai" sung in a variety of speeds and styles. However, there is still considerable delay before we finally see a cremation, though we see everything associated with it: we see wood being stacked, weighed, and thrown down to the cremation ground; we see smoking pyres; we see women, a young boy, and a dog picking among charred embers; and we see stretchers of corpses being washed in the river and lined up awaiting treatment where a cow nibbles tentatively at them (hinting here at yet another theme in the film, namely, that of "organic circularity"). We see lamenting mourners from a distance and a close-up of the doleful expression of a water buffalo whose symbolic role in this film appears to be to epitomize melancholy.

Even when the chief mourner takes a smoldering straw torch from the Dom Raja's hearth and walks down toward the cremation ground, we are not immediately vouchsafed a clear view of the cremation itself. Instead, there is a very long shot, taken from a boat of the kind used for hauling the firewood, now empty and almost imperceptibly pitching off-shore. The empty boat itself takes up most of the image, while the chief mourner is barely visible among a knot of other mourners at the top right of frame. Here he circumambulates a pyre with the now-flaming torch and then finally sets light to it. The sound track is rather muted compared to the previous tumult of chanting, but there is a low howling of dogs, the ever-present acoustic markers of the frontier between life and death.

Gardner explains that throughout the editing, he was dubious about whether he would use this shot but finally decided to do so because it pulls together a number of threads:

> Now, I don't know whether this really works, but it certainly contains all the elements I was looking for: namely, the boat, the river, the fire, and a soul being dispatched. The boat seems to be waiting on the shore for the crossing. It's a kind of summary shot which, if inspected at all carefully, contains a tremendous amount of information. (Gardner and Östör 2001, 106)

Even then, remarkably, we still do not cut back straight to the pyre. In between there are two shots, first of a water pipe emptying into the river and then of a boy drinking from it. These shots, Östör points out, are there to remind the viewer that in Benares the ordinary is combined with the extraordinary. But the sound of the splashing water runs into the crackling of a fire, and we at last see a close-up of a shrouded head licked by flames at what is almost exactly the three-quarters point of the 89-minute film.

Gardner says that he found this part of the film more difficult to cut than any other. Even while shooting, it had occurred to him repeatedly that he should avoid "simply documenting cremation." He felt that he had an obligation to preserve the dignity of the corpses while at the same time making the subject of death itself interesting. He was convinced that simply showing a long shot of a burning body would be "pretty tedious" and was not therefore the way to achieve his objective (Gardner and Östör 2001, 95). So now, having finally arrived at the culmination of the event toward which the whole film has been moving up until that moment, he quickly withdraws. After a single shot of the burning corpse, he returns briefly to the mourners lamenting and to the Dom Raja counting his money as the pathetic material goods left by one of his clients are kicked into the dust. Then he wraps up the whole sequence with a montage of the later stages of the cremation, moving very quickly over some of the more grisly moments, such as when the skull is smashed to release the spirit and the brains fall out.

It is evident that Östör is not entirely happy with this very brief treatment, and he expresses surprise since Gardner had been so uncompromising in showing corpses in the river earlier in the film (Gardner and Östör 2001, 107). But there is a clear similarity here with the way in which Gardner treated the cremation of the boy killed in *Dead Birds* some 20 years previously: there too, although Gardner had been totally uncompromising in the buildup to the climax of the funeral, we do not actually see the corpse committed to the flames. Once it has been enclosed within the funeral pyre, the scene is elegantly and swiftly brought to an end. It is also highly characteristic of Gardner that he should not really be very interested in faithfully documenting the phenomenon of a dead body and its ritual processing per se but rather in interpreting their significance. As he puts it,

> The whole Manikarnika [cremation ground] episode in the film had to end in a way that resulted in some understanding and that also created some useful mystery. I worked a long time to get it to satisfy these two requirements. (Gardner and Östör 2001, 106)

If I understand Gardner's intentions correctly, these requirements are met not by the documentation of the cremation itself but by its juxtaposition with the shots immediately before and immediately following—that is, by the conjunction beforehand with, first, the shot from afar in the boat of the circumambulating mourner, suggesting tranquillity and the imminent dispatch of a soul; then with the shot of the boy drinking water, indicating the everyday nature of the event; next by the conjunction with the shots underlining the insignificance of the material possessions left behind; and finally and perhaps most important, with the serial montage of shots that follows the cremation ground sequence. This montage consists of a veritable flurry of metaphors of transition—birds descending to the river and alighting on driftwood, dogs circling one another, various boats now moving downstream from right to left, and, on the sound track, the ever-ambiguous tolling of bells and cawing cries of birds.

The final quarter of the film, covering the period from sunset to sunrise, is largely "redemptive," as Gardner terms it, intimating that life goes on, not despite death but in association with death since the two are connected cyclically. The continuation of life is represented in the children flying their kites and playing other games on the ghats, by a brief return to the marigold gardens and the theme of organic circularity, by the devotional ritual in a nearby temple, and eventually by a return to Ragul Pandit chanting at dawn. But in the midst of this predominantly life-affirming final quarter, there is a disturbing and ambiguous sequence in which the healer-trickster, apparently in trance, is shown chanting over a flaming pit. The section is also regularly punctuated by memento mori: by the burial of a child in the river, by the burning funeral pyres and the tolling of bells at night, by dogs on the shore at dawn, and by further boatloads of wood for the funeral pyres. Finally, in a classical editorial "bookend" of the kind also used, incidentally, in *Rivers of Sand,* the film returns to where it began, to the river with a boat disappearing into the mists to the sound of the grating rowlock ropes.

MEANING AND EXPERIENCE

Through the gradual, unrelenting, almost overwhelming accumulation and superimposition of symbolic juxtapositions, it seems that Gardner aspires to move the spectator of *Forest of Bliss,* in a manner analogous to the participant in a religious ritual, that is, without consciously understanding all the connections, toward the master tropes of Hindu eschatology: if opposites are necessarily connected as dogs are to marigolds, as birds in the sky are to wood on the river, and as day is to night; if bliss can exist amidst squalor; if the river

Ganges is both a place of pollution and of purification; if the fire of the funeral pyre both consumes and releases; if in life we are in death, then in death we are necessarily also in life, and the committing of the body or its ashes to the waters of the holy river is not just the end of a cycle but also a beginning.

It seems that Gardner intends this to be not so much a film *about* a rite of passage as *to be* a rite of passage. Through the narrative of the film, he aims to engage and carry the spectator down to the cremation ground to confront his or her own mortality. But then, having forced the spectator to look into the void, he offers the possibility of redemption in the form of Ragul Pandit:

> He will give the final benediction here at the end of the film, not just to the people who are in the shrine but, if it isn't too presumptuous, to everyone who is watching the film. People in the audience have been through a relatively unsparing account of some of life's fundamental issues, and they deserve it. (Gardner and Östör 2001, 115)

Gardner is clearly aiming, then, to communicate an experience, but the meaning that he offers of this experience is highly mediated through his own subjectivity. It is in this respect that both he and his critics consider that his work may be in conflict with the some of the foundational tenets of anthropology. Reflecting on the report that certain world-renouncing saddhus would go to the cremation grounds to lie down on the pyres in anticipation of their own immolation, even engaging in cannibalism to transgress beyond all social convention, he comments,

> I think that everybody who goes there is something of an apprentice saddhu, insofar as there is any living through these preoccupations. I don't see how you can escape it. And then the question is what happens to a film that is connected with or even driven by that concern, and I guess that's what we have here. I suppose I'm asking the usual question of how the non-fiction film can survive the presumed conflict between personal issues and informational or anthropological ones. (Gardner and Östör 2001, 97)

Providing an adequate or appropriate context of meaning is a problem that attends not only all forms of filmmaking in the name of anthropology but all forms of textual representation in anthropology as well. Here it is instructive to compare and contrast Gardner's way of dealing with this issue with the means employed by practitioners of observational cinema. The latter, while recognizing that subjectivity is the means by which one engages with the world and therefore necessarily integral to every act of representation, nevertheless seek to adopt what David MacDougall (1998b, 156) has called a "stance of humility" before the world, recognizing that the story that the subjects may wish to tell about that world may be both quite different and also more valuable than the story that the filmmaker has in mind.

Therefore, the making of an observational film, at least in the participatory variant of the form, typically consists of a process of dialogue and collaboration with the subjects. These subjects are usually idiosyncratic characters whose experiences of the world provide the guiding narrative thread of a film, while their interpretations of these experiences, usually presented verbally in sync and emerging from within the body of the action, often in interaction with the filmmaker, provide the principal framework of explanatory exegesis. In short, it is the meaning of the experience of the subjects' world to the subjects themselves that is typically the principal focus of interest in an observational film. In contrast, in Gardner's films, it is the meaning of the experience of the subjects' world to the filmmaker that is the most significant. In this particular regard, I would suggest that Gardner's sensibility is closer to that of an artist than it is to that of a mainstream social or cultural anthropologist.

The prominence given to the indigenous voice in observational cinema, both literally and metaphorically, is one of the main reasons why there is such a ready compatibility, I would argue, between this approach and that of many social anthropologists.[15] Conversely, it is the absence of this voice in Gardner's films that many anthropologists, including myself, find challenging. For while one might indeed acknowledge that recent developments in cognitive science have demonstrated the significance of nonlinguistic modes of cognition and that there are many "things that go without saying" about social and cultural life, it is another thing altogether to assert the principle that indigenous speech and indigenous exegesis of experience are of merely secondary or no importance.

It is in this connection that I have some considerable sympathy with Gardner's critics, particularly when they point out that the significance that he attributes to particular phenomena are sometimes not merely oversimplified but completely at variance with indigenous interpretations. Such would appear to be the case, for example, with Mithai Lal, the "healer" character in *Forest of Bliss* who appears to be more of a diviner than a healer and whose ministrations are concerned more with petty marital squabbles and minor illnesses than with major eschatological issues of life and death, as is suggested by his role in the film (see Parry 1988). Similar doubts about ethnographic accuracy or at least adequacy have also been expressed about a number of Gardner's other films (see, among others, Mishler 1985; Strecker 1988; Ruby 2000).

However, where I am entirely out of sympathy with Gardner's critics is when they suggest that in *Forest of Bliss,* he has simply "let the camera roll" and as a result has produced "a jumble of incomprehensible vignettes." Whatever reservations one might have concerning Gardner's particular interpretations or the accuracy of his ethnography, no one could justifiably deny that the material captured by his camera has been profoundly and imaginatively manipulated in the edit suite. On the contrary, as I hope my preceding analysis has shown, this film represents a bold attempt to offer an insight into the meaning of an exotic cultural reality by means of entirely nonverbal symbolism and the principle of metaphorical association. Of all people, one might have thought that anthropologists, well versed as they often are in the analysis of nonverbal ritual metaphors, would be well disposed to appreciate such an endeavor.

Yet, even while one might appreciate such an endeavor, one need not necessarily adopt Gardner's methods in every particular or for every subject matter. Rather than engage in either uncritical praise or uninformed criticism, all anthropologists interested in using film as an ethnographic medium for the communication of meaning and experience could only benefit from studying Gardner's remarkable works in depth in order to explore in what ways the techniques such as those so ingeniously deployed in *Forest of Bliss* could be adapted to meet their own particular objectives.

PAST AND FUTURE

Peter Loizos (1993, 139–40) has characterized Robert Gardner's work as "experimental" because he sees it as going beyond current realist orthodoxies. Yet, while it may be true that Gardner's work holds promise for the future in this sense, it also represents the continuation of an older tradition of documentary filmmaking largely displaced by the congeries of word-driven realist approaches based on portable synchronous sound technology that have developed since the 1950s. As both critics and admirers have pointed out, there is an echo in *Forest of Bliss* of the "city symphonies" of the 1920s and 1930s (see particularly MacDougall 2001, 72). Gardner himself established the connection between his own approach and that of an earlier generation of filmmakers even more directly in his obituary of Basil Wright, who died in 1987, not long after *Forest of Bliss* had been released. For, apart from the use of a structuring voice-over, Gardner's account of Wright's editorial technique in *Song of Ceylon* could almost be a description of his own technique in *Forest of Bliss*. This technique, he suggested, consisted of

> …making relationships through editing which were most courageous and amazing in the way new perceptions emerged from the actualities observed. It did not matter that these actualities were commonplaces. In fact, their humanity drew strength from the fact that this is what they were. I am reminded in this connection of the almost literally transporting spirituality he evoked in the Buddha segment…where stone, birds, air and water are joined to create an overwhelming atmosphere of holiness…when looked at assembled by such a masterful cutter…and hearing the tintinnabulation of those relentless bells guiding the senses into novel excitations, the effect is transfiguring. We are in his grip and we are changed forever. (Gardner 1988, 24)

So too is it with *Forest of Bliss*. For no one who has watched this film with an open mind can fail to be enchanted and transformed by it. By studying the works of the "masterful cutter" who made it, anthropologist filmmakers too may learn how to enchant and transform their audiences.

NOTES

1. A more critical perspective is offered by Jay Ruby (2000).
2. In this sense, my use of the word "technique" has connotations akin to those of the original Greek term *techne* as defined by the *Cambridge Dictionary of Philosophy:* "a human skill based on general principles and capable of being taught. In this sense, a manual craft such as carpentry is a *techne,* but so are sciences such as medicine and arithmetic" (Prior 1999, 904).

3. In the interview with Barbash, Gardner explains that the unusual camera angles that are such a notable feature of *Deep Hearts* were actually shot by the other cinematographer on the credits, Bob Fulton, a longtime friend and collaborator.

4. To the best of my knowledge, the only case of direct verbal address to the camera in Gardner's films is the monologue by Omali Inda, a senior Hamar woman, in the opening sequence of *Rivers of Sand*. A somewhat different instance is the interview with Gerardo Reichel-Dolmatoff that features in *Ika Hands,* though here the subject is not directly addressing the camera but is filmed slightly in profile, directing his remarks offscreen, presumably to Gardner.

5. This quote is an excerpt from material in the new version of *Dead Birds* on DVD, *Dead Birds* by Robert Gardner (film, 1961; DVD, ca. 2004), Film Study Center.

6. Although it was not published until 2001, the conversation was first recorded in 1987.

7. "I think you certainly can appreciate the possibility of carrying over the burden of meaning in one film to another," Gardner comments to Östör. "I can't help thinking of the shots in *Dead Birds.* Also, I suppose, if it looks good and it seems to work, I just will not pass up a chance to put a bird in a film. Birds, for me, are wonderfully cinematic" (Gardner and Östör 2001, 20).

8. There is also a rather different use of extradiegetic sound that occurs only once in the film. This occurs in a traveling shot of a ghat, ostensibly as seen from a passing wood-carrying boat on its way up to the cremation ground. As the camera travels along a line of washermen at work at the edge of the river, two donkeys appear very briefly and barely discernibly in the background. Their fleeting presence is marked by some determined braying, out of all proportion to their importance in the shot. Gardner explains that this braying (and, incidentally, a similar braying at the beginning of *Rivers of Sand*) represents a "gesture" to Luis Buñuel and the donkeys that featured so memorably in his films *Land without Bread* and *Un chien andalou* (Gardner and Östör 2001, 75). Gardner met Buñuel in person and was evidently much influenced by his views on filmmaking (see chapter 5 in this volume).

9. Gardner seems to have been influenced here by the comment made to him by one of his local production assistants, Baidyanath Saraswati, who said that when he was a child growing up in a rural village, whenever he heard the sound of mango trees being chopped down, he knew that a death had occurred (Gardner and Östör 2001, 25).

10. One alternative that did exist at the time was the one employed by Jean Rouch in the making of *Jaguar* and *Moi un Noir,* that is, to record the commentaries of the protagonists postsynchronously in reaction to the screening of a mute assembly. But Gardner has never used anything resembling this technique.

11. A possible exception here is *The Nuer* (1971), in which some individuals do speak and the content of what they say is translated in voice-over. However, although Gardner coproduced this film and is credited with "additional photography," he did not direct it (nor is it clear who edited it). This would account, I suspect, not just for this particular feature but also for the many other stylistic features of this film that are distinctly untypical of Gardner's work as a whole.

12. See Gardner and Östör's (2001, 68–70) discussion of this sequence. When Östör raises the issue of what the disposal of animals in the river means in terms of sanitation, Gardner acknowledges

that this is a serious problem that should be addressed. "But," he continues, "that was not what interested me at the time, nor does it today...my feeling is that the metaphysical stairs will always be there, even if dead donkeys are disposed of in the electric crematoria they were talking about getting."

13. The association was also clearly understood by Oppitz (1988, 211).

14. See his discussion of the film with Ross McElwee that is reproduced in the supplementary material offered as part of the "package" on the DVD release (2004).

15. This is a point that I have discussed at length in a recent article. See Henley (2004).

REFERENCES

Barbash, Ilisa, and Lucien Taylor. 1997. *Cross-cultural filmmaking: A handbook for making documentary and ethnographic films and videos.* Berkeley: University of California Press.

Chopra, Radikha. 1989. "Robert Gardner's *Forest of Bliss:* A review." *Society of Visual Anthropology Newsletter* 5 (1): 2–3.

Gardner, Robert. 1972. "On the making of *Dead Birds.*" In *The Dani of West Irian: An ethnographic companion to the film* Dead Birds, ed. Karl Heider and Robert Gardner, 31–35. New York: MSS Modular Publications.

———. 1988. "Obituary: Basil Wright." *Anthropology Today* 4 (1): 24.

Gardner, Robert, and Ákos Östör. 2001. *Making* Forest of Bliss: *Intention, circumstance, and chance in nonfiction film.* Cambridge, MA: Harvard University Press.

Hayward, Susan. 2000. *Cinema studies: The key concepts.* 2nd ed. London: Routledge.

Henley, Paul. 2004. "Putting film to work: Observational cinema as practical ethnography." In *Working images: Methods and media in ethnographic research,* ed. Sarah Pink, Laszlo Kurti, and Ana Isabel Afonso, 109–30. New York: Routledge.

Loizos, Peter. 1993. "Robert Gardner in Tahiti, or the rejection of realism." In *Innovation in ethnographic film: From innocence to self-consciousness 1955–1985,* 139–68. Manchester: Manchester University Press.

———. 1995. "Robert Gardner's *Rivers of Sand:* Toward a reappraisal." In *Fields of vision: Essays in film studies, visual anthropology, and photography,* ed. Leslie Devereaux and Roger Hillman, 311–25. Berkeley: University of California Press.

MacDougall, David. 1998a. "Visual anthropology and the ways of knowing." In *Transcultural cinema,* 61–92. Princeton, NJ: Princeton University Press.

———. 1998b. "Whose story is it?" In *Transcultural Cinema,* 150–64. Princeton, NJ: Princeton University Press.

———. 2001. "Gifts of circumstance." Review article of *Making* Forest of Bliss: *Intention, circumstance and chance in nonfiction film: A conversation between Robert Gardner and Ákos Östör.* Cambridge, MA: Harvard Film Archive. In *Visual Anthropology Review* 17 (1): 68–85.

Mishler, Craig. 1985. "Narrativity and metaphor in ethnographic film: A critique of Robert Gardner's *Dead Birds.*" *American Anthropologist* 87: 668–72.

Oppitz, Michael. 1988. "A day in the city of death. *Forest of Bliss* (by Robert Gardner)—A film review." *Anthropos* 83: 210–12.

Parry, Jonathan. 1988. "Comment on Robert Gardner's *Forest of Bliss,*" *Society for Visual Anthropology Newsletter* 4 (2): 4–7.

PRIOR, William J. 1999. "Techne." In *The Cambridge dictionary of philosophy,* 2nd ed., ed. Robert Audi, 904. Cambridge: Cambridge University Press.

REISZ, Karel, and Gavin Millar. 1999. *The technique of film editing.* 2nd ed. Oxford: British Academy of Film and Television Arts/Focal Press.

RUBY, Jay. 2000. *Picturing culture: Explorations of film and anthropology.* Chicago: University of Chicago Press.

STRECKER, Ivo. 1988. "Filming among the Hamar." *Visual Anthropology* 1 (3): 369–78.

3 THE BURDEN OF SYMBOLS
FILM AND REPRESENTATION IN INDIA

MARCUS BANKS

During the course of their conversation about the film *Forest of Bliss* (1985), Robert Gardner says to Ákos Östör, "Considering all the different ways it is seen or alluded to, it is obvious that water has a pretty extensive meaning [in the film] ... [but] I don't think that anything of the kind we have been discussing ever gets surfaced [*sic*] by people watching films. We are being very precise about our associations. The average viewer won't be" (Gardner and Östör 2001, 65). A similar concern with what symbolic allusions an audience will or will not grasp is expressed at several other points in their conversation. Although the comments pre-date much or all of the subsequent commentary on the film,[1] it is clear that Gardner, if not Östör, was well aware of the burden that he was placing on both the film itself and its viewers.

My concern in this chapter is not to provide yet another comment on *Forest of Bliss,* or even to comment on the numerous commentaries on the film, except in passing.[2] Rather, I wish to bring together two broad themes that discussion of the film—and others like it—have revolved around: the presence of a symbolic dimension within ethnographic film representation and the notion of India as a cultural system that is in whole or part "unknowable." In a rather arbitrary fashion and governed as much by my own research interests as anything else, I do this through a broad comparison of early (colonial) filmic representations of India from a variety of genres and postwar ethnographic filmic representations of India, with a particular emphasis on films concerned with religion and the realm of the spiritual more widely.

POETICS, THE EXPRESSIVE, AND THE UNKNOWN

From a realist point of view, Gardner's concern, cited previously, is a question of whether the audience will "get it." Throughout the conversation with Östör, he uses phrases such as "My intention was...," "I hope that...," and both men refer to particular episodes within *Forest of Bliss* where experience has shown that an audience has either "got it" or has not.[3] At an empirical level, the audience's ability to read the film correctly could be tested (and it has been in other contexts—see Martinez 1990), but as clearly neither Gardner nor Östör can have been present at every single screening of this or any other film, doubts would still remain. One possible solution, again from the realist perspective, would simply be to make the film—this film, any film—more direct, more transparent in its communication of meaning. Unfortunately, this solution is misguided for two reasons. First and more trivially, such action would reduce the film to the form of an illustrated lecture in which an authoritative "voice-of-god" narration describes and explains exactly what is going on while the images float vaguely in the background, mute in their attempt to present anything other than surface form. This does not seem to be a particularly productive use of the medium. Second and more seriously, there is almost no realm of human communication that is not symbolic as well as pragmatic.[4] The speech used in a voice-of-god narration carries symbolic associations in delivery (tone, accent) as well as in vocabulary, though these are doubtless unintentional at the time. More important for anthropologists, the unfolding action on the screen carries symbolic associations for those who perform it. This is true in the realm of the mundane—a harshly rather than a softly spoken word, a tender rather than an admonishing gesture—but is richly true in the realm of ritual and religion, a point to which I turn later.

While anthropology prides itself on privileging the symbolic dimension in human action (e.g., as opposed to behaviorism), this itself is the cause of an epistemological tension, one that is again manifest in the realm of the mundane but strongly in evidence in the overtly symbolic realms of religion and ritual. As Larsen (1992, 20) points out, "classical epistemology" (as seen within anthropology) holds that an object is known to a subject through its representation. A modernist notion of truth allows anthropologists to compare representations (ethnographic monographs, films) to the objective reality they represent and to judge them as more or less accurate (19). This was very much the case during the interwar and immediate postwar heyday of anthropology, especially British social anthropology. Debates concerning, say, the various representations of so-called Virgin birth beliefs among Melanesian peoples could be conducted along these lines (e.g., Leach 1966; Spiro 1968). An epistemological shift since then, however, has led to what Larsen calls an "aesthetic turn" in the discipline. The grand narratives and empiricist-realist bases of ethnography, within which the forensic, black-and-white claims of truth could be made have, for whatever reason, become weakened.[5] In their place have arisen critiques based on the representation itself, on the premise that there is no knowable reality, or at least no independent access to that reality, only the representation. This is not to advocate hyper-relativism, though these are indeed the premises on which hyperrelativism rests, or even to endorse a milder form of relativism. It is simply to acknowledge that this, by and large, is the current state of ethnographic reporting and reception within the discipline, one in which the anthropologist is concerned equally with the empirical reality she experiences in the field, her recognition that her observational activity is simultaneously a meaning-making activity, and her knowledge that meaning will be made by those that consume her representation. To that extent, documentary or nonfiction film has always had an ethnographic advantage over ethnographic writing since at least the time of Grierson's definition of documentary as "the creative treatment of actuality" (Hardy 1966, 11), a treatment that specifically invoked the poetic.[6] The recognition of the representational process in filmmaking is (almost) inevitable.

This much is acknowledged in much of the recent writing on documentary and ethnographic film; or, put another way, it would be difficult to find any scholar within the past 10 years or so who unambiguously endorsed a straightforward empiricist-realist approach to film of the kind advocated by Heider's classic monograph on the topic (Heider 1976). The question still remains as to how, once the aesthetic dimension and its entailed relativism are acknowledged, can one judge or assess ethnographic films? How do we deal with the burden of symbols they carry?

One strategy, mentioned more than once by Gardner and Östör in their conversation, is a form of loose phenomenology. Even if the audience of *Forest of Bliss* (or any other film intentionally deploying a symbolic mode) might not be able to comprehend all the intentional symbols in detail, the hope is that they would come away with a rough, cumulative sense of them. For example, of a scene in which cremation fires are being prepared, Gardner says, "The sound of wood falling on the ground is meant to refer back to the earlier [sound of] wood splitting. If not, then at least these new sounds make one that much more intimate with wood as a substance" (Gardner and Östör 2001, 84).[7] It is certainly true that this film, as with some others,[8] is extremely effective in communicating or transferring sensory experience: the sounds of wood being chopped and of oars creaking in rowlocks and the feeling of lightness and openness given by shots of circling birds and fluttering paper kites.[9]

Phenomenology alone, however, is not sufficient to allow us to deal effectively with the copresence in a film of both familiar and unfamiliar symbols. We need to go further, to understand the poetics of documentary, especially the poetics of the nonrealist ethnographic documentary. In seeking to outline a theory of documentary, Michael Renov (1993, 21) outlines a typology of four rhetorical or aesthetic functions manifest by documentary representation that constitute the poetics of documentary or nonfiction film[10] while acknowledging that they are not mutually exclusive and indeed may be in conflict with one another. Of the four—to record, to persuade, to analyze, to express—the one that is most relevant to a discussion of films with an overt symbolic content is that of expressiveness. Renov asserts that the expressive dimension in nonfiction film has, over the years, simultaneously been present yet denied or undervalued (32). It thus occupies the inverse analytical space to that of the realist epistemology identified by Larsen for ethnographic writing: while realist epistemology is constantly asserted yet constantly undermined, so the expressive is always present yet frequently denied. In both cases, as Renov notes, this is due to a persistent dichotomization between art and science, between truth and beauty.

An explicit recognition of and engagement with the expressive has been raised by a number of visual anthropologists and others in recent years, not least because it seems to offer some way out of the dilemma, a means of reconciling truth and beauty. Edwards (1997), for example, considers the work of a number of photographers whose work lies "beyond the boundary" of conventional anthropology. It lies "beyond" not merely because the creators are not professional anthropologists but because the images deal in subject matter that some anthropologists might consider to lie exclusively within their own territory, and hence there is a hint that some might find the work to be "beyond the pale." What renders the work problematic, at least from a realist perspective, is the explicit acknowledgment of an aesthetic dimension, the overt presence of the expressive. As Edwards notes, an aesthetic or expressive dimension is of course inevitable (58), and the issue then becomes one of what one does with this. The strategy that Edwards upholds for anthropological purposes and that she finds present in the work of certain photographers is one that "maintains the integrity of the subject matter" while allowing for revelatory potential, as opposed to self-conscious formalism and "*self*-expression" (58).

A striking and particularly cinematographic example of this is seen in the work of the Finnish photographer Jorma Puranen, discussed by Edwards (1997, 72–73). For the series "Imaginary Homecoming" (Puranen 1999), the photographer gathered a number of photographs of Sami people taken in 1884 for ethnological purposes and then either superimposed them onto contemporary images of his own making or had them printed on to Plexiglas panels that he then photographed. The intention in both cases was to reinsert the long-dead Sami people back into the landscapes of the north from which they had been existentially exiled. In one particularly arresting image, a barbed-wire fence cuts diagonally across an open landscape of low snow-scattered hills. Perpendicular to and transversing the fence is a line of Plexiglas panels bearing the ghostly imprints of Sami faces, the majority looking straight out to the viewer. The crosscutting lines of the compositional elements and the black-and-white landscape that constitutes the image content combine to give a dual perspective, a double exposure made solid, that collapses the Barthesian therethen, here-now distinction. Although the innocent viewer cannot know that the original

1884 images were made for ethnological purposes, anthropological viewers who do know this—or deduce it—are immediately forced to question the form and structure of anthropological knowledge. Puranen's images are not merely political slogans ("Sami land rights now!"), nor are they romantic-nostalgic gestures (bringing the Sami home at last). They are challenges to the epistemological premises of both past and current anthropological investigation. Puranen's images ask the anthropologist to consider the status of "scientific" knowledge as contexts shift and force us to consider the political aspect of such a shift (Renov 1993, 16–17).

In his printing onto transparent Plexiglas and darkroom superimpositions, Puranen's images—staged, contrived, manipulated—show a preoccupation with surfaces, a point taken up by Bill Nichols (1992) in a further endorsement of the anthropological potential of the expressive within visual representation. Taking a cue from Trinh T. Minh-ha, Nichols suggests that "perforating" the surface of things by the camera to extract underlying concepts and categories is a form of violence, not so much in a moral sense (Trinh's apparent objection) as in an epistemological sense (60). Like many others, Nichols advocates a phenomenological and experiential approach toward ethnographic film production but one grounded in a firm poetics. Drawing on MacDougall and his suggestion of "employing repetition, associative editing and non-narrative structures" (60), Nichols goes on to discuss a number of films that "step beyond" realist conventions, works that draw inspiration from beyond the boundary (69). While this might facilitate the communication of the "body-to-body" experience that Nichols and indeed MacDougall advocates, we remain in the phenomenological dilemma outlined previously: how can we be sure that the audience "gets it"? In addition, can we even be sure what the "it" of the embodied experience actually is?[11]

The dilemma becomes particularly acute when we move to consider the realms of symbolic communication and transcendent experience, areas where realist and materialist representations know their limitations, as it were. Realist representational strategies after all make no claims to presenting anything other than what is there to be observed or described. An image can show the viewer a temple and its furniture, and a written account can explain what the function of religious practice is in that society, but neither seeks to translate or interpret the experience of religious belief or transcendence.[12] Going beyond the boundary and invoking the expressive can indeed take us to these realms, but what do we find there? In the following sections, I wish to consider first some early and then some later filmic attempts to express religious belief and sentiment in the Indian context.

EARLY FILM VIEWS OF INDIA

Early and, indeed, later travelers in and scholars of India quite often did not "get it."[13] While some early continental commentators were happy to revel in the ineffable nature of Hindu thought, early British commentators, as Inden (1990, 90) notes, shone the harsh light of Enlightenment reason and rationality into Hindu thought allowing them to dismiss great tracts of thought, action, and experience as irrational, imagination-based fantasy.

Early visual representation of India shares much of this stance, as Pinney (1997, chap. 1) demonstrates in his work on official colonial photography, not so much by penetrating the surface of the symbolic and transcendent as by simply ignoring it for the most part.[14]

Something rather similar can be seen in early uses of the cine camera in India. Cinema came early to India in terms of both production and consumption. Lumière shorts were screened in Bombay in the summer of 1896, and the U.S. Vitograph company arrived with a program of its own at the start of the following year; locally made shorts were quickly added to the programs (Chabria 1994a, 4).[15] It was not long before both foreign and local filmmakers embarked on feature-length productions, both fictional and nonfictional. D. G. Phalke's *Raja Harishchandra* (1913), a mythological film, is generally credited as the first indigenous fiction feature, although only a fragment now survives, and is followed by his rich dramas about the young Lord Krishna, *Shree Krishna Janma* (1918) and *Kaliya Mardana* (1919). Among the many foreign fiction productions, both Franz Osten's *Light of Asia* (1926) and the amateur missionary production *The Catechist of Kil-Arni* (T. Gavan Duffy and R. S. Prakash, 1923) are notable for their length and ambition. Foreign amateurs had been filming in India well before these dates, of course, though the only substantial work before 1920 is probably the Dorsey Expedition film (Doctor Dorsey's Travel Pictures) *Native India* (1916), a documentary that runs for 27 minutes.

Gavan Duffy and R. S. Prakash's *The Catechist of Kil-Arni* (hereafter *Catechist*) is particularly distinctive. Shot with amateur actors from a village of untouchable Christian converts in Tamil Nadu, the film tells the story of two cholera epidemics several years apart. In the village touched by the first epidemic, all the villagers are Hindu. As the sickness falls, those who are still healthy run away from the village, all except Ram, a drunken reprobate who proceeds to loot the fleeing villagers' homes. Ram is caught and imprisoned but on his release four years later discovers that his orphaned children (his wife Sita had died in the outbreak) have been cared for by the Fathers and Sisters of the Catholic Mission. Impressed by their selfless charity, Ram asks to be baptized and is rechristened Joseph. His deep faith leads him to train as a catechist, although he is many years older than the other catechists in training. Once trained, he is sent to the village of Kil-Arni,[16] where he converts the villagers and settles down. After a few years, cholera strikes again, but this time the now Christian villagers stay to help those who are sick, in due course aided by the Fathers and Sisters from the Mission. Joseph's son, who has become a priest, celebrates Mass at the end of the outbreak, and the film closes with Joseph garlanded and kissing a Bible.

Produced at the suggestion of Mgr. McGlinchey of Boston, *Catechist* was intended as a fund-raising film for American Catholics (the film closes with an intertitle urging the viewers' charity to raise funds for further catechist training). Father Duffy enlisted the help of Raghupati Surya Prakash, "the pioneer director and cinematographer of the film industry in Madras" (Chabria 1994b, 44) and, as mentioned, enlisted local villagers to play the roles of Ram/Joseph, Sita, and the rest. The narrative—which is more intricate than the summary given here, with numerous subplots—is told through relatively static camera shots and explanatory intertitles. Although at one point during the second cholera outbreak statues of the Virgin Mary and another saint are paraded through the village, apparently in some kind of propitiatory gesture, the conversions of Ram/Joseph, his wife Sita (who is baptized on her deathbed during the first cholera outbreak), and the villagers of Kil-Arni happen remarkably quickly and with remarkably little fanfare. Obvious signs of religious belief or action are also few and far between. On the Christian side, along with the procession of the Virgin Mary, Joseph's son's first Mass after the second outbreak is featured; the scene in fact seems to be actuality rather than staged and is in long shot down the aisle to the alter. On the Hindu side, we see even less. During the first cholera outbreak, the villagers initially respond by burying a live suckling pig in the ground up to its neck and then dance and drum around it and leap over it in an apparently vain attempt to avert the sickness. Apart from the fact that drumming at funerals is one of the traditional occupations of southern Indian Untouchables (today known as Dalits), the scene appears to come from Duffy's imagination.

Joseph's conversion of the villagers of Kil-Arni begins with him wiping a sacred symbol from the forehead of an elephant. A minor scuffle ensues until Joseph (presumably) explains why he did this and in the space of moments has converted the villagers to his point of view. Of course, there was no perceived need for the American Catholic audience to be educated in the rituals and practices of Untouchable Hinduism, and the rituals and practices of Catholicism would have been familiar to them anyway. Nonetheless, for a film about religion, made by and for those who professed religion, the film is remarkably prosaic.[17]

Equally prosaic but in a very different way is Osten and Rai's *Light of Asia* (1926) (hereafter *Light*). Based on a poem by Edward Arnold, the film tells the story of the life of the Buddha and seems to have been shot in and around Jaipur in Rajasthan. Although sometimes seen as a foreign production, *Light* is really a collaboration. Osten, a German filmmaker, was conscripted by Rai, who had come to Munich in search of Western but specifically non-British (i.e., non-colonial) technical help in his desire to develop a strong local industry. Together they returned to India and began work on *Light*, the first of several collaborations (Schönfeld 1995).

In a technique presumably intended to draw Western viewers into the story, the film opens in the present day with a group of tourists visiting the major sites of northern India, eventually arriving in Bodh Gaya, where they wonder (their thoughts represented through title cards) what the significance of the place is. At this point, they encounter an old sage with flowing white beard who begins to tell the story of the Buddha. The film's closing scene returns to the tourists and the sage in the present as the sage concludes his account. In between, most of the story centers on the Buddha's early life in his father's palace and finishes with his first post-enlightenment sermon. For a film directly concerned with religious experience, the style is remarkably naturalistic and contrasts sharply with Phalke's wholly Indian religious dramas from the same period. Indeed, the opening title card claims (slightly inaccurately) that the actors—a troupe calling themselves "The Indian Players" and dedicated to a renaissance of Indian theater—used no props, studio sets, or lights in the making of the film. There are some non-naturalist scenes, however, created by post-production laboratory effects. The first instance is Gotama's father's dream at the time of his birth, in which ghostly superimposed images of an empty throne and a burning canopy appear to him, a prediction of the future in which Gotama will renounce his inheritance. The second instance is in two parts, both at the time of Gotama's decision to leave the palace and his wife. He wakes in the night and sees that he has two choices: to be a great king or to wander alone in search of truth. The choices are presented to the audience by title cards but also to Gotama. As he stares out of a window at the night sky, the words of the choices are written on cards painted with a backdrop of a stormy nightscape, almost as though the character of the film had stepped out of the frame and could see from the audience's perspective. Following this, an earlier scene of Gotama's wedding procession is repeated, this time in a vignette indicating the family life that Gotama will be rejecting.[18]

Some Indian critics are highly critical of *Light*. Chabria (1994b), for example, despite using the film's title for a 1994 retrospective of Indian silent cinema and its accompanying book, declared it to be "narrated as the western tourists would imagine [the story], and not as the Indian story teller would. Osten's claim that he had made the first specifically Indian film is throughout undercut by the all-pervasive orientalism and exoticising of India and Indians" (58). In some ways, quite the opposite seems to be the case—the film is relentlessly occidentalizing or at least universalizing, casting the "Eastern" story in plain, naturalistic terms. In the final scenes, as the Buddha delivers his first sermon, he appears as a nineteenth-century rationalized Christ delivering the Sermon on the Mount—essentially as a humanist ethicist whose divine linkages are underplayed. *Light* nonetheless has a very clear and largely consistent aesthetic, far more so than *Catechist,* which is muddled in its representational modes (some good acting, some poor acting, some staged mise-en-scène episodes, some actuality sequences). But as with *Catechist, Light* banalizes religion and renders it quotidian. For the filmmakers involved, the truths of Christianity and early Buddhism were presumably self-evident and required little or nothing in the way of cinematic work for them to be communicated. Even in analytical mode, the only surface penetrated is that of Untouchable Hinduism in *Catechist,* which reveals an emptiness within. *Light* hopes to engage with early Buddhism rather than penetrate it analytically but can do so only by rendering the Buddha in Western form.

Foreign-made documentaries and short actuality films of the period tend to engage even less with symbolic and transcendent imagery, however, and certainly have no truck with the expressive. Films made by travelers and others merely passing through India quite often concentrate on the architectural or historical detail of religious buildings rather than their spiritual purpose. For example, in one travelogue from 1913, a scene of the Jain temples in Calcutta (memorably evoked half a century later by Lévi-Strauss in *Tristes Tropiques* [1963]) is cut with the intertitle "the temple is inlaid with mosaic and colored glass in various designs," but nothing is said about the Jains or Jainism (*Picturesque India* or *In and about Calcutta* [1913]). Films made by those with more experience of the country and with an explicit or implicit moral or religious agenda can lapse into disparagement. Rosie

Newman's otherwise quite entertaining films from the 1930s, *Glimpses of India* (1936) and *Further Glimpses of India* (1936), contain some elements of explanation (e.g., a title card introducing a scene inside a Delhi mosque reads, "Those rags hung about a Mohammedan priest's tomb represent peoples' prayers which they hope will be granted") but also inaccuracies ("These monkeys are worshipped by the Hindoos" on a title card relating to a Durga temple in Banaras) and condescension (the title card accompanying a scene of pilgrims circumambulating a temple, also in Banaras, reads, in part, "... in even savage bosoms there are longings, yearnings, strivings for the good they comprehend not").

Alternatively, the surface of religious life is skidded across, carrying the viewer into another unrelated arena. For example, in Dorsey's 1916 *Expedition* film, mentioned previously, a scene of elephants carrying Hindu icons during a festival is immediately followed by a scene of the elephants forced to fight (for sport) in a palace compound (possibly in Udaipur, Rajasthan), in turn followed by scenes of a cheetah hunt in Hyderabad.[19]

INDIA, RELIGION, AND ETHNOGRAPHIC FILM

With one exception (Dorsey's *Native India* [1916]), none of the films discussed previously were made with any kind of anthropological purpose,[20] and very few were to be so over the next several decades. By the end of the 1930s, foreign-made travelogues and amateur fiction features begin to be displaced by more professional productions, often sponsored by the government of India, especially as World War II got underway. After the war, and more particularly after Indian Independence, foreign film production in the country was much more tightly controlled, as was indigenous documentary film production.[21] Films deemed to be offensive to independent India's self-image, such as Louis Malle's *L'Inde fantôme* (1969), only added to the climate of difficulty. Under Nehru's leadership, India had embarked on a secular and quasi-socialist political path for several decades during which the state constantly asserted that it knew best for its citizens. While there were many positive aspects to this—such as Indira Gandhi's call to "abolish poverty" in the early 1970s and the stress on economic self-reliance—there were also repressive aspects, culminating in the state of emergency in the mid-1970s, during which many civil rights were suspended. *L'Inde fantôme*, despite the international renown of its director, offended for several reasons but most notably in its depictions of poverty and of caste exploitation that, for Malle, undermined democracy. Whether accurate or not, these were not images that the Congress government wished to be seen.[22] Given the difficulties foreign camera crews had in filming in India, it is not surprising that it is not really until the early 1970s that one can identify self-designated ethnographic films shot by foreign visitors to India,[23] and it is to a sample of these that I now wish to turn, a sample specifically focused on films concerning religion.

One of the first films from this period to engage with matters of religion and spirituality is Gardner and Staal's *Altar of Fire* (1975). Seen against the rest of the Gardner film corpus, this is a curious piece. The film documents the re-creation of an ancient Vedic ritual in Kerala, southern India. Supposedly conducted by local Brahmans periodically for the past

3,000 years, the *agnicayana,* or fire sacrifice, is a long, complex, and highly technical rite that took 24 hours of film to document, cut down to a 45-minute film (Schechner 1981, cited in Winston 1995, 174). One of the problems with the film is an uneasiness as to whether this is a re-creation or a contemporary event. The principal consultant was Frits Staal, a historian of religion, not an anthropologist, and while the Brahman participants are obviously performing the rite "for real," little is shown or said that concerns their lives beyond the ritual. They are in a sense actors, paid to perform.[24] In one way, this accords well with more recent anthropological theories of ritual (e.g., Humphrey and Laidlaw 1994) that seek to resolve the tensions between ritual's "archetypal" qualities (a prescribed set of actions and behaviors not created by the performers) and the participants' agency and self-awareness of the actions they are performing. However, *Altar of Fire* offers little insight into the latter aspect, the self-awareness of the ritual participants. Toward the end of the film, when the large temporary shelter under which the ritual took place is set ablaze, the viewer has a slight sense of breaking the frame, as villagers who have presumably had nothing to do with the *agnicayana* ritual gather to watch what is undoubtedly a dramatic spectacle. For a moment, we the audience are in historical time at a specific location, not the nontime, nonplace of ritual.

Ten years later, Gardner is filming in India again, this time with Ákos Östör, his collaborator on *Forest of Bliss.* The trilogy of films under the "Pleasing God" series title were all filmed and produced by Gardner, but only one was directed by him. The difference shows. All three films were shot in the West Bengal town of Vishnupur, where Östör had previously conducted fieldwork. Two of the three films, *Loving Krishna* (1985) and *Serpent Mother* (1985), concern, respectively, Vaishnavite devotionalism centered on the person of the playful but essentially benign child Krishna, and the snake-handling rituals at the center of the cult of Manasha, the more ambiguous goddess of the earth. Manasha can be a terrifying and dangerous goddess but offers protection to her followers. By handling snakes, the followers play with this dual aspect of the goddess's nature.

In theory, this ambiguous tension (resulting in what the film's publicity blurb refers to as "at first glance, exotic and inexplicable behavior") ought to provide a filmic springboard into the expressive. Indeed, some of the scenes of the snake handlers caught up in the frenzy of their activities, their appearance of disconnection perhaps enhanced by the pain of the repeated bites they suffer (and indeed encourage), do offer fleeting insights into transcendence. The effect is heightened by Gardner's camera work: several sequences of the swaying cobra heads and the weaving motion of the handler's hand that "charms" them shot against the empty sky, indicating the divine orientation of the actions perhaps, and equally many similar sequences of snakes and hands in sharp focus against an out-of-focus crowded street scene, indicating social transcendence perhaps. At another point in the same festival (of Jhapan), Gardner films a sequence in which a clay vessel is prepared to act as a container of Manasha's divinity. Three times, in tight close-up, a hand containing a little water moves across the screen and deposits the drops next to the clay pot; the brief sequences, separated by cuts, are almost identical (on the fourth movement, the hand instead places a spray of jasmine flowers on the pot) and create a small moment of visual rhythm and repetition that echoes the repetitive singing and drumming on the sound track.

Such moments in the film are relatively rare, however, and Östör's own influence, at least as evidenced from his earlier publication on ritual activity in the town (Östör 1980), seems to militate against them.[25] Östör's published anthropological analysis is largely structuralist, and although he often mentions his desire (following David Schneider and also Dumont) to work within local categories (e.g., 10–15), this does not extend to any sustained attempt to engage with local experience. Indeed, for this form of analysis, the very faithfulness of conformity to local categories would preclude drawing on expressive allusion from without. Consequently, both *Loving Krishna* and *Serpent Mother* are constrained from the start by an exegetical commentary that, while giving verbatim chunks of myth and devotional prayer drawing on the kind of sources used by Östör in his earlier written work, is in large part devoted to rendering the behaviors observed comprehensible. The overall effect is to indicate verbally that there are realms of experience open to the participants but that the viewer must ultimately observe from without: the experience cannot be shared, nor is the possibility of common ground offered. The surface is forensically pierced, and the contents are examined.

The third film in the trilogy, *Sons of Shiva* (1985), while maintaining a clear stylistic and structural continuity with the other two, is nonetheless slightly different. It is also the only one of the three directed by Gardner (with Östör) as well as produced, shot, and edited by him. From the outset, we have the signature Gardner shots: open waterscapes and landscapes with tiny figures in the distance, walking legs shot from a low angle, short close-ups of hands engaged in intricate tasks. Formal composition abounds—a shot of the devotees' loincloths drying in the breeze, for example, where blocks of color ripple across the frame. Gardner is perhaps aided by the fact that there is a great deal more structured activity involved in the Shiva *gajan* (festival). All the male devotees featured in the film temporarily renounce their secular lives, setting aside caste and other worldly statuses, to become a brotherhood of ascetics. Consequently, they perform their religious work together as a group, dressed nearly identically, often performing the same ritual actions in coordinated fashion. This is in marked contrast to the snake handlers of *Serpent Mother* who, while showing their devotion to Manasha at the same time and in the same space, are essentially a cluster of individuals, none really paying attention to any other. It is possible to use filmic language to convey the transcendent experience of the individual—Gardner indeed does this very effectively three years later in sequences of Ika (Colombia) bead-and-water divination in *Ika Hands* (1988)—but the choreography of the collective lends itself well to a more poetic, aestheticized representation.

Ideas and symbols of transcendence—wide-open skies, repetitive ritual movement, images of order and symmetry—abound in *Sons of Shiva* and seem to chime with the experience of the devotees, who through their initial renunciatory rituals and ascetic practices must be highly self-conscious of their own devotional state. An extended slow-motion sequence evokes the temporary suspension of this self-consciousness, the devotees lost in a trance-dance during which some of them actually lose consciousness. There are also images of impermanence that hint not only at the impermanence of earthly existence but also at the transience of the devotees' ascetic state: water running through fingers, an open fire suddenly and violently torn apart by a devotee's hands and the ashes scattered. These actions happen, of course, as do the trance-dances, as do the orderly lines of devotees in prayer. What Gardner does is to invest them with symbolic significance through shooting and editing. One question to ask at this point, however, is: are we the audience of (presumably) non-devotees and the subjects of the film experiencing the same symbols in the same way?

To address this more fully, I want to consider a final film. Perhaps surprisingly to the reader, this is not Gardner's most well known (some would say notorious) Indian film, *Forest of Bliss* (1985). For one thing, the film is much discussed elsewhere. More particularly, while the film carries an obvious burden of symbolism and co-opts the expressive to draw the viewer beyond the empirical, it is, I think, relatively overt in its aim to convey a universal set of experiences rather than a locally particularistic one.

Jouko Aaltonen's *Kusum* (2000) seems to owe a debt to *Forest of Bliss,* not least in the use of enhanced and nonsync sound (on which see chapter 2 in this volume).[26] The film's narrative concerns the search by a Delhi rickshaw driver and his family to find a cure for his young daughter, Kusum, who is at times unable to swallow and is prone to fugue-like states. After an unsatisfactory encounter with practitioners of Western medicine, the family turns first to a local traditional healer and then finally to a well-known healer at a temple in Mehndipur, Rajasthan, famous through northern India for offering cures and relief for the supernaturally afflicted.[27] Much of the film is set at this temple, and as the events unfold, various other family members who have accompanied Kusum on her search for a cure also fall prey to spirit possession. As a whole, the film presents the events as a grand psychodrama in which the changing relationships between the family members structure the narrative. However, as a piece of theater, this drama appears to have two directors. The first is Aaltonen himself, of course; through the use of highly saturated color, non-sync sound, and non-chronological editing, Aaltonen orchestrates the images into a coherent yet strongly non-naturalist whole. The girl Kusum is the central character for this director, a still, passive, and largely silent center around which the other characters revolve. Kusum has unusually large, liquid eyes, and the camera stares into these often, drawing the viewer into contemplating her inner state. The crackling sound of fire, which Kusum says she feels within, often accompanies such contemplative moments.

The other director of the action is Bhagatji, Kusum's healer at the Mehndipur temple.[28] A dark, brooding, and clearly charismatic man, he orchestrates events at the temple and through his female medium addresses not just the human participants but also the spirits that reside within them. Just as Aaltonen edits and manipulates his material, so Bhagatji "edits" and rearranges the social and spiritual relationships of those around him. There is no central character in Bhagatji's drama, just a field of action that he manipulates through ritual form. Bhagatji holds a *darbar* (a royal court) at the temple once a month. Spirits are brought into the court through the medium, who acts as a mouthpiece for them. They are then chastised or exorcised by Bhagatji, who, with the power of Balaji (Hanuman), the temple's powerful deity, behind him, remains unpossessed and in complete control throughout.

Aaltonen's film manages to contain both sets of directorial intentions and actions. The film's expressive dimension is not external to the understanding of the film subjects but is derived from them, not so much from their life in the mundane world as from their experiences beyond it. Of course, an audience cannot know that the afflicted experience the world of possession in hypersaturated color, for example, but through the film the audience comes to know that the supernaturally afflicted somatize unusual sensory experience, for which hypersaturated color seems to be as good a symbol as any. Equally, an audience knows from the film that Bhagatji choreographs the afflicted and their kin in a dance of encounters and separations—with himself, with one another, with the spirits. This dance can be—and to some extent is—presented in a realist fashion in the film in the sense that the audience hears the words, notes the gestures, and observes the response. Yet, although there are points in the film in which Bhagatji does this verbally and explicitly, at other points there is only silence. In one scene, for example, Bhagatji and Kusum's father sit silently on a rooftop. The father seems to be meditating or maybe just lost in thought while Bhagatji leans casually back in a chair, observing him. Not a word is spoken, yet in the narrative structure of the film, this is the point at which Bhagatji wrestles the father for control of his daughter and wins. *Kusum* thus succeeds in marrying an aesthetic expression of image and sound/silence with an equally aestheticized (in the sense of value creating—see Morphy 1994) local experience of spirituality.

CONCLUSION

The films I discussed from the early part of the twentieth century generally failed to address Indian religious experience; within their admittedly unsociological framework of inquiry, these films perfunctorily penetrated the surface of symbol or experience and cursorily analyzed the contents. The more anthropologically informed films from the latter part of the twentieth century engaged more seriously with religion, ritual, and symbol, sometimes through analytical mode but increasingly by evoking the expressive. As the "aesthetic turn" became more widespread in ethnographic writing—or at least in writing about writing—so filmmakers involved in the production of films generally categorized as ethnographic[29] could come out of the closet, so to speak; they could become more explicit and more bold in their aesthetic adventures. Films about India, however, prove particularly difficult in this respect, especially when they deal with the transcendent. Films "about" religion face the same problems whatever society they deal with, but as mentioned previously, India seems to pose a particularly intractable problem. The history of British and other foreign observers' failure to "get" India, particularly Indian religion, while at the same time persistently meddling in its affairs and probing into its culture and society provides a particularly dense backdrop to all nonfiction filmic endeavors there.

At the beginning of this chapter, I outlined an approach toward the poetics of nonfiction film, one that saw the expressive dimension as more than merely aesthetic self-indulgence on the part of the filmmaker but that instead could derive from or echo the society or culture depicted and help effect an engagement with—rather than merely an analysis of—that society or culture. This is many ways is similar to MacDougall's (1999) idea of a "social aesthetics" or what he otherwise calls the "range of culturally patterned sensory experience" (5; reprinted in MacDougall 2005). This is a universal quality, of course, found in all societies at all times, though some may be more attuned to it and self-aware than others—MacDougall (1999, 6) cites Japan and Bali—and it is particularly evident in small, self-contained social environments, such as boarding schools. Religious groups and communities of believers would also seem to be ideal loci not merely for a study of social aesthetics but also for letting their social aesthetic inform representations made of them and their experiences. If, as Firth (1996, 10, 50, and passim) argues, religion is best understood humanistically as an art—a creative response to the human condition that itself produces art—then the justification for an aestheticized filmic response to religious experience seems self-evident. The "problem" of depicting Indian spirituality then dissolves. It is precisely those films that do not simply seek to explain or analyze that work best in this capacity. Films such as *Catechist,* or *Light of Asia* are unsatisfactory not because they do not analyze sufficiently but precisely because they seek to analyze at all, however shallowly. *Altar of Fire* and, more particularly, the "Pleasing God" series (particularly *Sons of Shiva*) represent a moment in ethnographic film history when the need to draw on the expressive comes up against the naturalist and explanatory. By the time of *Forest of Bliss* and *Kusum,* the shift to the expressive is complete. Hinduism is not a mysterious essence, a jungle of

luxuriant plants, or a sponge, as characterized by earlier observers (Inden 1990, 87), nor is it an error, easily reducible by post-Enlightenment rationalization to a set of philosophical practices overlain with folk superstition and pragmatism. For filmmakers like Robert Gardner, it is, like all other religious forms, an art, a mode of creativity, best represented by an equally creative venture.

When talking about *Forest of Bliss,* Gardner and Östör worried whether the audience would "get it." They need not have worried. What they and other recent filmmakers have done is present an expressive and creative response to an aesthetic system. The deployment of symbols as an introduction of the expressive by the filmmakers and the manifestation of symbols in the speech and action of the film's subjects are necessary aspects of this response but not burdens to be shouldered. The symbols are rather a means to an end, a challenge to anthropological and other epistemologies of knowing. As Östör notes, anthropologists can write about these issues or about the relationship between images and words (Gardner and Östör 2001, 81), but only films like Gardner's can present them as a form of experience.

NOTES

1. Although the transcript was published in 2001 and thus postdates the flurry of articles surrounding the film, the conversation took place in April 1997 (Gardner and Östör 2001, 6), and Östör claims to have made only "minimal" changes to the text (7).

2. I have commented on the commentaries elsewhere (Banks 2001, 18–22).

3. Not "getting it" can operate at a fairly crude level, far removed from associative chains of symbols. For example, in one sequence a dying woman being ministered to by a ritual specialist moves her hands in a fluttering fashion. Apparently, some viewers had interpreted this as a gesture of rejection of the ministrations—"That is amazing," comments Gardner, "I wouldn't have thought for a moment that someone could come up with the idea that she is trying to ward off something. It seems so unmistakably welcoming as a gesture" (Gardner and Östör 2001, 63).

4. The exceptions to symbolic-as-well-as-pragmatic communication would include involuntary body responses to communicative acts of others, such as being unable not to turn around when someone taps your shoulder to get your attention. Nonetheless, most of us, most of the time, simply experience life—and our interactions with one another—rather than interrogate each encounter for meaning.

5. Setting aside those anthropologists and others who insist that this ("postmodernity" for want of a better word) is no more than a passing fashion, there are disagreements as to when the shift actually took place. Larson (1992, 21) seems to think the criticism of classical epistemology in anthropology has been present "since Boas," that is, since the start of the twentieth century. Others date it to the publication of Asad's (1973) collection *Anthropology and the Colonial Encounter,* Geertz's (1975) essay on the Balinese cockfight, or Clifford and Marcus's (1986) collection *Writing Culture.* A critical strain against the fixity of subject, object, and representation has probably always been present but refashioned by each generation.

6. In truth, we can go back further to Vertov or further back again to 1898 and the Cambridge Torres Strait expedition, where we find Alfred Haddon sitting up one night making ritual masks out of cardboard and crayons, to be used by the Islanders in a dance that he will film the next day, the original masks having been destroyed earlier under Christian missionary influence. Haddon's brief film did not treat actuality poetically, but he had already intervened in the real prior to filming (Griffiths 2002, 138)

7. To be fair, at various points in their discussion, Gardner also explicitly references aspects of the film's symbolism that are deliberately posed as puzzles for viewers, to be resolved later in the film. One good example is the sound of wood being chopped early in the film, with no visual reference (Gardner and Östör 2001, 25).

8. Within the context of religious experience in India, see, for example, Pankaj Butalia's *Salvation* (1993) on the lives of Hindu widows in Vrindavan, West Bengal, effectively incarcerated by their families in religious institutions, or Nilita Vachani's *Eyes of Stone* (1990) on gender and spirit possession in Rajasthan.

9. David MacDougall (1998, chap.1) makes a more explicit investigation into (ethnographic) film's phenomenological capacities, with specific reference to the body (see also MacDougall 2005). Drawing on Merleau-Ponty and others, MacDougall argues that what holds our attention and permits identification with the film subject is not the mere visibility of the body but the vitality of those bodies, the "quickness" as he terms it (as in the phrases "the quick and the dead" or "cutting to the quick"). This experience of and therefore empathy with quickness is not primarily visual but synesthetic—as Merleau-Ponty (1992) says, "The senses are different openings to the world that co-operate as a *unified system* of access. The lived-body does not have senses. It is, rather, sensible. It is, from the first, a perceptive body" (77). Following this, MacDougall argues that we-the-audience make contact with film-subject-others via the camera as a probe, not by a quasi-linguistic understanding of meaning but by a process of bodily mimesis, or what Merleau-Ponty calls "a postural schema," in a double synchrony with both the film-subject and the filmmaker, whose own embodied "quickness" is already present on the screen. For MacDougall (1998), filming other people "celebrates the common experience of consciousness, including the very differences between us" (55). These differences may, of course, be negatively evaluated though still experienced bodily: Nichols (1992, 56) cites Tambs-Lyche's account of the Norwegian students who vomited when shown Harris and Breidenbach's *The Nuer* (1970).

10. Gardner prefers the term "nonfiction film" to documentary, and indeed in much writing on this film form there is a great deal of slippage between "documentary" in the Griersonian sense and Renov's identified tendency of "record[ing]" and "reveal[ing]."

11. Of course, it is in the nature of haptic experience that it cannot be spoken of directly but only felt. I am grateful to Lucien Taylor for pointing this out.

12. There is, of course, plenty of anthropological and other writing on what symbols mean and indeed on religious experience. My point, however, is that such texts do not aim for a

phenomenological identification on the part of the reader, merely an intellectual apprehension. Writing and images produced by devotees or those who have experienced the transcendent, of course, do seek to communicate in this way, but then these are not generally intended to be analytical.

13. See, for example, Inden (1990) for scholarship on India generally or Mitter (1992) for responses to Indian art, including religious art. More accurately, Inden's thesis is that early scholars of Indian society and culture certainly "got it" in the sense that they constructed an image of India that was comprehensible to them; his point is that these images say more about how Europe thinks about itself than how India really is or was.

14. As Pinney (1997, 91) goes on to demonstrate, some Indian uses of photography at the time did seek to get beyond the surface, not by piercing it but by letting the surface itself act as a trace of a much larger project that could not be contained within the frame. Although dismissive of some claims that Indian photography is a direct successor to earlier painting styles and can thus reveal an authentic Indian visuality, Pinney acknowledges that in both the colonial and the post-independence periods, some forms of Indian photography do reveal an attempt to harness the technology to refashion a personal and perhaps collective sense of self. Indian photography seeks not to summarize or categorize the self but rather to extend it into other arenas (see also Pinney 1992).

15. As far as I am aware, none of these locally made shorts survive or have been identified as such. The Indian National Film and Television Archive holds an unidentified fragment apparently shot from a boat traveling down the Hoogly River in Calcutta dated to 1899. The British National Film and Television Archive holds a similarly unidentified fragment (Indian Procession) that may have been shot at the 1903 Delhi Durbar in the presence of the Duke and Duchess of Connaught; the Archive also holds a Walturdaw fragment (Native Street in India) from 1906. Any or all of these might have been shot for and exhibited as part of these commercial programs.

16. The village name is spelled this way on title cards throughout the film. Apparently, there really was a village of this name—or something approximate—nearby, and the name was selected because of its similarity to Irish place-names and therefore appealing to the intended audience of Boston Irish Catholics (Chabria 1994b: 45).

17. A feature documentary shot for the Salvation Army two years later is equally prosaic (Salvation Army work in India, Burma and Ceylon 1925, 62 minutes, National Film and Television Archive). Only in the final reel is there any sense of emotion or engagement, in a shot where a young girl is persuaded to give up her bracelets and jewelry as a renunciation of worldliness but is clearly unhappy about doing so.

18. There is also one instance of a nonnaturalistic production effect when flowers fall "from heaven" (i.e., from above the camera) onto Gotama's mother as she dies after giving birth.

19. That is to say, a hunt where a previously captured cheetah is the hunter, not the quarry, continuing the slippage into the mundane. The next scene is of a tiger hunt—a popular scene in amateur films of the period made by the British elite—where, of course, the tiger is the quarry.

20. The opening title card to *Native India* states that Dorsey was a curator of anthropology at the Field Museum, Chicago.

21. Briefly, official documentary film production came first under the control of the Film Advisory Board (Central Office of Information) and then after independence under the Films Division (Ministry of Information) and in both cases was strongly influenced by the Griersonian tradition (Mohan 1990; Ray 1991). Access to stock and materials was difficult for those not working through official channels until the 1970s.

22. While generally received positively outside India, some nonetheless saw *L'Inde fantôme* as a cop-out, as insufficiently political and critical (e.g., Gitlin 1988).

23. See, for example, the Contemporary South Asia Film Series produced at the University of Wisconsin in the 1970s under the project directorship of Joseph Elder. Ethnographic film in general cannot be easily identified as a category much before this date either (Loizos 1993). Anthropologists from Haddon on had film cameras in the field well before this, but the self-conscious impetus to make an ethnographic film—as opposed to recording footage for ethnological purposes—is a relatively late development.

24. As far as I know, Staal and Gardner did not pay the *agnicayana* ritual participants any kind of wage as such; they did, however, fund the high costs of the ritual itself. Some, such as Richard Schechner (cited in Winston 1995, 174), seem to see this as a problem, but to do so ignores the fact that anthropologists quite frequently contribute to the cost of expensive ritual activities and compensate their informants for their time in a variety of ways. More significantly, the objection indicates an adherence to a realist observational mode as the ideal for ethnographic film, one in which the camera mutely and passively records spontaneously occurring action and in which the filmmakers themselves adopt a strictly hands-off approach.

25. I have no privileged information on the respective contributions of Gardner and Östör—or indeed Allen Moore, the third contributor—and perhaps my presumption of Östör's analytical influence is overextended. Nevertheless, Östör seems to allow Gardner much more freedom in the shooting and editing of *Forest of Bliss*. For example, Gardner suggests at one point in their conversation that there is "a fair amount of [anthropology] stored away in nearly all the images we've seen," a point with which Östör agrees, but he indicates that writing would the medium with which to convey it (Gardner and Östör 2001, 81).

26. Aaltonen studied social science at university and co-founded a documentary production company with the Finnish anthropologist Heimo Lappalainen. Antti Pakaslahti, a Finnish psychiatrist who acted as academic consultant for the film, has extensive research experience of spirit possession and mental illness in India. My reading of the film is indebted to background research and analysis conducted by a former Oxford visual anthropology student, Hugo Whately.

27. The famous Balaji temple is not in fact identified by name in the film, nor is its location or even proximity to Delhi made particularly clear. Aaltonen, however, confirmed to Whately in a personal communication that this was the location and indicated that he had drawn some of his understanding from Sudhir Kakar's (1982) ethnopsychological research there. A more recent

ethnography by Graham Dwyer (2003)—but based on fieldwork conducted a decade earlier—provides a great deal of material about the temple and its rituals and offers a critique of Kakar's approach.

28. A *bhagat* is a type of healer, the suffix *- ji* being an honorific, but this man is known by this title to his clients and in the film. For details of his life and work, see Dwyer (2003, 128 ff.).

29. The reason for this rather awkward turn of phrase is that by some criteria there are few if any ethnographic filmmakers. There are, however, sufficiently large numbers of arenas devoted to the screening and discussion of ethnographic film (festivals, journals, instructional screenings) that this particular category of nonfiction film exists in a nominal sense whether or not the makers of such films consider themselves to be ethnographic filmmakers or their intentions informed by the academic discipline of anthropology (see also note 21).

REFERENCES

ASAD, Talal, ed. 1973. *Anthropology and the colonial encounter.* London: Ithaca Press.

BANKS, Marcus. 2001. *Visual methods in social research.* London: Sage Publications.

CHABRIA, Suresh. 1994a. "Before our eyes: A short history of India's silent cinema." In *Light of Asia: Indian silent cinema 1912–1934,* ed. S. Chabria and P. Cherchi Usai, 3–24. New Delhi: Wiley Eastern.

———. 1994b. "Notes on the Indian silent cinema retrospective, Pordenone, 1994." In *Light of Asia: Indian silent cinema 1912–1934,* ed. S. Chabria and P. Cherchi Usai, 41–66. New Delhi: Wiley Eastern.

CLIFFORD, James, and George E. Marcus, eds. 1986. *Writing culture: The poetics and politics of ethnography.* Berkeley: University of California Press.

DWYER, Graham. 2003. *The Divine and the demonic: Supernatural affliction and its treatment in North India.* London: Routledge Curzon.

EDWARDS, Elizabeth. 1997. "Beyond the boundary: A consideration of the expressive in photography and anthropology." In *Rethinking visual anthropology,* ed. M. Banks and H. Morphy, 53–80. London: Yale University Press.

FIRTH, Raymond. 1996. *Religion: A humanist interpretation.* London: Routledge.

GARDNER, Robert, and Ákos Östör. 2001. *Making* Forest of Bliss: *Intention, circumstance, and chance in nonfiction film.* Cambridge, MA: Harvard University Press.

GEERTZ, Clifford. 1975. "Deep play: Notes on the Balinese cock-fight." In *The interpretation of cultures,* 412–53. London: Hutchinson.

GITLIN, Todd [1974] 1988. "Phantom India." In *New challenges for documentary,* ed. A. Rosenthal, 536–41. Berkeley: University of California Press.

GRIFFITHS, Alison. 2002. *Wondrous difference: Cinema, anthropology, and turn-of-the-century visual culture.* New York: Columbia University Press.

HARDY, Forsyth. 1966. *Grierson on documentary.* London: Faber and Faber.

HEIDER, Karl. 1976. *Ethnographic film.* Austin: University of Texas Press.

HUMPHREY, Caroline, and James Laidlaw. 1994. *The archetypal actions of ritual: A theory of ritual illustrated by the Jain rite of worship.* Oxford: Clarendon Press and Oxford University Press.

INDEN, Ronald. 1990. *Imagining India.* Oxford: Basil Blackwell.

KAKAR, Sudhir. 1982. *Shamans, mystics and doctors: A psychological inquiry into India and its healing traditions.* Delhi: Oxford University Press.

LARSEN, Tord. 1992. "The aesthetic turn." In *Ethnographic film aesthetics and narrative traditions,* ed. P. Crawford and J. Simonsen, 17–24. Aarhus: Intervention Press.

LEACH, Edmund. 1966. "Virgin birth." *Proceedings of the Royal Anthropological Institute* 1966: 39–49.

LÉVI-STRAUSS, Claude. 1963. *Tristes tropiques: An anthropological study of primitive societies in Brazil.* New York: Atheneum.

LOIZOS, Peter. 1993. *Innovation in ethnographic film: From innocence to self-consciousness, 1955–1985.* Manchester: Manchester University Press.

MACDOUGALL, David. 1998. "The fate of the cinema subject." In *Transcultural cinema,* 25–60. Princeton, NJ: Princeton University Press.

———. 1999. "Social aesthetics and the Doon school." *Visual Anthropology Review* 15 (1): 3–20.

———. 2005. *The corporeal image: Film, ethnography, and the senses.* Princeton, NJ: Princeton University Press.

MARTINEZ, Wilton. 1990. "Critical studies and visual anthropology: Aberrant vs. anticipated readings of ethnographic film." *CVA Review,* spring, 34–47.

MERLEAU-PONTY, Maurice. 1992. *Phenomenology of perception,* trans. Colin Smith. London: Routledge and Kegan Paul.

MITTER, Partha. 1992. *Much maligned monsters: A history of European reactions to Indian art.* Chicago: University of Chicago Press.

MOHAN, Jag. 1990. *Documentary films and Indian awakening.* New Delhi: Ministry of Information and Broadcasting, Publications Division.

MORPHY, Howard. 1994. "The anthropology of art." In *Companion encyclopedia of anthropology: Humanity, culture and social life,* ed. T. Ingold, 648–85. London: Routledge.

NICHOLS, Bill. 1992. "The ethnographer's tale." In *Ethnographic film aesthetics and narrative traditions,* ed. P. Crawford and J. Simonsen, 43–74. Aarhus: Intervention Press.

ÖSTÖR, Ákos. 1980. *The play of the gods: Locality, ideology, structure, and time in the festivals of a Bengali town.* Chicago: University of Chicago Press.

PINNEY, Christopher. 1992. "Montage, doubling and the mouth of God." In *Ethnographic film aesthetics and narrative traditions,* ed. P. Crawford and J. Simonsen, 77–105. Aarhus: Intervention Press.

———. 1997. *Camera Indica: The social life of Indian photographs.* London: Reaktion Books.

PURANEN, Jorma. 1999. *Imaginary homecoming.* Oulu: Pohjoinen.

RAY, Mriganka Sekhar. 1991. "Social documentary in India—An overview." In *The short film scene in India,* ed. P. Maitra, 1–7. Calcutta: Nandan Publications, West Bengal Film Centre.

RENOV, Michael. 1993. "Toward a poetics of documentary." In *Theorizing documentary,* ed. M. Renov, 12–36. New York: Routledge.

SCHECHNER, Richard. 1981. "Restoration of behaviour." *Studies in Visual Communication* 7 (3): 2–45.

SCHÖNFELD, Carl-Erdmann. 1995. "Franz Osten's *The Light of Asia* (1926): A German-Indian film of Prince Buddha." *Historical Journal of Film, Radio and Television* 15 (4): 555–61.

SPIRO, Melford E. 1968. "Virgin birth, parthenogenesis, and physiological paternity: An essay in cultural interpretation." *Man,* n.s., 3: 243–61.

WINSTON, Brian. 1995. *Claiming the real: The documentary film revisited.* London: British Film Institute.

4   GARDNER'S FIRST SHOTS
VECTORED LANDSCAPES

KARL G. HEIDER

> There is an enormous amount to be said about something as singularly important as the
> first shot of a film.
>
> —Gardner and Östör (2001, 16)

Thus Robert Gardner begins his discussion with Ákos Östör in their illuminating book-long explanation of Gardner's 1985 film *Forest of Bliss.* In this chapter, I take up Gardner's implicit invitation to examine his own first shots. We will see that, generally, he uses these opening shots to set the stage in complex ways. They can be characterized as establishing landscapes, physical and symbolic. Then, for contrast, I compare them with first shots in other ethnographic films, films that use a different sort of opening shot.

In their book *Making Forest of Bliss,* Gardner and Östör have produced a unique document. I can think of no other instance of a filmmaker and ethnographer exploring in such detail their own collaborative intentions in making an ethnographic film. They go through *Forest of Bliss* shot by shot, Gardner explaining, Östör adding comments, and often finding that they disagreed about what was going on. Even for someone who is quite familiar with Gardner's ethnographic films, there are many revelations. For example, we learn the extent to which Gardner deliberately makes visual references to Greek myths, to his own earlier films, and to classic films of Buñuel and others. In a sense, this book was necessary because the film, at first viewing, strikes most people as deliberately obscure. Where Gardner's earlier films, like *Dead Birds* (1963), had a dense ethnographic narration, designed to bring the viewer along toward Gardner's understanding of that culture, *Forest of Bliss* has no narration, and the only English at all is an enigmatic epigraph from Yeats: "Everything in this world is either eater or eaten, the seed is food and fire is the eater." But even this is more allusive than revealing. Gardner's position throughout the book is one of expectation that the astute viewer would grasp his visual and aural allusions, at least on a subconscious level.

The first shot of *Forest of Bliss* shows a dog trotting along a featureless sandy plain. Gardner explains that this is "the far shore," across the Ganges River from Benares (Varanasi) (Gardner and Östör 2001, 16). During his several visits to Benares before he began shooting, he had been developing his ideas about the city. This other shore gave him a sense of "a quite forbidding mystery" (16). In fact, here the "first shot" really includes the first 11 shots, which form a sort of prologue to the film before the title and credits come on. Most of these 11 shots are of the far shore or are views from the far shore back to the burning ghats—the cremation sites on the steps of Benares proper. We are introduced to many of the most important motifs of the film: dogs, birds, boats, kite and sun, and a human corpse. None is yet elaborated, but we are meant to store them in our memory and to appreciate them as they recur again and again in the film.

There is indeed much to be said about these first 11 shots. It takes a knowledgeable and attentive viewer to appreciate them on a first viewing. When I teach this film to undergraduates, we go over the prologue shot by shot with help from the Gardner–Östör conversation. Certainly, this violates Gardner's original intentions, but it does wonders for the students' appreciation of the film.

A quarter of a century earlier, Gardner had introduced his New Guinea film about the Dani, *Dead Birds* (1963), with a similar concern for both the physical landscape and the symbolic context. In *Dead Birds,* however, the very didactic narration had seemingly left nothing to the imagination.

The very first shot of *Dead Birds* (for a shot list, see K. Heider 1972) is an extraordinary pan taken from a hill looking down on a large bird as it glides almost 180 degrees around the base of the hill. Out of focus below the bird, we make a first pass over Dani compounds, fallow sweet potato gardens, and the auracaria grove, all of which will be important locations in the film. And even as we are visually located in the Dani landscape, the narration is telling us the Dani mortality myth, a myth that Gardner evokes visually and verbally throughout the film:

> There is a fable told by a mountain people living in the ancient highlands of New Guinea about a race between a snake and a bird. It tells of a contest which decided if men would be like birds and die, or be like snakes which shed their skins and have eternal life. The bird won and from that time, all men, like birds, must die.

A short time later, the twelfth shot, again taken from the hill, shows us the compounds and gardens but this time in focus. Then, suddenly, the shot opens up to look across the entire valley toward the mountains beyond the valley. Now the narration locates the no-man's-land and a battle field that we will see at close quarters later in the film. But Gardner is not finished with setting the geographical stage. In the twenty-first shot, we begin at the compound of the hero, Weyaklegek, and trace his path out to his watchtower, giving us a third overview of the landscape of the film.

Meanwhile, after that first key shot, Gardner introduces the key theme of death with a funeral (the second and third shots, under the titles). In fact, there are references to death in half of the first 21 shots. We also meet the two main characters of the film, Weyaklegek the war leader (the third through the seventh shots) and Pua the swineherd (the eighth through the eleventh shots).

It would seem that *Dead Birds,* with the explicitness of its narration, is totally different from *Forest of Bliss,* which demands considerable acuity on the part of its viewers. But this is not quite the case. For all of Gardner's apparent transparency in *Dead Birds,* one

important motif is never really explained. The birds in the film's title, pictured in so many of the shots and alluded to in so many more shots, seem for most viewers fairly trivial. Even Peter Loizos (1993, 144–52), who has given the most insightful and sympathetic reading of *Dead Birds,* has missed the significance of the birds.

As it happens, Gardner had originally made a 40-minute-longer cut of *Dead Birds,* but various friends advised him that a two-hour documentary was unwatchable. So he edited it back to its present release length of 83 minutes. I had seen the longer version when Gardner returned to Netherlands New Guinea in 1962, and I remember it as being more satisfying than the shorter version because it expanded on the bird motif. Actually, at the time I told Gardner that he had exaggerated the human–bird theme. I had stayed on with the Dani after Gardner, and the other members of the Harvard-Peabody expedition left New Guinea in 1961. Then I came down to the coast when Gardner screened that long version of the film in the Dutch governor's residence. When I returned to my fieldwork, I immediately followed up on this problem and soon established, to my surprise, that my Dani informants endorsed his insights. If anything, Gardner had downplayed the bird symbolism. Of course, he had been trained as an anthropologist at Harvard. Although he spent most of his time with the Dani behind the camera, his ethnographic eye picked up much of Dani symbolism far faster than my own (I was concentrating mainly on material culture at that time).

Gardner did write about the bird motif some years later, but it was in a somewhat ephemeral source that is not easily available (Gardner 1972, 35). So we are left with, at best, the allusion to the fateful identification of humans with birds described in the narration over the first shot. But the implications of this probably do not register with most viewers.

Briefly, the Dani mortality myth sets up a Jungian triad of bird, snake, and human. Bird and human are linked and each is more or less explicitly opposed to snake. Each Dani is a member of a patrilineal descent group—a sib—that is identified with a particular bird species. The feather ornaments and wands and even the clay-smeared shoulders of people at rituals and battles are explained by the Dani as a manifestation of their identity with birds. (In the narration for the ninth shot, Gardner [1972] says, "The patches of color around the eyes and shoulders help to complete their image of themselves as birds" [39].) And the film's title, *Dead Birds,* is a phrase referring to trophies taken from enemy warriors during battle. These are sometimes called "dead people" (see K. Heider 1997, 126–28).

So far, on the basis of these two films, we can characterize Gardner's first shots as being specifically geographic. But these are not simply geographic, and they are more than just landscapes. Gardner sees these landscapes as being directional, as being vectored. In *Forest of*

Bliss, the Ganges flows from south to north (at that point), and in the film it is significant whether boats go upstream or downstream; the far side of the river is death and foreboding, the near side is the side of life. In Gardner's words, they are "the world of death as against the world of life" (Gardner and Östör 2001, 16). There is an apparent contradiction in calling the burning ghats, where the cremations take place, "the world of life." I assume that Gardner is thinking of the Hindu concept of death as release from the wheel of suffering. The title of the film itself reflects this thought: the forest produces the logs for the funeral pyres, which bring the blissful rebirth. And it must be recognized that this vectoring of the landscape is Gardner's interpretation and not necessarily in the minds of the local people. Östör, who was, after all, the ethnographer of the film, says that "the significance of the farther shore for me was one of peace and, in a sense, of relief to be away from the confusion" (16).

The landscape of the Grand Valley of the Balim in *Dead Birds* is also vectored, most explicitly in the twelfth shot, which first shows us the peaceful compounds of the Dani, then takes us quickly across the sweet potato fields to the no-man's-land and the battlefields where we shall later see battles fought between our friends and the enemy Witaya across the valley. In this case, Gardner very accurately represented the Dani sense of vectoring. As the warriors approached the grounds where they would engage the enemy, the danger palpably increased. We see this clearly in the film, where the relaxed tone of men at home changes into blustering aggressive demeanors as they reach the scene of battle.

A parallel to the "vectored landscape of war" was described by the Gestalt psychologist Kurt Lewin (1917). Lewin had served in the German army during World War I and he described how, as soldiers approached the front, the landscape took on special meanings according to how exposed the soldiers were to danger. This change was not so much simply an awareness of danger as it was an awareness of the landscape itself: "it is experienced as a feature of the objective landscape" (F. Heider 1959, 113).

In *Dead Birds,* Gardner's constant references to the landscape of the Grand Valley intensify this sense of a vectored war landscape. In part, this was quite intentional, as in his choice of opening shots and narrative lines. Serendipity also played a role. That hill, which rose above our campsite, stuck out into the Grand Valley and afforded a magnificent panoramic view of the valley. In addition, toward the end of the film, there are two deaths. These are presented as they actually happened. During the time that Gardner was filming in 1961, we saw some eight battles on the battlegrounds in the no-man's-land. Surprisingly, no one was killed outright in any of these battles. But there were two killings in the neighborhood where we lived. One was the ambush of a young boy, and the other was the killing of an intruder from the enemy area. Both were the outcomes of fatal misjudgments. Each victim seemingly ignored what seemed to us to be obvious dangers, ignoring the vectoring that should have been firmly set in their minds. In *Dead Birds,* Gardner's explicit focus is on the symbolic, emotional, and ritual aspects of the two deaths and their aftermaths. But the cognitive vectoring of the landscape, introduced in his opening shots, is a strong implicit theme throughout the film.

At first, the viewer does not yet understand all the meanings of the landscapes in these two films. However, these meanings are clearly in Gardner's mind, certainly as he edited the films and probably in some form as he shot the footage. And the meanings are revealed later in the films. To test this reading of vectored landscapes, we need to look at more films—earlier films that Gardner was involved with and other films that he made between *Dead Birds* and *Forest of Bliss* and even ethnographic films made by others.

Let us go back just a few years to *The Hunters* (1957), John Marshall's first Kalahari film, which was edited by Marshall in collaboration with Gardner. It is hard to work out now how much of a role Gardner played in the editing, but the opening shots are very different from those that we have discussed so far. They present a diffuse impressionistic feeling. There are some two dozen short shots of flowers, trees, fauna of all sorts and sizes, people in close-up, people at a water hole, and people walking across the landscape before the memorable first line of narration: "The northern Kalahari is a hard, dry land. In this bitter land live a quiet people who call themselves !Kung or Ju/'hoansi . . ." This is landscape, of course, but it is not vectored in nearly the same way as we have seen in the first two films under discussion. In a sense, this is surprising because the Ju/'hoansi, as superb hunters and gatherers, know their landscape as well as the Dani know theirs. John Marshall has given us a fine picture of Ju/'hoansi hunting knowledge, and we see how their Kalahari landscape must be vectored not in terms of safety but in terms of water and food resources. However,

Marshall does not present their landscape as vectored in the same way that Gardner was to do with the Dani and the Hindus of Benares.

It is worthwhile to look at *Blunden Harbour* (1951), Gardner's first film. It was photographed by W. H. Heick and P. Jaquemin, but Gardner has credit for writing and direction. It concerns a small Kwakiutl (Kwa Kwaka' Waku) village in British Columbia. The first shot shows the title, *Blunden Harbour*, followed by credits, all superimposed on the image of a totem pole. On the sound track, we hear what turns out to be the chugging of a boat motor. The second shot is of a placid river, and the narration draws on a Kwakiutl myth that carries on over further shots from the motorboat passing along the front of a village stretched along the riverbank:

> Now I think of Heleste my master, my dear one
> The chief at the beginning of the world
> Went spouting around our world
> and he went ashore from his traveling canoe
> killer whale mask
> he liked the place because of a sandy beach
> and now my ancestors had for their chief Heleste.
> When he had finished his house a canoe came in sight
> And he called his four visitors
> Then my ancestor gave them seal to eat
> And when they had eaten ...

This joining of myth and landscape anticipates the first shot of *Dead Birds* although not nearly so richly and without the deep appreciation of the vectoring that Gardner visualized later.

Next we can look at *The Nuer* (1971), which was shot mainly by Hilary Harris and George Breidenbach among Nuer living in Ethiopia at the time Gardner was in another part of the country filming the Hamar. Gardner visited the site and shot interview footage in sync sound that was used in the final cut. The film's credits read "Produced by Robert Gardner and Hilary Harris," "Additional footage by Robert Gardner," and "A film by Hilary Harris and George Breidenbach."

The opening shot of *The Nuer* is a long view of flat land simmering in the heat with a few people walking about, a bird walking, and the sound of cattle mooing. The next 50 or so shots before the titles and narration examine men, cattle, villages, birds, and a few women. Taken together, this set of images effectively sets the mood appropriate to Evans-Pritchard's seminal monograph *The Nuer* (1940) of men and their cattle. But Hilary Harris, a filmer of dance in New York, was interested primarily in the people and the ways in which they moved. He did not develop the landscape to any great extent.

Rivers of Sand (1974) was shot and edited by Gardner. It focuses on Hamar women and their difficult lives with their husbands. The first shot is a close-up of a woman's face. The second is of a woman walking and the third of a woman beating one rock with another. The narration over these shots says,

A time comes when a Hamar woman leaves her father's house
to live with her husband.
It's like smoothing the grindstone with a piece of quartz.
The quartz is his hand, his whip
and you are beaten and beaten.

In these opening shots, there is no hint of landscape, vectored or otherwise, but rather domestic intimacy in both visuals and narration. There is no myth but a powerful figure of speech, illustrated in the third shot, which powerfully prefigures the wife-beating theme that runs throughout the film.

Deep Hearts (1981) is Gardner's film of how Bororo Fulani men sensuously celebrate their own beauty. The first shots are of men dancing in lines in very dim light, and then the shots become gradually clearer until we are in broad daylight. After the title, "*Deep Hearts*. A film by Robert Gardner," comes a shot of a long string of camels bearing veiled men. The narrator says,

Each year, after months of nomadic herding across
the Sahel of central Niger
the Bororo Fulani and their beloved cattle
converge in great numbers at temporary ponds
which catch the uncertain rain between endless dead dunes.
They come to enjoy
and to celebrate their vision as chosen beings.

Here the landscape is incidental in the framing of the first shots but is vividly pictured in the narration.

In this brief look at Gardner's opening shots, we see that he has used several different strategies. In these films (I have omitted his films of American artists) with the partial exception of *The Hunters,* each has always gone directly to the main subject of the film. But it is *Dead Birds* that is most intense as it presents the vectored geographic setting together with the mythological setting and hints at the symbolic human–bird theme.

We can also contrast Gardner's films with those of Jean Rouch. There may be no opening shot of Jean Rouch's as loaded with import as the one that begins *Dead Birds* (here I am at a disadvantage, for I have seen only the few Rouch films easily available in the United States). Rouch's *The Lion Hunters* does present a Lévi-Straussian dualistic landscape, opposing the village to the bush, with a story line hinging on events triggered by a lion crossing the line from bush into village. But it is more striking that each of the three most famous of Rouch's African films revolves around a trip: in *The Lion Hunters,* the Land Rover drives across the landscape into "the bush that is farther than far." In *Les Maîtres fous,* the Hauka leave their regular jobs for the weekend and drive into the bush to stage their ceremonies; and, of course, *Jaguar* is the story of a grand trip of the young men known as "jaguars" from the upper Niger to the coast at Accra and back again.

There is indeed much to say about the first shot—or shots—of a film. In Gardner's first shots, he can combine settings, geographic and symbolic, while Rouch was the Zen-ish guide of the path, the trip. Of course, any such generalization risks being simplistic, and both Gardner and Rouch were too much the auteur, exploring many ways of making ethnographic films, to be trapped in formulas.

REFERENCES

GARDNER, Robert. 1972. "On the making of *Dead Birds.*" In *The Dani of West Irian: An ethnographic companion to the film* Dead Birds, by Karl Heider, 31–35. New York: Warner Modular Publications.

GARDNER, Robert, and Ákos Östör. 2001. *Making* Forest of Bliss: *Intention, circumstance, and chance in nonfiction film.* Cambridge, MA: Harvard University Press.

HEIDER, Fritz. 1959. "On Lewin's methods and theory." In *On perception, event structure, and psychological environment: Selected papers, psychological issues* 1: 3, 108–19. New York: International Universities Press.

HEIDER, Karl G. 1972. *The Dani of West Irian: An ethnographic companion to the film* Dead Birds. New York: Warner Modular Publications.

——. 1997. *Grand Valley Dani: Peaceful warriors.* 3rd ed. Fort Worth, TX: Harcourt Brace.

LEWIN, Kurt. 1917. "Kriegslandschaft." *Zeitschrift für Angewandte Psychologie* 12: 440–47.

LOIZOS, Peter. 1993. *Innovation in ethnographic film: From innocence to self-consciousness 1955–1985.* Chicago: University of Chicago Press.

5   OUT OF WORDS
A CONVERSATION WITH ROBERT GARDNER

ILISA BARBASH

In the spring of 1999, the University of Colorado, Boulder, hosted a retrospective of the works of Robert Gardner in conjunction with his appearance at the last annual Conference on World Affairs of the twentieth century. I spoke with him at length the morning after the screening of *Rivers of Sand,* which was the first time in more than two decades he had seen the film together with an audience. The screening had shaken him up a bit, and it provided the impetus for him to reflect back on his original intentions as a filmmaker, to criticize, forgive, and compliment himself for decisions he had made, strategies he had undertaken, and plans he had conceived for the future. We discussed both the style and substance of quite a few of his works, his cinematic influences, and his thoughts on anthropology, art, and nonfiction.

Ilisa Barbash: Many of your films seem to depart from the observational norms of documentary and ethnographic realism. Could you talk a little bit about your work's relationship to reality and what such a concept means to you?

Robert Gardner: I have always been interested in indicating things by suggestion rather than direct statement. Yet I don't think this is because I have insufficient faith in unvarnished realism. Perhaps my tendencies arise from an interest in, among other things, surrealism. In my view, many of my films are far too content with a plain and ordinary way of looking at the world for me to be taken for an unrepentant surrealist but there are clear signs in almost all them of a soul straying from the paths of documentary orthodoxy. Maybe I'm a repentant surrealist.

In this regard I'm reminded of some sequences I shot for *Dead Birds* almost 40 years ago. I remember thinking then how important it was to find ways of heightening the Dani reality going on around me with such predictability. I kept hoping for situations and individuals that were somehow deviant and could take me to the edge for a better view of the whole. So one day I enlisted a young man I knew who had a sort of strange look in his eye, one which seemed to betoken a willingness to run certain kinds of risk. I had the idea of filming him in a dream sequence where he would act out his fantasy of being a great warrior. I borrowed a beautiful bird of paradise headdress, the kind worn only by the most important and successful fighting men, and put it on him. I then shot a sequence in, of course, slow motion in which he danced with a spear as though he had just wounded or killed an enemy. Fortunately, this sequence lies buried in the outtakes with some other failed attempts to bring about clarity through an altered reality.

There are places though even in *Dead Birds,* a film regarded I suspect as one of my more conventional efforts, where the reality presented is shaped through my interventions. A small example of what I mean is the nightjar or owl-like bird in the forest when the little swineherd Pua comes to drink at the spring. I had captured that bird when it was very young and later tethered it to the branch from which I filmed it looking down on Pua. It was a prop that I shamelessly, even excitedly, used to convey a sense of mystery and enchantment. The bird had been our companion in that grove for many weeks and all through that time had been witness to our own and the Dani's coming and going. My using it this way was simply an idea of how to represent a commonplace actuality in cinematic terms. I have never thought I was violating any canons of documentary probity. In fact, I even thought I might be extending the expressive range of the genre.

IB: Peter Loizos has called you a "symbolist." Certainly many of your films revolve around abstract concepts, that are part and parcel of the fabric of the human condition per se: conflict, gender relations, beauty, death, and so on. Both metaphor and metonymy figure prominently, though in your hands these are devices as visual as they are literary. In any event, I have wondered how you arrive at your symbolism, and what has motivated your choice of visual symbols throughout your work?

RG: I knew at some point Peter had used that word to describe what I was doing but I am still unsure if it was meant approvingly. I also am not sure whether, if he had the nineteenth-century literary movement in mind, I would approve myself, though I can't think of better company than Proust or Eliot.

But to try and answer your question more directly, I should say something about how the symbolic devices that show up in my films come to be chosen. This is hard for me to say with much precision but I don't think the answer is particularly complicated. As a small child, the stories invented by the Greek imagination filled me with fear and trembling. That they crop up in this particular imagery made when I had become an adult can, I suppose, best be explained by my parents' ideas about what children should read. But they also may help explain where some of these things come from, why this imagery gets used instead of some other.

In *Dead Birds* there are some scenes near the beginning in which Weyak, the important adult male in the film, is busy weaving what turns out to be a long, thin band on which he ultimately sews some cowry shells and bits of fur. These decorated bands are presented to appropriate individuals at a funeral ceremony. I spend what appears to be an inordinately long time showing this activity in pretty explicit detail, including lengthy close-ups of orchid fiber twine being endlessly manipulated by knowing fingers. The thread being woven is intended as a symbol standing for life itself. Its choice and prominence derives, in a very personal manner, from my exposure as a child to the Greek myth of the threads which measured the length of human lives being cut by, I think, the Fates. So, Dani weaving had built into it some powerful meaning and I simply grabbed it for its latent meaning and whatever else it might express.

Quite apart from the thread and weaving, the funeral bands themselves have a meaning of their own which was to represent the passage of time. The editing establishes Weyak starting to weave a band in the opening minutes of the film and shows him finishing it at the end. When it is finished, the film is over and the life of a person is likewise over because the band had been made for the purpose of being given on the occasion of a death. The occasion of death, I should add, is a major concern of the film.

Finding small and insignificant items to draw from the actual world, like the thread used by the Dani in weaving, that can signify more than themselves has seemed to me one of the few ways there are to convey meaning pictorially in films. In *Rivers of Sand* the same thing happens. In the Dani world only men weave funeral bands, itself a minor piece of irony considering our own gender distinctions. In the Hamar world only women use a grindstone. In *Rivers of Sand* the grindstone becomes a key symbol denoting a wide range of meanings. Elizabeth Hardwick told me when I was searching for a name for this film that I should call it "Women at the Grindstone." For her I had made this item of the Hamar environment centrally important despite its utter plainness. She was right about its importance but I always thought her idea for a title too banal. She might have been kidding except that she was in the grip of feminism herself at the time. There is also something about the choice of titles which needs explaining, isn't there?

The use of symbolic imagery of the kind you have asked about is even clearer in *Forest of Bliss* where there are no words at all to help with the rendering of meaning. In that film a number of mundane articles found in actuality play major roles in getting an understanding of the world in which they are imbedded; things such as wood, marigolds, ladders, boats, kites, to name some of the most important.

IB: Could you say a little more about the titles you choose for your films?

RG: A title often serves to organize my thoughts and guide my attention. The title *Dead Birds,* for example, was extremely important in the way it channeled my thinking about the world I was trying to comprehend. The moment I heard the expression in a conversation about something I had seen, I knew it conveyed much of what I was feeling but had not yet been able to put in words. I was surrounded by elements of violence and death in the form of ceremonial battles, funerals, watch towers, weapons and even children's games of war and I looked upon my Dani friends as victims of a cruel set of circumstances. On reflection, I thought these circumstances had a great similarity in their meaning to my own concerns. I found the concept of us all being identifiable as Dead Ducks or Birds very convincing. It was really a shorthand way of saying the utterly obvious, that people are mortal, but it was saying it in a way that permitted me to look at our circumstances from a new perspective.

Many, if not most, nonfiction films seem to have very plain and unambiguous titles: *Granton Trawler, Night Mail, The Hunters, High School, Rain,* and so on. These kinds of titles give evidence or, in some ways, a guarantee that the film in question is going to be about something identifiable and limited. Other kinds of titles are more suggestive and indicate possibilities of a different order, for example *Sans Soleil.*

IB: Your films distinguish themselves from most ethnographic documentary not only because of their largely nonexpository, narrative structure, but also by their sensuousness, and the pride of place you accord to the visual. Although the styles of *Rivers of Sand* and *Forest of Bliss* are very different, they both have extremely evocative landscapes, portrayed (more so in *Forest of Bliss*) with a long lens peering through the dust or the mist. On the other hand, one of the most striking aspects of *Deep Hearts* is your use of extreme camera angles, both high and low. This and the use of a wide-angle lens serve to further elongate the tall, statuesque bodies of the Bororo. In addition, you include an extraordinary number of fragmentary close-ups—of the devouring eyes, the mouths, and other body parts—calling attention to their practical, symbolic, and above all, their aesthetic significance. I wonder if you could talk at all about the aesthetic of your cinematography? And perhaps also, more generally, about how you see the relationship between visual perception and knowledge itself.

RG: Let me try to speak here at least to the part about camera style and then try to say something about the much more difficult and weighty business of visual perception and different kinds of knowledge.

I was never taught the camera in anything like the way one learns the piano or even handwriting. At a certain point I wanted to make film and so I needed to use a camera. In the early fifties there were very few places in this country where filmmaking was taught with any seriousness and so most of us just started with an instruction book. I had two, one for a camera called the Filmo and another for the Bolex and I think this mattered quite a lot in stylistic terms. The Filmo was Eastman Kodak's basic 16mm camera. It had a turret for three lenses and a way to change the frame rate. That was about all. You wound it up, rotated the turret to get the right lens, looked through a viewfinder simulating what the lens saw and pushed the button. It held 100 feet of film, or about three minutes of screen time. It was very direct and simple. The Bolex was different. It had a turret for three lenses but at least my model had a reflex viewfinder. You saw what the lens saw even if only faintly. It also had a fading shutter which meant you could increase and decrease the shutter speed to control sharpness and exposure. There was a handle which allowed you to rewind the film and reshoot to get superimpositions, dissolves and other effects. It also had a single frame setting for pixilation and, as I remember, a high frames per second speed setting which allowed for pretty dramatic slow motion. The Bolex was a camera with considerable pictorial resourcefulness and made it possible to learn the language of filmmaking, not just to document actuality. I see the Filmo as having played a part in developing documentary sensibilities and the Bolex as having opened up some aesthetic possibilities. Maybe I am a child of both potentialities.

Neither camera was well designed for hand holding but that is because the tripod was virtually obligatory at the time. You can tell this by the look of the nonfiction films of the period. You saw a static camera in almost everything except a few astonishing experiments which were my other most important means of instruction. We looked at films from everywhere all the time. I think the greatest influence on me was Wright's *Song of Ceylon,* along with Grierson's *Granton Trawler* and, of course, Riefenstahl's *Olympia.* These films told me the camera didn't have to be on a tripod in order to interrogate the world. The Bolex and other cameras like it belong to the domain of non-synchronous filmmaking. That is, they are used independently from tape recorders. Of course, the Aaton can be used that way too and most often that is how I work. What is clear to me is that the camera itself influences the imagery.

For some reason, I think I have always felt obliged to find new ways to use the camera. I once heard Buñuel say he could not let the screen go black in a fade because he regarded it as giving up on the image. I feel badly when I let the camera stand back and be passive.

In answer to your observation about the camera-work in *Deep Hearts,* it should be said that some of the more extreme angles are those in a few shots made by my old friend and frequent helper with sound, Robert Fulton. It is also Fulton who has taught me most of what I know about the Bolex, a camera of which he is surely one of the few undisputed masters.

Now, as to the hard part where you ask about the relation between visual perception and different kinds of knowledge, I must honestly say this kind of question really daunts me. What I know about visual perception is terribly limited. I have read some of the major theorists and felt the shock of recognition coming across in their thoughts but I can't say I have ever really understood what was giving me those fleeting pleasures.

Still, I'm tempted to think there is a difference in what motion pictures provide in the way of understandings and what comes out of reading and even painting or music though somehow I suspect music and film share similar powers over the mind. I would also venture that some of the special strengths of film reside in its appeal to our kinesthetic natures, especially to our capacity for empathy. Many years ago I watched Len Lye show an audience how we perceive motion by dropping an unfolded piece of paper he was holding over his head and following its progress to the floor. He rightly, for me, predicted that we "see" it with the whole body; we "feel" the paper as it slips and dips through the air.

What I take from this is that in film experience we kinesthetically incorporate actuality or its fictional equivalent and almost relive it in the process. Maybe new and different understanding arises from these felt experiences. Lye's demonstration was also the inspiration for an exercise I used to give in my filmmaking course. It was given in the Autumn semester and I asked the students to make a shot of a leaf falling from a tree. I hoped it would give them a chance to see how hard it was to do something incredibly simple and also how meaning could be gotten from something so elementary: tension, rhythm, time, finality, melancholia.

IB: I wonder if you might discuss your philosophy of film editing? While written ethnographies are highly synthetic, when it comes to film, anthropologists seem to distrust any form of montage that isn't contained within a single shot—between different moments of the shot, or parts of the frame—in other words, they would seem to wish that editing emerge, naturally as it were, almost as a given, from the pro-filmic itself. Whereas the contrasts and implications you create through juxtaposition take full advantage of the cinematic medium. Correspondingly, you don't as a rule have much time for long takes, another staple of ethnographic film and some documentary Vérité. Why do you think that is? Do you think you distrust the looseness of long takes, their digressions, or their dead spots?

RG: As you know I have already gotten into trouble saying anthropologists can be less than astute as film critics and so to hear you say they prefer editing to be contained within the shot does not surprise me. I'm pretty sure they are not talking about radical filmmaking like that of Miklós Jancsó who has created entire features using no more than a dozen camera setups. In fact, some of his most vivid and memorable work unfolds within a continuous, repeatedly rehearsed, 10-minute take of extraordinary complexity. They are talking about the opposite, an anticinema, using a camera which reveals only what happens within 10 minutes and in range of the optics chosen to define the space under observation. I remember such a strategy being seriously advanced by Margaret Mead in one of her more doctrinaire moments.

I don't think there is anything wrong about Mead and others wanting to do surveillance filming. It might even result in some interesting discoveries. But it is surely only one of a great many different ways to employ this medium. I am not aware of there being only one way or even a preferred way to write about the world around us and so I would suppose the same can also be said for filmmaking. (When I say "filmmaking" I mean the whole range of expressive means that word includes both in regard to making images and to their combination through editing.)

You have asked about my indifference to long takes, especially the kind associated with the Vérité manner of shooting. In reply, I would say what seems important is what is being filmed not so much how it is being done. There are times when because what is in the eyepiece is so compelling it feels absolutely wrong to end a shot and there are other times when it feels equally wrong to have thought it necessary to start one. I have no formula for determining what is and what is not "filmic," to use a slippery term, by which I mean subject matter that has some convincing affinity to the medium. I am quite sure there are no rules which govern in these matters. Everything depends, it seems, on some combination of knowledge, insight, inspiration and talent. These scarcely measurable and mostly unteachable attributes tell me that film, whether we like it or not, is an art form and that we should welcome, not despair of the fact.

IB: You have said that "nonfiction filmmakers with the interests and scruples that require them to follow rather than to lead the action need a sixth sense of what is about to happen just to get onto something visually interesting. The life of a nonfiction filmmaker is really a search for ways to be there before something happens."

And you have also spoken of the roles of serendipity and extreme vigilance in capturing particularly profound moments on film, like the coincidence of the little boy and the kite dropping into the Ganges in *Forest of Bliss*. How would you distinguish between subjectivity and a sixth sense? How much of knowing when to turn on the camera comes from what's actually going on and how much from your knowing ahead of time that this is what you want to put in your film?

RG: I think that chance, circumstance and inventiveness all play a part in these matters. Vigilance also, of course, is important in nonfiction filmmaking. It's necessary to keep all these things in mind in order to maximize what comes out at the other end. I don't know any formula that assigns a value to them individually and says that one has to be in greater proportion than another but, as between filmmakers, there probably are differences.

I think I was using the words "sixth sense" in what you quoted because I didn't know how else to account for something I know only from experience. What I am speaking of is a feeling that tells me something interesting is happening. How this becomes apparent is what I can't easily explain except it seems likely that you are right in suggesting that I'm seeing what I had wanted to see all along. Often though, I have found myself totally unprepared for what I was shooting but sure of its rightness. In these instances, I suspect it has to do with the way I was using the camera, the way the scene was unfolding pictorially. This tells me that style has something to do with content. Image making can reveal and it can obscure.

Now this brings up the question of talent and what part it plays in the final outcome of these endeavors. Talent is an unfortunate word because the inference is people are unequally endowed. If we were talking about musicianship, the issue of talent would always be part of the discussion. If we talk about almost any performance art or the performing of any art, even finger painting, talent is a major factor in achieving ends agreed upon as desirable. Of course, if there is no agreement upon what ends are desirable, then it may not matter how much or how little talent there is.

IB: Jean Rouch speaks of going into a "cine-trance" when filming. How would you describe your state of mind while shooting?

RG: I heard Jean talking about this trance state of his once when he came to Harvard to teach in the summer school. It was in the midst of a week-long program during which he showed his Dogon films from morning to night. I confess I may have fallen into trance myself as I watched what seemed might never end. I think I understood that he meant that when he began to shoot he entered a state which made it very hard for him to stop. I have spoken of a related experience of my own in which, rarely but with immense certainty, the mood would come over me that what I was seeing in the viewfinder was in every respect of form and content so absolutely right I was obliged me to film it at all cost. The cost, however, never went beyond whatever length of film was left in my camera. It has always been a seizure of the moment, an occasion when visual and aural stimuli concatenate in some commanding way.

IB: Could you speak generally about your relationship to words, and particularly speech, in your films? As I see it, your films have progressively withdrawn from language. You seem increasingly interested in a mode of representation that is non-linguistic or which precedes language in some sense.

RG: I must say there was a time when I thought words were very important. I am a great admirer of writers and writing and would have been one had I more talent and courage. For me *Dead Birds* was a huge job of writing and at the time I was very much under the influence of well spoken, lyrical kinds of commentaries, but in that film I now feel that although there may be some poetry there is not enough. It reveals the conflict I felt between my obligations as a conscientious observer and impressionable filmmaker. *Rivers of Sand* prolongs the conflict but moves a little more in the direction of personalization. So do *The Nuer* and *Deep Hearts.* The breakthrough was *Forest of Bliss* where the radical departure took place and I completely abandoned the voice-over device. I did this in part because I mistrusted the authority of voice-over but I also wanted to allow mystery and ambiguity to play a part in the larger understanding of what I was putting in the film.

IB: Can we talk about your use of narration? Why did you decide to narrate your early films? And how do you feel about your voice or narration now?

RG: I suspect "voice" is at least as important as the words of a commentary and maybe more. I know that when I hear someone speaking in a film, I make all kinds of judgements about what they are saying and much depends on how I feel about their voice. Sometimes I will stop looking at a film if I'm sufficiently put off by the voice and sometimes I will just sit there being entranced. This happens whenever I hear Lionel Wendt's voice speaking Knox's text in *Song of Ceylon.*

When I was making films with a narration, the voice was very important. In *Blunden Harbour,* I wrote the text but looked high and low for another voice than my own. I thought I found it in a young poet friend whose voice seemed to resonate with just the right amount of melancholia. Then and even later, a voice was a way to insert something affective into the solemnity and seriousness of tone in nonfiction.

I started doing my own "voicing" with *Dead Birds* which came fairly fast on the heels of *The Hunters* which I had helped John Marshall complete. He did the writing and the voicing as you know, and I always thought that made perfect sense inasmuch as the story was so much his own personal odyssey. I thought he put tremendous feeling into that track despite what he might more recently be thinking.

As I have already said here, the writing part of making *Dead Birds* involved a major effort and when I was finished doing it I had only to decide who would speak the words. It happened that many of my friends of that time were poets or writers of other kinds. Everyone I knew seemed to be involved with words and I dwelled in considerable awe of their accomplishments. It also happened that among their number were some wonderful readers of verse, Dylan Thomas especially but also others. I was impressed and wanted, I think, to borrow some of their strengths for my own medium. I thought by treating the text I had done as a literary thing and providing as thoughtful a reading of it as I could, it might result in achieving a tone I felt it wanted.

I don't think for a moment that my reading is what I most hoped for the text of *Dead Birds* or for the film for that matter. In fact, in recent years I have been greatly tempted to both rewrite the text and "re-voice" the narration. I have gotten nowhere in accomplishing this task but the desire has not abated.

IB: In your earlier work, *The Nuer* and *Rivers of Sand,* you translate some dialogue for the audience. Could you talk about the process of working with a translator, and perhaps about issues of translation more generally?

RG: It is true that there are translations of some of the things said in *Rivers of Sand* and *The Nuer.* For both films there was someone with me who knew the language far better than I but there was no one I was able to consult about language in the editing of either film. When I asked Omali Inda in *Rivers of Sand* those questions about her life as a woman in Hamar society, I got a pretty good idea of what she was saying from the rough translation given me right after she answered them. These rough translations led me almost immediately to formulate new questions or variations on those already asked. There was a sort of exchange between the two of us and Ivo Strecker who translated for me. When I thought I had asked enough questions, the next thing I wanted were literal translations to have when I started editing. As soon as I had those literal translations, I began to read them as a text needing its own translation. In the end, what Omali Inda says in the film came out of a pretty literary process. I used to think of it as being similar to what happens when writers translate poems written in languages they hardly know. It happens all the time with sometimes remarkable results despite what Frost says about poetry being that which is untranslatable.

There are problems and benefits in doing things this way depending on what it is that an author thinks is most valuable in the end. The way I worked in *Rivers of Sand* meant that I could interpret what Omali Inda was saying by putting her words through the filter of my own sensibilities. It might be more correct to say we were co-authors with a significant assist from Ivo Strecker. What might not be fair is that I did my part without asking Omali Inda's permission. For some people this may be one of the problems. On the other hand, had it not been my film, there might not have been any words to give meaning to at all. As it stands, the words are there and anyone can translate them any way they want. It happens with texts all the time.

IB: Trinh Minh-ha has insisted that all translation is interpolated by ideology, and that it can never be objective or neutral. She understands translation in the wider sense of the term—as a politics of constructing meaning. "Whether you translate one language into another language, whether you narrate in your own words what you have understood from the other person, or whether you use this person directly on screen as a piece of 'oral testimony' to serve the direction of your film, you are dealing with cultural translation." What do you think of this? What responsibilities or problems might this imply?

RG: I am in total accord with these notions though I might not put such exclusive reliance on "ideology" as the determining factor. Ideologies are important but surely not singularly so. As she says, all translation may indeed be "interpolated by ideology" but surely other filters are at work as well, like religion or even personality. I think the important thing is that knowing this about translation, whether in the narrow sense of rendering verse from one language to another or in the larger sense of portraying an entire culture in images, should not paralyze the effort to do all these things in the most discerning and sensitive way possible. Strictures like Trinh's can be helpful in recognizing the limitations on crossing cultural frontiers but they should not be reasons for not trying. Besides, it seems doubtful that there is any "ideology" which will satisfy all of Trinh's implied requirements for neutrality much as she or anyone else might wish.

In the faulty manner in which anthropology and all the related humanities work toward better understanding the human condition, I see more hope than despair. Each

additional insight gained in our observations seems to me worth the effort and worth the risk of being wrong or being boring which can also be the case. I am content to think of not just myself but of the whole of Nature as a piece of very unfinished business to which, one way or another, we keep attending by a variety of means.

IB: Since you have chosen not to translate indigenous speech in your films, could you talk a little then about the alternative means you do use to get inside your subjects' heads, or if that's too tall an order, at least the ways you go about understanding what their lives are about, and communicating that to your viewers?

RG: There does seem to be an immediate reason for using Vérité shooting in which the capture of language and other sounds is as or even more important than visual material. There are many sequences and even whole films that demonstrate this nicely. But this seems to me only part of the larger business of finding out what is going on "inside people's heads." The larger business being the meaning of the feelings expressed or the thoughts related. This is the hard part but it is where I think the peculiar nature of film can be helpful in that it has an uncanny capacity to isolate and, through comparison and contrast, to examine the meaningfulness of behavior.

Let me start with asking the question of why a person has a particular expression on his face or why hands are used to make some gesture. Could it not be in order to say something about what they are doing or feeling? Why is this happening and does the form it takes tell me something about the meaning of the act being performed? I think it does and I look for those visual matters, those clues that are indicative of something, that point toward something like meaning.

As far as technique is concerned, it's up to me holding the instrument to collect this evidence that I think is there to find. It has a lot to do with some faculty that's not a hand/eye thing as much as it's an internal, intuitive business connecting me with this event in some informing way. I think intuition is important in rendering the meaningful image, the image that gives meaning to what is going on. The camera is there to ask questions and even to create ambiguity as much as to give answers. This ambiguity and these questions arise from trying to satisfy a curiosity about what things mean. Directing the camera in some intuitively felt direction in an effort to see things more clearly satisfies this curiosity.

The only film in which I used an interview was *Rivers of Sand,* with Omali Inda, and that was more than just an interview. She was an actress in the film, in the sense that she took it over in many ways. I wish I'd let her take it over more. I wish I'd let her direct the film—maybe—I don't really mean that because I'm not one who thinks that by giving cameras to the "Other" you're going to unlock their secrets. But then that may depend on where you are trying to "get." Giving the Dani a camera would not have helped in this quest though it might have given us some ideas about what interested them as they looked around at themselves. I think [John] Adair showed us something about the Navajo when he let them use a camera. But I don't think what the Navajo did expanded on Adair's self-knowledge. Filmmaking is a language it takes time to learn and talent to use well. I don't see a camera as a device which can produce insights just because it gets turned on.

IB: Last night you screened *Rivers of Sand* in front of an audience for the first time in over twenty years. How did you feel about it? Would you have wanted to have done anything differently?

RG: No, I don't think so though I might have been less intense about last night if I had seen the film more often and more recently. At bottom, I still look at *Rivers of Sand* as a piece of work in which I put a good deal of private feeling along with reasonable attention to being a responsible observer. At the time I was making it, I thought, "Even if people don't really understand what I'm trying here, I do and hopefully they will too, sooner or later." But as I told you, I was a little shaken last night because I saw it was not as fully realized as I had thought. It was clear to me I was holding back in places where I shouldn't have been. I was making stylistic choices that went with a kind of filmmaking I thought I was leaving behind. It seems now that I felt compelled to proceed by first showing I could hit singles when I should have just gone for the home run. I spent too much time touching too many bases.

IB: What were the bases?

RG: Mostly, I think, they had to do with conventions like narration. For example, I don't think the *Rivers of Sand* narration should have dealt with factual matters as much as it did. I wish I hadn't thought: "I shouldn't make everybody mad at me by withholding information." So I put a lot in. Well, now I think most of that information is pretty inappropriate for the film I wanted to make. It may have assuaged some ethnographers' misgivings or it may not have. In the end, I don't think it helped really because ethnographers are the ones who like the film the least anyway.

I also think I may have made too many concessions in the cutting or editing. In some places, I can say I still love the cutting. At times, it seems to really work and has the audacity I wanted. The film was intentionally conceived as a collection of impressions of a frequently fragmentary nature threaded together to comment on the notion of sexual injustice. It clearly is not a story I found there or imposed through the editing as was the case with *Dead Birds.* So I did not have to provide as many conventionally edited sequences as there came to be in the film. It could have been less discursive. I don't think, however, I would ever want to give up such familiar devices as the very long takes, which amount to whole episodes contained in one shot such as the ones of the man who leads the praying as they drink coffee or the conversation between two men who are just out for a walk. Those I liked when I put them in and I like them now.

Last night I also saw many technical imperfections I have apparently ignored for 15 or 20 years, especially things to do with the shooting. Even so, I liked seeing it. I thought in the end it had all been worth it as I sat looking at it after all this time. I felt an interesting human situation had been rendered with at least some coherence.

It's also true, I suppose, that everything we saw last night has probably vanished in the last 25 years. But the depiction of life to be seen in *Rivers of Sand* is very much still there in the film to look at if anyone wants to see how imaginative human beings have been in inventing lives for themselves. But maybe that is just being incurably romantic when in fact that life is not nearly as imaginative as it is oppressive and mean-spirited.

Unhappily, we have the merest fragment of the larger human chronicle to look at when all is said and done. There is almost nothing to indicate what it was like to be a Kwakiutl Indian for example although we can admire the majesty of that world in their accomplishments in the myth and art which remains.

Somebody asked me a question last night that I thought was wonderful. It was something like: "Now that you've been all over the world what have you learned from it?" I was not expecting to be asked anything like that at an event like this. It made me feel as though the whole premise of what I have been doing was being questioned and about all I could say was: "I'm not sure but I think, in the end, I know a little more about myself than about those others in my films." What I meant is that I think I have learned something about my own humanity and if my audiences have learned something about the people in *Rivers of Sand* that is an added benefit. In the end, though, I think what transpired was something quite personal.

This element of private gain is hard to explain. It sounds enigmatic and very selfish. What can I possibly mean by saying that going to the ends of the world has been a way for me to understand myself better? Hidden in this answer are ideas such as it is presumptuous to try and explain other people without bothering to explain oneself. Also hidden are my thoughts about going to the "ends of the world." What importance does doing that have?

At a certain point, I began to think that a lot of what I'm doing, going wherever I go, might be doing the next best thing to getting inside heads. This is not only a struggle— it seems a hapless task in that it is obvious you cannot get inside people's heads. But is that really the end of the matter? Maybe the capability we all have for getting into our own heads is what provides us with sensibilities like empathy that help in comprehending things vicariously?

So for me going to distant cultures leads to self-examination which in turn refines sensibilities for detecting meaning in the lives of others.

IB: Two of your early films, *Dead Birds* and *The Nuer* seem to concentrate mainly on the lives of men. And then, in 1974 at the height of the Women's Movement in the United

States, you made *Rivers of Sand*, which focuses on the lives of women and the spectacular rituals of Hamar patriarchy. Was your choice of subject matter a conscious reaction in any way to your earlier films? How about its relation to the historical moment of 1970s feminism? Do you see it as motivated by changes in your own life at all? A process of, as you say, "self-examination"?

RG: Well all of those things are factors in it. There was definitely a reaction to what was seen by some as an imbalance in *Dead Birds* between what was shown of women's lives as opposed to men's lives. Yet, if one were to do a shot by shot analysis of the film, I'm not sure that the number of scenes in which women are doing something versus ones in which men appear are significantly fewer. I do think that there's an awful lot about women in the film.

IB: You have to look for it, but I know what you mean.

RG: What is important is that the central concern of the film—the issue of mortality—is explored largely through the lives of men. They were the ones who went to war and did all the spectacular stuff even though both women and children of both sexes were potential victims of the deadlier business of ambushes and raids. It was also true that women were the ones who did the main grieving. It was they who lost their fingers when a relative died. They were the major sufferers of repeated anguish and bore the greatest part of its burden. Despite this, as you say, the film has a masculine flavor in that what is seen has mostly to do with men. Speaking of which, it is not irrelevant to what you are asking to note that the film's major figures are boys or men. No woman gets quite the same billing as Pua, the young swineherd, and Weyak, the warrior.

But, even if I don't think *Rivers of Sand* is any more exclusively about women than *Dead Birds* is exclusively about men, there is a switch of emphasis from men to women. This switch is pretty evident in my choice of a very strong female figure in the film: Omali Inda.

Indeed, *Rivers of Sand* does owe something to the climate of thought about the situation of women in the late 60s, but it also owes something to what was happening in my own life as a father and husband. Here I would like to say I think this film is not just about how women feel or behave but also about what happens to men as they make their lives with women. I made the film at a time when my own long-standing marriage was coming to an end and when there were accusations, if not good evidence, of certain kinds of abuses—I don't mean physical abuses—I mean troubling circumstances which were distorting our life together. I would go off for a long time to make a film. For example, I left everyone at home for six or seven months when I went to do the shooting for *Dead Birds*. And that's not fair. It caught up with me and it seemed quite natural and helpful to be going about the making of *Rivers of Sand* at that particular time.

The material I was working with made a huge impression on me. What I mean is that I really disliked those Hamar guys. They were pretty hateful in the flesh and in the images and I don't think I would have felt any different had there been no Women's Movement. I just don't think anyone can escape thinking the same way once they see the film, which is a serious thing to say because there were a few Hamar men who were quite sweet and gentle but there were many others who were just monstrous. As a culture it seemed intolerable both for women and for men. So why not say so? I don't think anthropology is doing its job by being value free. I honestly don't. I think it's just avoiding its responsibility to find larger truths.

IB: The other day we talked briefly about *An American Family,* and you said that you felt that the lives of the subjects of the film had been deeply affected by the presence of the camera crew. How do you feel you may have affected the lives of the subjects of your films? How would you characterize your relationships with your cinematic subjects, both during and after filming?

RG: I had always understood that the outcome of the *American Family* project was quite devastating to the "family" most concerned but I have never talked with any of those in front of or behind that camera so what I have heard is only secondhand. I can speak a little though about what I think the effect my own filmmaking may have had on those involved, both in front of and behind the camera.

I suspect that the longer I have stayed in a community to make a film the greater the impact has been. After living more than half a year in very close proximity to about 20 or 30 Dani, there were some among this number to whom I had become inextricably attached and who had themselves made me and my companions important figures in their own lives. By this I mean that when I went away, I felt as though part of my life was being left behind. I suspect that there were some Dani who felt that part of their future was leaving with me. I knew this to be true from the many dreams and memories which filled my thoughts in all the years following that first leave-taking.

As for the Hamar, I was so out of harmony with the male ethos of that society that I could not enjoy their company, not that of the men at least. Much of the time I was trying not to appear unsympathetic which was not at all easy. In some ways the difference between how I felt in Ethiopia and how I felt in New Guinea is that I regarded the Dani as people who had much to teach me and with the Hamar it was they who might have had something to learn from me. This much oversimplified scheme of things puts everything on a very different footing and promises very different results in terms of one's affections. I felt genuinely fatherly and brotherly to several Dani and would have liked it if there was any way to provide for some of their many needs but I never had this feeling for any Hamar with the exception of Omali Inda with whom I felt an immense, conspiratorial, almost illicit, camaraderie.

IB: In writing about *Forest of Bliss,* one critic complained that it was unclear to him why you preferred to use non-Western people to pursue your interests. But obviously you haven't done just that. Do you think there are thematic affinities between your Western and non-Western films? Is it an accident that your Western films are all about particular individuals, while your more classically "ethnographic" films tend to focus more on a collectivity, as well as being more overtly about culture?

RG: I sometimes wonder myself since I do not think my "interests" can be served only by going to the ends of the earth. There is a story I want to make into a narrative film which is set on a remote ledge in the North Atlantic but it is one that is populated by citizens of France who are not exactly exotic or primitive. It is a lonely place and the life there is rudimentary which I suspect are the qualities which interest me. When I think about it, I have been to some pretty rudimentary places—the Kalahari, the thorn jungle in Ethiopia, the Sahel in Niger, the high Sierras in Colombia—but I have also gone to Benares which is a very rich and complex city. I think it is true that somewhere remote and even alien is what I look for and, in some way, I think artists fill this bill quite well.

Benares may seem an exception but I am reminded that when I went to India my intention was to make a film about a Saddhu or holy man. This would have meant being with a person or a group of like-minded persons who had basically rejected society and its conventions, as rudimentary a set of conditions for filming as there is. It turned out that I couldn't find what I wanted so I had to take on something very different. Had I found the Saddhu and had I gone to his cave in the hills and had I stayed with him long enough to make a film, the "interests" you ask about would have been amply served I'm sure. Staying in Benares and trying to make sense out its chaos served perhaps related interests while engaging the same film sensibilities and techniques.

Another reason for going to these places and finding the people I have filmed in them might have to do with a certain despair about my own culture. I grew up thinking that much of what America stood for was not particularly noble or uplifting. These feelings were exaggerated by events like the war in Viet Nam, various assassinations and so on. Going far away was cowardly but attractive in that it offered the prospect of refuge.

There is also something of the chronicler in me. I don't think I mean historian so much as someone who collects tales and other accounts of human life across the planet. I don't think I'd ever be an historian but I do like the idea of paying attention to what is happening in the world. When I was being trained as an anthropologist, I often felt drawn to documenting what it was anthropology did and what it learned about people and places. It had something to do with what I took historiography to mean, the anthropology of anthropology or the assembling of the chronicle of human life. Methodological disciplines such as structuralism and functionalism never interested me much.

IB: In writing, or filming, the great chronicle of human life, which filmmakers have most inspired you? Do you feel you have any cinematic "totemic ancestors"?

RG: Some that come to mind are Jean Vigo whose *Zero for Conduct* I think wonderfully understands the inner life of the child, also Lasse Halstrom's *My Life as a Dog* and *What's Eating Gilbert Grape,* a film which for me perfectly evokes American life in the Middle West. These people along with such others as Kurosawa in *Dersu Uzala* and much more obscure figures like the man who made *Freeze, Die, and Come Alive,* about the experience he had as a prisoner in a Soviet gulag, all work in so-called fiction film. The figures I most admire belonging to the arena of nonfiction would include Basil Wright for his *Song of Ceylon* and Flaherty, especially for *Man of Aran.*

I think, if I could choose my genetic inheritance cinematically speaking, I would ask for equal parts of Andrei Tarkovsky and Basil Wright. Both these filmmakers took creative chances almost no other figures inhabiting their genres were up to. If there is a more wondrous opening to a film than that of Tarkovsky's *Andrei Rublev,* I haven't seen it and, if there are more meaningfully lyric passages in nonfiction than those to be found in *Song of Ceylon,* I have not seen them either. It seems to me that both these filmmakers are primarily concerned with finding ways to illuminate the human spirit in moving images and I am more than content with that as an ultimate goal for filmmaking. After seeing their work, I am more certain of my own humanity and that, for me, is the real test of a higher anthropology.

IB: You've written of your affection for comedy—and I think you once said that Charlie Chaplin's *Modern Times* is one of your favorite films—but your own work is distinguished by its moral earnestness, its seriousness of tone. How do you see the role of humor in your work?

RG: Indeed, you are right, "moral earnestness." That is a kind way of putting it. Somewhere I have confessed to a tendency to preach but I think I said in the same breath that I tried never to point to a moral. As for humor, I think it is very difficult. I'm too shy and reticent to even think of using humor and I have never done so except once in the only exclusively Vérité film I ever made, called *Marathon.* I can't think of anything more embarrassing than being unfunny. Still, I do appreciate humor and welcome it wherever it can be found, in *Modern Times* for example. Yes, Chaplin was, I think, a marvelous observer but no keener than Gary Larson for example. Larson is uncanny. What is more penetrating than his Far Side? Maybe it's the blackness, even the bleakness that I enjoy in the images which people like Larson and a handful of others use to depict our humanity.

There is an honorable role for humor in describing human affairs but the idea of a funny ethnographic film has its own laughability. Being funny and knowing when someone else is being funny are two pretty different things. As I think about this, I can't remember many times when I was amused by the Dani, the Bororo or any of a number of peoples into whose lives I have inserted myself. Once, though, a 10- or 12-year-old !Kung Bushmen boy imitated the way I walked by firelight one night in the Kalahari and I was shaken by laughter along with a number of others who were watching.

Most of the time I have been excluded from whatever mirth was present among those with whom I was sojourning. I am sure the reason was that I could not speak their language well enough for them to see in me someone who could appreciate the fact they were being funny. It was easy enough to know when they were being serious and this probably accounts for the fact that humor does not show up in my films. It may also account for the generally matter of fact tone of most films about other cultures. Come to think of it, how many monographs are there with anything particularly comic about them despite the enormously important role humor plays in human life?

IB: Thomas Cooper has said that none of your films indulge in "the pleasures of the flesh" and that when "bare breasts or buttocks are shown, it is because they are customary in a native society, just as suits or skirts are in ours." On the other hand Peter Loizos has spoken of the potential for audience titillation and voyeurism in *Deep Hearts.* How would you relate these comments to some of the scenes in *Rivers of Sand,* for example, such as the close-ups of the men bathing and the women grinding grain? More generally, I wonder if you could consider the role of the erotic in documentary and ethnographic film?

RG: I'm not sure Tom Cooper is right about bare breasts and buttocks. To be sure, there seems to be nothing sensual for the Dani or Nuer about their own nakedness but that does not prevent Westerners from exercising their own views on such matters. Nor does it mean that I or anyone else portraying these people in their nakedness can escape the inevitably erotic meaning attached to exposed flesh. I would say Peter is nearer the mark though I don't like to think the only effect of bare breasts on people watching *Rivers of Sand* is titillation. For me being naked is being stripped bare and results in some combination of vulnerability and innocence. It removes a layer of protection and civility and gets us to a more rudimentary state of affairs.

I have said that I had hoped in India to make a film about a Saddhu. Saddhus are characteristically without clothes. I have seen them walking naked through the snow and ice on the approaches to the sacred town of Baidranath in the North. I don't think for most people there is much that is inherently erotic about a naked holy man but I do think that being exposed to the elements in such an unprotected way can be a disturbing view of what has been invented as a way of life. As such it would be my expectation that we could gain some better understanding of human limits from seeing this.

Further to your question about nudity in *Rivers of Sand,* I should say that in the scene of the man using a small calabash of water to bathe, which must be the scene you have in mind, I was acutely aware, especially in the editing, of its sensuousness without knowing much about what the man doing the bathing felt. As I remember that scene, he was also fondling his rifle and this combination of activities, caressing himself and his weapon, interested me as a way of putting an audience in mind of what I thought was a widespread narcissism affecting the entire population of Hamar males.

In fact, this scene was meant to illustrate one of the major themes I tried to develop in the film: the damage done to the male personality as a result of their suppression of women. My feeling was that their physical domination of women exacted a psychological price in that its effect was to depress them and elicit from them a self regard bordering on narcissism. I grant you my reasoning is based on intuitive responses to what I saw not on any disciplined study of Hamar psychodynamics. My point is only to say that Hamar nudity, both male and female, was a fact of life in that society and one which I understood to have meaning both for our eyes and theirs. It was our eyes that mattered most to me as I made the film.

IB: Part of the magic of film's powers of mechanical reproduction is that it captures, or locks, what it portrays in time forever, or at any rate until the print, tape, or data disintegrates. So that, when I see *Dead Birds* or *Rivers of Sand* today, I experience Weyak and Pua and Omali Inda today as they were then, in your eyes, but 40 and 25 years later. How do you feel about reviewing, and about being made accountable for, images you created decades ago?

RG: How do I feel about what I did twenty-five or more years ago? There's really nothing you can do about it, is there? As filmmakers we are burdened with an apparatus capable of such permanence and fidelity there is no mistaking the content which can be justly regarded as composed of fragments of lived time. As you say, this is part of film's magic but being so faithful and so precise also means that film cannot escape being imbued with an underlying melancholy. I first came across this idea reading John Berger on photography and I was struck dumb with his insight. As I see it, the melancholy arises from the fact that these fragments, these unalterable moments arrested in time, are constantly referring to what once was and yet, at the same time, are telling us everything and everyone can only change, get older and eventually die.

So, to the question about what it's like to see these faithful, if fragmentary, representations years later, I would say there is certainly that latent melancholy of which I have spoken but many years later that sensation can easily give way to outright sadness knowing, for example, as I do today, that Pua is dead and so is Weyak. What was "predicted" in the frames I shot in 1961 has come to pass. What is true about these two individuals is also true about everything else in *Dead Birds* or *Rivers of Sand.* The culture represented in the events portrayed in those films has also changed, almost to the point of extinction. What remains then is something full of wonder, full of possible meanings to be supplied by those who see it. What remains, despite change and even extinction, stands for something more than the "itness" of the moment of its creation.

What I think is left, long after the act of filmmaking, is a form of fiction composed of these magical, quasi-real fragments. The fragments have an authority that comes from the manner in which they were made but their arrangement into what we call a film is arbitrary and unique. But this is what provides coherence and what makes it possible to find meaning even if that meaning varies according to the viewer. To try and answer your question, I feel I am accountable for the particular arrangements called *Dead Birds* and *Rivers of Sand* but not for the meanings they engender.

IB: You have made quite a few nonfiction films in Europe and North America that are less well known to anthropologists. Can you talk about these?

RG: I have made a number including one about the Boston marathon and another about an atomic physicist. I have also made a few films about artists. I have just completed *Passenger,* about the painter Sean Scully. I've done two films about Mark Tobey, also a painter, and a film about Alexander Calder. I did one about Miklós Jancsó, the Hungarian film director and I started a film, which I may never finish but hope I will, about Joan Miró.

I don't know exactly why I've done these except that in many cases they were people I greatly admired or knew well enough to impose upon them. Also, I think, the world of art and artists has similarities to the sorts of places and people I've been drawn to otherwise. I'm not saying that Tobey equals the Dani, or that Miro and the Hamar are the same but that they all present sets of circumstances that interest me in similar ways and make me want to try to extract something meaningful by aiming my camera at them. When I was very young and had just moved back to Cambridge from Seattle, I had the idea of making a film about Robert Frost who lived nearby. I managed to get a time to see him and we talked about the possibility. A film had never been done about him and it was already 1955. He asked me what he would have to do and I could think of nothing except to say he would just pretend he was Nanook and I would pretend I was Flaherty. He must have thought this was really quite amusing because the story kept coming back to me from people who had seen Frost. I never got to be Flaherty and Frost became the subject of an ambitious public television film not very long after my visit with him.

When I look at an artist I see a whole, coherent world. They get up in the morning, pick up their tools and go about their business of making sense, better sense, out of what they see around them. The "sense-making" is in how they work and the "sense" is in their results, their paintings, movies or whatever. In *Passenger* I wanted to see how Sean Scully made a painting, how he looked for and sometimes found sense with the marks he made on the canvas. I doubt that anyone who is not a painter can say much about this act. Maybe there are not many painters who can say much either but there is reason to think there is something to say if only the right words or, in my case, the right images can be found. Scully in his studio with his paint, canvases, brushes, music etc. comprise a miniature culture which can be looked at carefully.

Of course, there is the old problem we have talked about concerning what one cannot see, the difficulty of getting at what is going on inside Scully's head. I thought my best chance of getting at that sort of thing was through his face and gestures. So, more than anything else, *Passenger* is a film about Scully's whole body and how it moves in relation to the canvas.

IB: Much of the power of *Passenger* has to do with the absence of speech, which is quite unusual in contemporary documentary. To my mind it invites a different engagement with the subject. Did you ask Scully not to talk? Were you aware beforehand that you wouldn't want any dialogue (or even monologue) in the film?

RG: When Scully and I started this project there was absolutely no talk about how it would be done. I met him early one morning at his apartment and we walked over to his studio which was only a few minutes away. He opened the door and began to get out whatever he needed to start painting. We set up one of the cameras which I had decided should be going in time-lapse mode during the whole time I was there and within a few minutes the project was underway without either of us saying practically anything at all.

Naturally we talked occasionally as we worked but I never felt that anything we were saying was of sufficient interest or consequence to record. I was far too engaged in the act of watching Scully and trying to put my camera into the flow of events to think about explaining what was happening with words. As it happened, Scully had no interest in talking about what he was doing either and so it was an exceptionally quiet scene. In fact, I worried most about various noises emanating from the small manufacturing enterprises which went on in the rest of the building.

Very soon I began to hear certain sounds which seemed to define the activity under observation. Other than the music which was there from the beginning, it was the sound of Scully's shoes on the smooth wooden floor which took on almost immediate meaning for me and which ended up being an important audio element in the mix of sounds. I quickly realized it would be a film with a few prominent sound effects, music and no words whatever apart from the lyrics in the songs being played as Scully worked. There was no phone ringing, no one paying a visit and least of all any extraneous personages with wise things to say off or on camera. It is a fact that there was quite a good deal of sound enhancing and manipulating as the film came together. Once the notion of shoe sounds being a sort of voice for Scully seemed right, I had to dub in many footfalls and scuffles which were not recorded when the scenes were shot. There were other things like brush sounds, sandpaper, spatulas in use etc. These kinds of sounds became the vocabulary instead of words.

IB: In some ways your earlier films are reflexive, not because they overtly address the process of representation or foreground the relationship between you and the spectators, or you and your subjects, but because their style expresses your own subjectivity or sensibilities. Each of your films seems to be a very personal response to a people or an environment—I don't mean intimate, necessarily, or overtly emotional, of course, but idiosyncratic, particular to you and your camera. Nevertheless, *Passenger* is the most overtly reflexive of your films that I have seen, both because it's about the process of creating art and because you include images of yourself shooting the video. Do you feel that the more explicit reflexivity in *Passenger* is part of a natural evolution in your work? Just what do you think about reflexivity in general?

RG: I used to think about this quite a lot. And I have been pondering it more recently because in the last year or so I have been transcribing the journals I kept over the years, journals which contain a good amount of personal feeling. I wrote or dictated in the evening reflecting on what had transpired during the day and now there are hundreds of pages of pretty dense and undigested material. This transcription process has given me the chance to think things over. Among other things I have asked is: why didn't I put myself in those films? It would have been so easy. Why did I leave something of such interest to me now out when it would have been so simple to do? I could also have imagery of the people who were with me. I could also have documented a process over time which is not uninteresting in itself about how I worked. But I was ultra scrupulous about leaving myself out, thinking it would compromise my intentions to preserve my objectivity.

I think all that was kind of silly, to have left all of that out. I don't think my films would have been any different had I not done so. I don't think I would have used any of it in the films because I was much too wedded to the lofty view and I wanted to avoid the slightest hint of the travelogue. I only wish now that it could have been part of the larger record.

The fact that I'm in *Passenger* is the chance result of having put a camera in the back of the studio set to shoot a wide angle frame about every 30 seconds while we were in the studio working. So, if I'm there filming, I'm going to be in the frame. But I never thought of doing this for any reason other than to be able to see the work emerge over time. I actually had in mind that wonderful film, *The Mystery of Picasso,* by [Henri-Georges] Clouzot where he shot from the other side of a sheet of glass as Picasso painted letting one see the painting emerge through a succession of brush strokes. I wasn't thinking in the Scully film of looking at the way he painted as much as at the changes the painting went through over time. But the moment I saw the material, I realized the process collapsed in time would be one of the major visual motifs in the film. I realized this quite quickly because I was able to see what the camera was getting as soon as the tape had been shot. There was no waiting for processing and printing.

The fact that I was flitting in and out of the frame may be of some interest from the point of view of filmmaking but it doesn't contribute much to the understanding of the way the painting is made. I didn't really think my presence was important except that it may speak to the filmmaking and to the dance between two artists as described by Stan (Brakhage). You might as well see who's dancing. It came out of what seemed to me the requirements of that particular undertaking and really had nothing to do with any theory or ambitions to be a self-reflexive filmmaker which I seem to have studiously avoided. I'm not sure why. I probably didn't like it because I wasn't doing it. I think if I had, I would have been more in favor of it.

IB: So how do you feel about the enthusiasm for first-person confessional films and explicitly reflexive documentaries today? I think that some filmmakers seem to feel that if they have a shot of the camera-person or the sound-person intruding into the frame then they have revealed their relationship to the subject. And in fact, that hasn't happened at all. One really hasn't gotten much closer to the process itself.

RG: No, and it doesn't seem a great leap of imagination to see the camera and sound persons as having had to intrude without having to be shown their faces. However, being in the frame and being given the information you get through speech and body language may put the viewer in closer touch with the "process" as you put it. In Ross McElwee's case his presence is that of an actor or presenter as much as a film practitioner and it makes perfect sense for him to "intrude." I'm not sure I can make as good a case for other Vérité filmmakers putting themselves deliberately in the frame. I tried doing this in one film, *Ika Hands,* where I had a little conversation with Reichel Dolmatoff, the Colombian anthropologist, and I'm not at all sure it worked. I also tried in *Deep Hearts* to do monologues about what it was I was trying to do in Niger with the Bororo but I tossed it out when I saw it in all its pretentious obscurity.

I wonder if the confessional approach might in some way be an effort to observe political niceties, an attempt to start off on a level playing field having assumed you were not on one to begin with. I'm not sure what's "unlevel" about being the filmmaker as against not being the filmmaker. I suppose some situations are unquestionably exploitative and shouldn't be tolerated but aren't those situations mostly confined to the commercial world? Being from the West and making a film in the East is not by definition hegemonic I hope. Most of the filmmakers I know are very sensitive and enormously caring about the people they have chosen to film, sometimes to the point of losing adequate perspective.

IB: Uniquely, I think, among filmmakers, your films have surely suffered from neglect, or at any rate misinterpretation, from both ends of the Art–Science spectrum. I know that Stan Brakhage thinks it an outrage that your films aren't at the Anthology Film Archives, while the open-endedness of and lack of translation in *Forest of Bliss* provoked the ire of a number of anthropologists. Where would you situate your films on the Art–Science continuum? Or, if you feel they resist simple categorization, why do you think that is?

RG: If Stan is at one end of a nonfiction Art/Science continuum and Anthropology at the other, I'm not sure where I end up. Stan is one of the few people championing Film as Art who leaves room in the canon for nonfiction. There are not many people who champion Film as Science who would leave room for Stan, yet I would argue he has done some wonderfully observant work. There really are too many competing standards and criteria to know where anyone or any particular piece of work belongs. I suppose it is safe to say that a reasonably generous view of nonfiction would find room for my films.

At the moment, though, I am trying to do a something which is not so easily categorized. I'd like to make a narrative film where I could really direct what would happen, rather than sensing what was happening. I think the big difference between fiction and nonfiction film is being able to ask for things to happen instead of not being able to ask because we want things to arise out of the actuality. As I think about doing something like a narrative project, I wonder whether there is that much difference between what I have been doing and what I might be doing in the future.

IB: What are the similarities?

RG: Your question makes me think about Flaherty who wanted to make a so-called feature for the last 10 or so years of his life. I remember his widow saying it was going to be a film incorporating some ideas about the American Indian. He'd been moving in that direction for a long time. *Louisiana Story* was, of course, a story. All the films were stories, including *Nanook.* He was a storyteller, wasn't he? I never met him but people tell me when he wasn't making a film he was telling endless stories wonderfully.

If I were to be asked to describe what I do in genre terms, I would say up until now at least I'm a story-finding filmmaker. I go out into the real world and find something I want to tell people about what I have seen and think is important. One of the ways I do this is in a story. There is a story about Omali Inda in *Rivers of Sand,* about Weyak and Pua in *Dead Birds* and about a city in *Forest of Bliss.*

As I think about it, almost everything seems locatable in some story. Maybe it's the story that gives everything its meaning. How do we come to know each other? Which is to say, how do we come to mean something to each other except by telling our stories to each other? It seems we are relating to each other narratively speaking all the time.

I think going to this, supposedly different, genre of feature making is stepping right into the central issue of telling stories. (An earlier version of this interview appeared in Barbash [2001].)

REFERENCE

BARBASH, Ilisa. 2001. "Out of words: The aesthesodic cine-eye of Robert Gardner." *Visual Anthropology* 14 (4): 369–413.

PART TWO: THE FILMS AND PHOTOGRAPHS

6 THE CAMERA IN THE STUDIO
ROBERT GARDNER'S *PASSENGER*

ANNA GRIMSHAW

> When I look at an artist I see a whole, coherent world. They get up in the morning, pick up their tools and go about their business of making sense, better sense, out of what they see around them. The "sense-making" is in how they work and the "sense" is in their results, their paintings, their movies, or whatever. In *Passenger,* I wanted to see how Sean Scully made a painting; how he looked for and sometimes found sense with the marks he made on the canvas.
>
> —Robert Gardner

The opening shots of Robert Gardner's film *Passenger* reveal an artist's studio. Light comes into the room from broad windows on left, there is a plain wooden floor, and a row of large striped paintings are propped up along the right hand wall. At the far end of the studio hangs a single gray canvas with a panel cut out of it. Sean Scully hovers close to his materials on tables beneath the window, shifting uneasily from one foot to another. Eventually, he walks across the room to stand in front of one of his paintings. He moves forward a step so that he almost touches the surface of the canvas. The relationship between the size of the painting and the physique of the painter is intriguing. Herein lies the tension of Gardner's film. For Scully, a burly man dressed in jeans and a paint-splattered T-shirt, is engaged in a complex struggle with the work. It is a struggle that is strikingly physical.

Passenger, billed as "a video in four movements," was shot by Gardner over a period of seven days in Scully's Barcelona studio. The film unfolds as a sort of choreography between the two men, almost a dance, in which moments of stillness are punctuated by energetic outbursts with a range of subtly modulated movements lying between them. *Passenger* is interesting for a number of reasons. Compared to the more well known films such as *Dead Birds* or *Forest of Bliss, Passenger* has not attracted much critical attention by commentators on Gardner's work. Moreover, his portrait of Scully appears to be on a different scale from many of his other classic films. It seems more modest in its ambition, limited in its scope and extension, and it is located in the context of Western culture. *Passenger* is also self-consciously reflexive in a way that Gardner's other films are not.

Beyond the immediate question about how *Passenger* might be understood in terms of Gardner's overall trajectory, the film raises a number of other important issues. These relate,

first and foremost, to Western constructions of the artist and *his* space of creative expression. Hence, following my discussion of *Passenger,* I seek to locate the film in the context of a broader, if undertheorized, genre of documentaries about art and artists. For, in *Passenger,* Gardner works with a particular image of the Western artist that was established—and popularized—through earlier films such as Hans Namuth's *Jackson Pollock* (1951), Henri Clouzot's *The Mystery of Picasso* (1956), and De Antonio's *Painters Painting* (1972). But central to the genre—and to any proper appreciation of *Passenger*—is the question of the film medium itself. What is distinctive about a *film* of an artist in his studio? What might film uniquely reveal—or not, as the case may be—about painting?

The second group of issues relate to judging *Passenger* as a work of visual anthropology. Robert Gardner has long been one of the most interesting figures in this field. In particular, he has consistently challenged the timidity of ethnographic cinema and the narrow conservatism of its objectives and methods. What makes Gardner such an exciting figure for some anthropologists—and such a problematic one for others—is precisely his commitment to art, understood as aesthetic experimentation inseparable from epistemological inquiry. *Passenger,* with its reflexive focus on the making of art (as painting and as film), suggests new possibilities for a bolder and more intellectually expansive visual anthropology.

I

PASSENGER

The Irish-born painter Sean Scully has been described by one commentator as having "singlehandedly taken Abstract Expressionism into the twenty-first century" (Carrier 2004, 17). He is known for his large striped oil paintings—the canvas often comprises different panels or a main panel and a "window." The relationships established within the painting—between its panels, its vertical and horizontal planes, its blocks of color and layers of paint—generate an unusual dynamic. What appears, at first sight, to be a canvas comprising solid and defined parts begins to dissolves as one looks more closely, until eventually the painting reveals itself to be a fluid, shimmering space of color and movement. We may recognize in Scully's paintings the linearity and control associated with grids of Mondrian, the sensitivity to color that marks the work of Matisse, the intense emotionality of Rothko and expansiveness and rhythm unique to Jackson Pollock.[1]

Scully's early work of the 1970s reveals his interest in exploring the possibilities of non-figurative painting, taking the texture of the urban world (its structure and rhythm) as his creative point of departure: "I don't think of my paintings as abstract, since they are not an abstraction of something that already exists. I think of them as real. I am always working towards a reality" (quoted in Carrier 2004, 64). Scully began experimenting with grids while training as an artist in England, but, not surprisingly, his work began to take decisive shape with his move to New York in 1975. Like many before him, Scully found the New World liberating. America gave him the context in which he could explore scale and abstraction, offering him the freedom to push beyond the limitations of an English training. Always passionate and engaged, Scully was impatient with minimalism and its cold, hard shapes and surfaces. Instead, he sought to infuse new life and movement into abstraction, to humanize painting without falling back on the figurative.

For Carrier (2004, 89), it was Scully's 1981 painting *Backs and Fronts* that constituted the "breakthrough." It followed a 10-year exploration with line and color until, finally, Scully articulated his own artistic vision. Critical to this transformation had been an earlier trip to Morocco in the late 1960s. There Scully found himself transfixed by strips of colored fabric that he found hanging on frames to dry in villages and towns. This experience became, literally, part of the fabric of his own painting, woven into his practice such that it eventually emerged as an integral and distinctive part of his creative personality. With *Backs and Fronts,* Scully announced the particular contours of his approach—his commitment to scale, to the stripe, to the juxtaposition of panels and planes, to the exploration of color and texture of paint.

By the mid-1990s, Scully enjoyed a considerable international reputation. He was hailed as an artist whose work expressed the ambition and expansiveness of the New World fused with a painterly sensibility deeply rooted in the European tradition. Once Scully had achieved recognition, defining and consolidating his reputation with each successive painting, he no longer based himself exclusively in New York. Increasingly, he moved between Europe and America, working from studios in London, Barcelona, and Manhattan. *Passenger,* Gardner's film of Scully at work on his painting of the same name, was made in his Barcelona studio.[2]

Gardner begins by establishing the space of the film, situating Scully in the studio and in relation to the canvas and his materials. He also suggests something important about the artist himself and how he works. There is a sense of anticipation, indeed apprehension, in the film's opening shots. Scully seems awkward and ill at ease. But it is perhaps the sound of his footsteps on the hard wooden floor of the studio that betray a sense of waiting, an uncertainty, a sort of limbering up, before Scully begins to paint. Finally, he moves over to prepare his materials that stand on the tables beneath the window.

Passenger has four parts. The first, "just a dreamer," shows Scully embarking on a new painting—a large grey canvas with a window cut out of it. It also reveals the techniques that Gardner uses as a videographer for this work.[3] He works with two cameras. One, a time-lapse camera with a wide-angle lens mounted on a tripod, is located at the back of the studio and captures the whole space in which Scully works. The second, Gardner's own handheld camera, actively explores the space between the artist, the canvas, and his tools. Working with both cameras, cutting between time-lapse footage and shots that unfold in real time, enables Gardner to expose the inherently temporal dimension of painting. As the filmmaker explains in his interview with Ilisa Barbash, "I wasn't thinking in the Scully film of looking at the way he painted as much as at the changes the painting went through over time" (chapter 5 in this volume, pp. 115–116).

Scully scrapes out congealed paint from a plastic bucket, he sloshes turpentine, and he mixes his oils. With a wide brush, he starts to paint broad black and red vertical stripes on his prepared canvas. There is purposefulness to his activity that contrasts with the earlier hesitation. Scully's body moves fluidly. Gardner draws our attention to the sensual quality of the entire process—the sounds of paint, of the footsteps, the artist's exhalations as he works, the messy process by which he prepares his materials. Scully's connection with the process is direct and unmediated—he is splattered with paint. Once the large canvas is completed, Scully hangs the smaller panel and begins to paint it in gray and brown stripes. Finally, he puts the two panels together, inserting the smaller into the larger one and hanging the canvas as a painting of horizontal stripes.[4] Scully goes over to his music player, and inserts a tape. He stretches his body and stands back to review his work. His body slowly moves in front of the canvas as if trying to grasp the painting's rhythm.

The second part of *Passenger,* "helpless, helpless," documents Scully as he undertakes the process of reworking, revising, reimagining the piece. He takes apart the canvas and repaints the small panel. Again Gardner underlines the way that Scully works with his painting—his hands on the canvas, the maneuvering of the panels, the rehanging, the scrubbing, the sanding, the mixing of new colors. Putting together the whole painting, the artist pauses, and, from a low wooden stool in front of the canvas, he once more studies his work. There is no closure yet. Scully, preoccupied and restless, moves to embark on the next stage.

There is a different dynamic to "the ocean is." Scully, now animated and still more purposeful, works on the large canvas with a renewed energy and vigor as if the painting is now within reach. Energetically, almost excitedly, he moves back and forth from the canvas, his whole body engaged as he uses a broad brush over the bold red and black stripes. In "letting go," the final part of Gardner's film, we see Scully continuing to repaint the large panel. The brown and cream stripes have now become black and white. Scully puts the two panels together and rehangs the completed canvas. There is a palpable sense of relief. Scully stretches, mops his forehead, moves away from the painting in order to judge the piece. Like all the other aspects of his creative practice, this too is marked by a heightened physicality. The artist is almost never still. It seems as though there is a tangible connection between Scully's body and the painting. At times, the engagement is intensely focused, at others it is revealed through small gestures and movements. Barbash and Taylor liken him to a dancer, noting that even when not painting, Scully is contemplating his work "from up close, at a distance, standing still, hanging sideways, swaying from one foot to the other, on his hands and knees, pacing, seated, lying on the floor, even using the canvas as a background for martial arts practice" (chapter 1 in this volume, p. 7).

Scully's reputation as a painter lies in the emotional quality that emanates from his simple abstract forms. Commentators have also noted the inherently musical quality to the work—its overall structural unity and yet individual variation. The artist always starts with the same basic element, the stripe. But each time he works differently with it, generating through a play of color, paint texture, and contrasting vertical and horizontal planes a finished canvas the surface of which vibrates with energy. Observing Scully in the studio reveals the rhythm of the paintings to be inseparable from the making of painting itself. For the movement of his body not only produces certain forms on the canvas but also affects the quality or texture of the paint on the canvas. Indeed, the fact that Scully *paints* is critical. It is at the core of his artistic persona. Gardner acknowledges this, drawing our attention to the demands that such a technique exacts. His camera shows painting as a direct extension of the artist's body, a completely unmediated process that takes hold of Scully as a kind of possession. What *Passenger* exposes is that Scully's discoveries as an artist take place within the moment of painting itself. They do not exist prior to it.[5]

In an interview with Kevin Power (2004), Scully explains that he never works without music unless he has to (Carrier 2004, 210). Music has long been central to Scully's practice—as an indispensable source of connection with the world and integral to the paintings themselves. During the painting of *Passenger,* the artist listens to a series of tracks from an album by Neil Young, and it is from Young's song titles that Gardner derives the film's section titles.

Gardner makes this music a dominant part of the film's audio track, weaving it together with other (heightened) sounds that emanate from Scully's studio as he works. The rich soundscape that Gardner creates is perhaps one of the most striking features of *Passenger.* It is interesting to consider it as partly a response to the camera's limitations. How can we see something that is essentially internal? What can a filmmaker reveal about human creativity, both a highly individual and a fundamentally interior process? Of course, there is an external manifestation—the painting itself—but Gardner reminds us of more subtle and nuanced aspects of creation evoked through sound and rhythm. In particular, Gardner documents the artist's creative process as a series of pauses, hesitations, and ruminations as much as it is a fluid, concentrated, and disciplined series of actions.

2

THE CAMERA IN THE STUDIO

> Heroic, affirmative, spiritual, transcendent, intense, emotive, charged, extreme, physical, enduring truths, passionate, volatile, vibrant, universal, romantic.

These are the terms used by curators and art historians in their commentary on Sean Scully (see, e.g., Carrier 2004; Danto 2004). He is portrayed as a self-made figure whose determination in the face of obstacles and setbacks eventually yielded a unique artistic vision that set him apart from his contemporaries. Moreover, his struggle to give expression to his creative personality is interpreted as bearing a particular burden of history. Scully represents himself and is represented as a figure who stands against the prevailing skepticism of much present-day art that has turned its back on the classical forms, particularly painting. This conception of the artist as *savior* resonates through Gardner's film. In *Passenger,* Scully's assertion of his creative will through the materiality of his painting practice is urgent. The undercurrent of tension that marks the film derives precisely from this. Pitting himself against his canvas, the struggle that unfolds in Scully's Barcelona studio is more than just personal. It is historically resonant too.

Gardner's depiction of Scully may be understood as part of a long, established tradition of images that represent the European or American artist. Beginning with Rembrandt's remarkable self-conscious fashioning of himself in around 75 self-portraits (Chapman 1990, 3) to the famous photographs of Jackson Pollock painting, we have become accustomed to a certain image of the artist understood to be a uniquely creative individual who works in special circumstances that separate him from society. This image is, of course, historically and culturally specific—and, as feminist art historians have pointed out, deeply gendered too (Jones 1996). Integral to it are notions of personal struggle, heroism, isolation, and genius. The studio, as an enclosed private space of production, is a critical site for the performance of this artistic subjectivity. With its origins in seventeenth-century Europe, the artist in the studio began to emerge as a compelling image as a part of changes in social and economic practice that rendered obsolete the older workshop system built around masters and apprentices. Rembrandt is widely viewed as a key figure in this transition (Alpers 1988; Chapman 1990), symbolizing the rise of individual authorship and the origins of the modern art market. Of course, this presentation of artistic self with its recognizably modern profile (e.g., the assertion of individual authorship) coexisted with Rembrandt's continuing practice as a guild master who supervised assistants and workshop production. What was as much an image as a reality became consolidated over the course of subsequent centuries—Picasso was an outstanding example. But, according to Jones (1996), it was the postwar American artists like Pollock, Newman, and Rothko who perhaps most completely inhabited the role. For they fused the spirit of American individualism with the traditional European image of artistic production—the isolated artist struggling to express his creative personality in the seclusion of the studio. Crucial to the consolidation—and popular dissemination—of this image were image-based technologies themselves (Jones 1996).

With *Passenger,* Gardner follows a line of distinguished photographers and filmmakers into the artist's studio. Picasso was famously filmed by Paul Haesaerts and Henri Clouzot, Pollock by Hans Namuth, while Alexander Liberman's (1988) lavishly produced book of photographs, *The Artist in His Studio,* documents his "pilgrimage" to the creative sites of both the living and the dead—Picasso, Dali, Giacometti, Cezanne, Matisse, and Bonnard, among many others.[6] The hushed, reverential tone of the narrative evokes the mystery of genius, communicating to an audience not just the author's sense of unique discovery but also his privilege in breaching the sacred threshold. Allowing the filmmaker and his cameras into what is usually a carefully guarded space is not without risk, however. According to Krauss (1993, 294–302), Jackson Pollock never fully recovered from permitting Namuth to film him at work on a painting.

If photographers and filmmakers have long been interested in exploring this secluded, semi-sacred space, anthropologists by contrast have rarely ventured into it. The ethnographic investigation of Western art practices is a relatively recent development within the discipline (see, e.g., Marcus and Myers 1995). Much work has addressed questions about the circulation and display of objects, and their changing value as they move across different cultural categories (Myers 2003; Steiner 1995).

Although anthropologists have become increasingly interested in how art is *made,* one of its most potent sites in Western culture—the artist's studio—remains largely overlooked. In *Passenger,* Sean Scully's studio becomes an anthropological field site—and, like Pollock, the artist takes a risk in admitting Gardner to the space of his creativity. The studio becomes highly charged, as painter and filmmaker must forge a collaboration that does not, at the same time, undermine the creative autonomy of each individual. The resulting piece is a powerful reaffirmation of the artist as romantic, male hero—the artist, of course, being both Scully and Gardner.

Passenger is about the performance of this identity. Scully is highly conscious of his responsibility as an artist, casting himself within the classic role that was once profoundly part of the tradition of Western painting. But painting no longer holds sway in the contemporary world. Hence, Scully's task is immense. For in the face of cynicism, play, and pastiche, he seeks to recover painting for art, to address the universal and the transcendent, to return the body and emotion to aesthetic experience.[7] The scale of his work, its directness, its texture, his method of painting (by hand and body), and his materials (canvas, oils, and brush) all serve to express his particular understanding of his role. Gardner's film becomes a site for its performance. Admitting the camera into his studio is then not such a dangerous move on Scully's part since it can be used to recuperate the image of the Western artist that Warhol and others destroyed.

In her discussion of what she calls "the romance of the studio," Jones (1996, 1) notes that, paradoxically, the proliferation of images coincided with a radical change in the role of the artist and the site of creative work. The camera entered the studio at the moment that the studio itself—and everything it symbolized—was being questioned. The work of the 1960s profoundly challenged assumptions about art—the site, methods, and objects of artistic production. The camera in the studio was part and parcel of these changes, even though this was not acknowledged within the work itself. With *Passenger* and with his other films, Gardner (like Flaherty) is seeking to recover a disappearing world. He uses his camera to re-present an image of the artist in the studio that such technology helped destroy—not least because it transformed the isolated artist as genius into the public artist as media celebrity.

3

THE FILM OF ART, THE ART OF FILM

The unabashed aesthetic sensibility that runs through all of Gardner's work sharply distinguishes it from other films in the ethnographic tradition.[8] Given his commitment to "art," it is perhaps not surprising to discover that in addition to *Dead Birds, Rivers of Sand,* and *Forest of Bliss,* Gardner has also made several portraits of artists. These include an early piece about the American abstract painter Mark Tobey (1952), a recent portrait of the filmmaker Miklós Jancsó (2001), and a work in progress about Joan Miró. At first sight, these films—and most notably *Passenger*—seem significantly different from Gardner's more well known contributions to ethnographic cinema. In particular, there is a disparity of scale. Placed alongside classic films like *Dead Birds, Rivers of Sand,* or *Forest of Bliss,* with their epic sweep, exotic location, and lofty ambition, this other body of work by Gardner is shorter, more modest, and limited in scope. For example, *Passenger* is 25 minutes in length. It is focused on a single person and confined to one location. Nothing intrudes from outside the space of Scully's Barcelona studio. There is no narration or opening statement other than the barest of details about when and where the filming took place. Gardner makes no claims for what he shows us beyond the relationships he establishes between the artist, his canvas, and his working materials.

Passenger's apparent modesty of ambition, however, is deceptive—or somewhat double edged. For, despite the film's narrow focus, it addresses the kind of overarching human themes that mark Gardner's classic work. If not concerned with violence, death, or beauty or the relationships between men and women, *Passenger* nevertheless makes an undeniably grand statement. This time it is about art itself. Gardner presents Scully as a heroic, anguished figure whose visceral struggle with his canvas symbolizes something fundamental about the human spirit. At the same time as the artist is elevated as hero, so too, by implication, is the filmmaker himself. Although *Passenger*'s reflexive dimension is described by Gardner as "accidental," a consequence of his decision to use a time-lapse camera as a way of documenting the transformation in the painting over time, it also serves to make manifest what anthropologists have long found problematic in his approach. Gardner has always understood his mission in terms that evoke an older project of inquiry—one that is idealist, intellectually ambitious, universal in scope, and contemplative rather than instructional. His commitment to "human uplift" is never crudely improving as in the case of John Grierson; rather, he is poetically engaged as a filmmaker in the spirit of Basil Wright (Gardner 1996, 173).

Passenger, the painting that absorbs Sean Scully during Gardner's film, is in many ways emblematic of his 1990s output. It shares with other pieces of the period a simple, abstract form that is animated by the dynamic relationship established between the broad stripes, between the larger and smaller panels, and between the layers of color that Scully's technique of multiple repainting generates. Ironically, despite the solidity and apparent definition of the work, its effect on the viewer is precisely the opposite. One becomes aware of movement and fluidity, as the spaces in between begin to dissolve the certainties of form and color. Scully has always described his concerns as an artist not with abstraction or formality for its own sake but with relationships and pairs and with what happens in between. Is it possible to interpret the reflexivity of the film in the same terms? For, as I noted earlier, the reflexivity of *Passenger* is one of its unusual features. Although Gardner clearly authored his other films, the relationship between himself and his subjects has not been previously foregrounded within the work itself.[9] This time it is enhanced by the careful positioning of the second camera. The feature that Gardner downplays as accidental, a consequence of its placement at the back of the studio recording timed interval shots, is, in fact, what makes his film interesting. It locates the filmmaker centrally within the ethnographic space rather than allowing him to remain on the edges of it. The camera frame comes to mirror the frame of the painting, drawing the viewer's attention to the proximities of creative endeavor. The complex choreography forged in the Barcelona studio between Scully and Gardner reveals *Passenger* to be as much about the art of film as a film about art.

An important precursor to *Passenger,* as Gardner himself acknowledges, is Georges-Henri Clouzot's 1956 film *The Mystery of Picasso.* Clouzot's film is a good example of the distinctive, if largely overlooked, genre of postwar films that documented the artist in the studio. This genre, most prevalent in the 1950s and early 1960s, gradually gave way to a different kind of film, one that was produced for television and explored art rather than artists (Jones 1996, 65–66). Critically, the new focus of this work reflected the shift in media production, as the filmmaker as auteur, like the artist himself, was replaced by a model of collective production characteristic of broadcast television. As I have noted, what Gardner shares with Clouzot and other filmmakers of the time is the classic image of the Western artist—the isolated white male who is engaged in an intense creative struggle within the enclosed space of the studio. By making Scully's body a dominant part of his persona as an artist, Gardner also follows Clouzot. For, in *The Mystery of Picasso,* Clouzot draws attention to the body of the artist. Picasso is shown working stripped down to shorts and a vest—by the end of the film, he has discarded the vest and appears bare chested.

Beyond these parallels, Clouzot's film is significant for a different—and perhaps more interesting—reason. Shortly after its release in 1956, the French critic André Bazin (1997) hailed *The Mystery of Picasso* as a watershed in films about art. In opening his review, he states that the film "doesn't explain anything"—we watch Picasso painting, but watching him paint does not reveal the secrets of his artistic gift. Observing the artist at work reveals the creative process as an elusive movement that cannot be understood in simple terms of cause and effect, one moment leading to another—for, as Clouzot's film reveals, Picasso confounds our expectations at every stage. The importance of *The Mystery of Picasso* lies elsewhere—intimately tied to the medium of film itself.

For Bazin (1997), Clouzot's achievement was to restore temporality to painting. "Pictorial duration," as he calls it, is integral to painting, but it is lost once a painting is completed: "all we knew until now were 'canvases,' vertical sections of a creative flow more or less arbitrarily decided upon by the painter himself, in sickness and in health. What Clouzot at last reveals is the painting itself, i.e. a work that exists in time, that has its own duration, its own life, and sometimes—as at the end of the film—a death that precedes the extinction of the artist" (212).

Bazin (1997, 213) was anxious to clarify that his notion of "pictorial duration" was *not* about *explaining* the process by which a painter achieved certain effects in his painting. What Clouzot reveals in his film is that "the intermediate stages are not subordinate and inferior realities, parts of a process that will result in a final product: they are already the work itself, but a work that is destined to devour itself, or rather to metamorphose, until the painter wants to stop." The film is about the paintings beneath the painting—not conceived of as sketches, preliminaries, or progressive stages of a single piece but, instead, understood as individual paintings in their own right—paintings that have to be discarded as the artist moves on to the next one.

The breakthrough that *The Mystery of Picasso* represented for Bazin (1997) hinged on Clouzot's insight into the creative possibilities of his own medium. Only film can render the temporality of artistic creation—and Clouzot, abandoning the usual conventions of narration, explanation, drama, biography, commentary, or contextualization, foregrounds pictorial duration in his 80-minute portrait of Picasso. Clouzot's camera does not stand outside what it is being used to explore. The film is not an animation of the painting process—rather, screen and canvas are fused within an unfolding creative process. As Bazin puts it, "Film here is not the mere moving photography of an a priori, external reality. It is legitimately and intimately organized in aesthetic symbiosis with the events pictured" (216).

Robert Gardner attempts something remarkably similar in *Passenger*. He, too, is seeking to effect a creative synthesis between his own medium, film, and Scully's artistic practice, painting—and, as he acknowledges, duration is at the heart of the matter (chapter 5 in this volume). If Gardner's portrait of Scully is deeply conventional, however, celebrating "the romance of the studio" and reclaiming a traditional image of the male Western artist—in its form, *Passenger* is much more radical. Indeed, it presents an important challenge to visual anthropology. For, like Clouzot, Gardner's attempt to fuse the object and medium of his inquiry raises questions that are critical to contemporary work in the field.

4

TOWARD A VISUAL ANTHROPOLOGY

Visual anthropologists often like to think of themselves as avant-garde, inherently radical and questioning of established disciplinary practices. Nevertheless, experimentation has been cautious and a certain kind of ethnographic film—documentary realism—has long dominated the field. Over the past three decades or so, with the academic consolidation of visual anthropology as a specialized arena of inquiry, there have emerged two constellations of interest. Banks and Morphy (1997, 1) identify the study of visible culture and visual systems on the one hand and the use of visual technologies in anthropological research on the other. The former (including the anthropology of art, culture and media, museums, and memorialization) has remained largely wedded to the conventional methods and forms of textual anthropology, while work associated with the latter has increasingly been concerned to break with these textual conventions as part of the articulation of a distinctive intellectual agenda. It is one in which vision functions as a metaphor for ways knowing located in the body and the senses (Grimshaw 2001; MacDougall 1997, 1998). Understood in these terms, visual anthropology is no longer a literal enterprise, a form of illustration or pictorialism. Instead, it becomes an expansive and reflexive exercise. It is concerned with new kinds of knowledge, with extending anthropological inquiry into areas of human experience that lie on the edge of language, as inseparable from a concern with the possibilities of such knowledge. This project is engaged both with the full complexity of the ethnographic encounter and with anthropology itself.

What remains a problem, however, is the divide between an anthropology *of* the visual and a *visual* anthropology. It is a problem acknowledged by other scholars working in related fields (e.g., art historian Barbara Stafford). The question increasingly posed is how to work analytically with the new, rapidly proliferating forms of visual culture without translating them into a different conceptual register. How can we avoid "cultural textology" (Stafford 1996, 6) or "linguification" (Taylor 1996, 86)? In a subsequent essay, Taylor (1997, 15) goes further. He warns that anthropologists' increasing interest in the visual threatens, paradoxically, to check the emergence of a fully visual anthropology. He suggests that the new concern with the visual as an object of inquiry might become a substitute for an exploration of the potential of the visual as a medium of inquiry rather than the basis for a rethinking of ethnographic method, epistemology, and form. This is why *Passenger* matters.

Robert Gardner is anthropology's enfant terrible. It is difficult to know whether the hostility provoked by his work has its origins in his commitment to aesthetic innovation or whether it is more about the grandiosity of his themes and ambitions. Whatever its source, the filmmaker tends to polarize anthropologists in rather predictable ways—those for "art" and those for "science," as if aesthetics and knowledge, form and content, can be separated. Indeed, any proper critical appreciation of the aesthetics of Gardner's films reveals them to be *precisely* about knowledge.

From the beginning of his career, Gardner announced himself as a filmmaker to be less interested in the explanatory and more in the poetic. He has always intended his work to be suggestive, allusive, contemplative, and he draws heavily on metaphor to effect the movement between cultural particularities and universal themes. This commitment to transcending the literal, what Loizos (1993, 140) describes as Gardner's "Symbolist" impulse, finds expression in the distinctive visual and aural textures that characterize Gardner's film aesthetic. There is a remarkable consistency to the work, shaped by a strong authorial presence asserted through the structure of the image, the resonance of the sound, and the urgency of the narration. Despite the clarity of Gardner's cinematic vision, it is also important to acknowledge changes in the filmmaker's sensibility as it has evolved over time. Specifically, the relationship between image and sound has changed—and this is intimately linked to the shifting epistemological ground of Gardner's work.

For many reasons, Gardner's early films like *Dead Birds* or *Rivers of Sand* are considered problematic by anthropologists. Certainly, the startling beauty of the images creates unease, but it is, perhaps, the sound tracks of these films that has generated more professional consternation. There is an irony here. If anthropologists have objected to the dominance of Gardner's commentary in *Dead Birds* (speaking for and imputing emotions to his Dani subjects), to his selective use of the subject's voice (that of Omali Inda) in *Rivers of Sand,* they have also objected to the complete abandonment of the verbal in *Forest of Bliss.* What is clear is that the filmmaker progressively discards the spoken in favor of a richer and more subtle understanding of sound itself. While never wedded to linearity or to audio as a passive accompaniment to the image, this change nevertheless frees Gardner to push his experimentation with narrative further. The retreat from language opens up new possibilities. But this expansion of aesthetic possibilities is not pursued for its own sake. Instead, it is necessitated by Gardner's commitment to exploring areas of human experience that, until recently, have remained outside anthropology's purview. Gardner's work can be understood as part of a broader phenomenological turn in the human sciences that has returned matters of the body, the senses, movement, the imagination, and knowing to the heart of intellectual inquiry.

Passenger may be considered to be representative of the new stage in Gardner's project. In significant ways, it extends the kind of experimentation that marked *Forest of Bliss. Passenger* explores the profoundly nondiscursive, abstract painting. Through images, sound, and editing, Gardner suggests the full complexity of artistic praxis, or what he calls "sense-making." But it also is different from *Forest of Bliss.* The latter is an elaborately constructed symphonic poem. *Passenger,* however, is forged through the collaboration between artist and filmmaker. It is an expression of the creative synthesis achieved between object and medium of inquiry. Gardner's film of Scully is, finally, not a commentary on an already existing, determined reality; rather, as Bazin (1997) says of *The Mystery of Picasso,* it is "legitimately and intimately organized in aesthetic symbiosis with the events pictured" (216). Moreover, Gardner's achievement of this synthesis hinges crucially on working differently with montage.

Montage or radical juxtaposition has long been considered central to Gardner's work (Loizos 1993). In seeking to transcend the literal, the filmmaker has consistently refused to approach reality as inherently continuous and meaningful. Instead, he fragments it as a preliminary to reconstituting it according to his own poetic logic. This approach was, however, at odds with the spirit of twentieth-century anthropology and the profound commitment to context. But the discipline's self-conscious turn has brought techniques of montage into new focus (Marcus 1994). Within both cinema and anthropology, montage is often regarded as inherently radical. It is understood as a method of interrogating the world as it presents itself, of exposing the conventional as the ideological. Within visual anthropology, too, it has come to be opposed to the realism of ethnographic film (Loizos 1993; Nichols 1999). But the techniques of neither realism nor montage are inherently radical—as Gardner's film *Passenger* reveals in a most unusual way.

In his classic essay "The Evolution of the Language of Cinema," Bazin (1967) unfavorably contrasted the "tricks" of montage, "the creation of a sense or meaning not objectively contained in the images themselves but derived exclusively from their juxtaposition" (25), with filmmaking approaches built around a "respect" for reality (understood not as any straightforward transcription of reality but created by means of a different kind of artifice). According to Bazin, by sacrificing an omniscient camera for a situated perspective, directors like Murnau and Flaherty revealed scenarios of remarkable subtlety and complexity. As he explains in his much cited remarks on the seal hunting scene in Flaherty's film *Nanook of the North,* "The camera cannot see everything at once but it makes sure not to lose any part of what it chooses to see. What matters to Flaherty, confronted with Nanook hunting the seal, is the relation between Nanook and the animal; the actual length of the waiting period. Montage could suggest the time involved. Flaherty however confines himself to showing the actual waiting period; the length of the hunt is the very substance of the image, its true object" (27).

Looking closely at *Passenger,* it is hard not to notice Gardner's resemblance to Flaherty here. His film is grounded in an exploration of the mise-en-scène constituted in the space between the artist, the canvas, his materials, and his studio. Its central concern is pictorial duration, the time of the painting. This emerges from the filming process itself, from the creative synthesis achieved between Gardner's practice and that of Scully. *Passenger* is unusual in that the filmmaker resolutely refuses to bring anything into it from outside. He deals solely with what happens over six days in Scully's studio. The breaking up of reality as a preliminary to its reassembly according to the poetic vision of the film director— exemplified in Vertov's cinema and characteristic of Gardner's other work—is replaced here with something infinitely richer and more suggestive. *Passenger* renders problematic the traditional opposition of Bazinian realism and Vertovian modernism. For, here, Gardner is not adding to reality. He interrogates it in such a way that the process of artistic creation is not made transparent but instead becomes ever more mysterious.

Robert Gardner has long been committed to a radical project that takes seriously the potential of the film aesthetic as a medium for anthropological understanding. His bold experimentation with form has always been matched by a grandeur of ambition. He has continued to hold fast to universal themes in an era of specialization and cultural particularities. Like that other self-styled romantic hero, Jean Rouch, Gardner is unafraid of breaching political sensitivities, his confidence and expansiveness serving as a refreshing antidote to the doubt and anxiety of contemporary anthropology. His film, *Passenger,* importantly reminds us that art properly belongs to the field of visual anthropology, posing questions about how, where, and by whom art is made in the West. But inseparable from the exploration of these questions is the method and form of inquiry itself. In *Passenger,* aesthetics and knowledge are inseparable. Critical to Gardner's achievement of synthesis is his relationship with the artist. One feels that in Sean Scully, Gardner finally meets his subject on shared ground.

I am very grateful to David Freedberg, Amanda Ravetz, and the editors of this volume for their constructive comments and editorial suggestions.

NOTES

1. The artist himself variously cites these influences in the evolution of his style. For example, see Scully's interview with Kevin Power in Carrier (2004) and Zweite (2001).

2. For a discussion of the titles given to Scully's paintings, see the artist's own comments (Carrier 2004, 107) and also Zweite (2001).

3. Gardner's use of more than one camera is unusual here. I am grateful to Ilisa Barbash and Lucien Taylor for reminding me that Gardner has not used multiple cameras in his other film work.

4. Scully works on *Passenger* as a series of vertical stripes, but it becomes clear, as the film unfolds, that the artist intends the painting to be one of horizontal stripes. Each time Scully reviews his work, he changes the plane of the canvas and window from vertical to horizontal. In his conversation with Keith Power, Scully explains, "Horizontals are the eternal horizon, where we see the edge of our own local world. Verticals are assertive, like us standing" (quoted in Carrier 2004, 211).

5. "I am not looking for clarity; I am looking for emotion. Therefore I work and work until it arrives. I am not, in a sense, making it, or forcing it, or controlling it: I am improvising and painting with feeling until it arrives. I feel as I am making the painting, though not controlling its destiny" (quoted in Carrier 2004, 212).

6. Liberman's book was first published without photographs in 1960. The later edition included the images that he had taken during the 1950s while visiting artists in their studios.

7. The terms he uses to describe himself include "romantic," "idealistic," "relentlessly emotive." He declares, "My work is affirmative. I want to affirm the expressive potential of the individual, to re-establish this in the face of the world order" (quoted in Carrier 2004, 211).

8. I am using the term "aesthetic" here to refer to the heightened sensory qualities of the Gardner's films rather than to notions of beauty and judgment. Howard Morphy's (1992) discussion of aesthetic effects is valuable here. For an anthropological debate of the cross-cultural issues relating to aesthetics, see Ingold (1996).

9. This is an issue that many anthropologists have found especially problematic. For example, see Loizos's summary (1993, 152–58) of the controversy surrounding *Rivers of Sand.*

REFERENCES

ALPERS, Svetlana. 1988. *Rembrandt's enterprise: The studio and the market.* Chicago: University of Chicago Press.

BANKS, Marcus, and Howard Morphy, eds. 1997. *Rethinking visual anthropology.* New Haven, CT: Yale University Press.

BAZIN, André. 1967. *What is cinema?* Vol. 1. Essays selected and edited by Hugh Gray. Berkeley: University of California Press.

———. [1956] 1997. "A Bergsonian film: *The Picasso Mystery.*" In *Bazin at work: Major essays and reviews from the forties and fifties,* ed. Bert Cardullo, 213–20. New York: Routledge.

CARRIER, David. 2004. *Sean Scully.* London: Thames and Hudson.

CHAPMAN, H. Perry. 1990. *Rembrandt's self-portraits: A study in seventeenth-century identity.* Princeton, NJ: Princeton University Press.

DANTO, Arthur. 2004. "Sean Scully and the art of painting." In *Sean Scully: Body of light,* 3–31. Canberra: National Gallery of Australia. Exhibition catalog.

GARDNER, Robert. 1996. "The impulse to preserve." In *Beyond document: Essays on nonfiction film,* ed. Charles Warren, 169–80. Hanover, NH: University Press of New England.

GRIMSHAW, Anna. 2001. *The ethnographer's eye: Ways of seeing in anthropology.* Cambridge: Cambridge University Press.

INGOLD, Tim. 1996. *Key debates in anthropology.* London: Routledge.

JONES, Caroline A. 1996. *Machine in the studio: Constructing the postwar American artist.* Chicago: University of Chicago Press.

KRAUSS, Rosalind. 1993. *The optical unconscious.* Cambridge, MA: MIT Press.

LIBERMAN, Alexander. [1960] 1988. *The artist in his studio.* New York: Random House.

LOIZOS, Peter. 1993. *Innovation in ethnographic film: From innocence to self-consciousness 1955–1985.* Manchester: Manchester University Press.

MACDOUGALL, David. 1997. "The visual in anthropology." In *Rethinking visual anthropology,* ed. Marcus Banks and Howard Morphy, 276–295. New Haven, CT: Yale University Press.

———. 1998. "Visual anthropology and the ways of knowing." In *Transcultural cinema: Selected essays,* ed. Lucien Taylor, 61–92. Princeton, NJ: Princeton University Press.

MARCUS, George. 1994. "The modernist sensibility in recent ethnographic writing and the cinematic metaphor of montage." In *Visualizing theory: Selected essays from V.A.R. 1990–1994,* ed. Lucien Taylor, 37–53. New York: Routledge.

MARCUS, George E., and Fred R. Myers. 1995. *The traffic in culture: Refiguring art and anthropology.* Berkeley: University of California Press.

MORPHY, Howard. 1992. "From dull to brilliant: The aesthetics of spiritual power among the Yolngu." In *Anthropology, art and aesthetics,* ed. Jeremy Coote and Anthony Shelton, 181–208. Oxford: Clarendon Press.

MYERS, Fred R. 2002. *Painting culture: The making of aboriginal high art.* Durham, NC: Duke University Press.

NICHOLS, Bill. 1999. "Dislocating ethnographic film: *In and Out of Africa* and issues of cultural representation." *American Anthropologist* 99 (4): 810–24.

POWER, Kevin. 2004. "Conversation with Sean Scully." In *Sean Scully,* ed. David Carrier, 208–14. London: Thames and Hudson.

STAFFORD, Barbara Maria. 1996. *Good looking: Essays on the virtue of images.* Cambridge, MA: MIT Press.

STEINER, Christopher B. 1995. "The art of the trade: On the creation of value and authenticity in the African art market." In *The traffic in culture: Refiguring art and anthropology,* ed. George E. Marcus and Fred R. Myers, 151–65. Berkeley: University of California Press.

TAYLOR, Lucien. 1996. "Iconophobia: How anthropology lost it at the movies." *Transition* 69: 64–88.

——. 1997. "Introduction." In *Transcultural cinema,* by David MacDougall, 3–24. Princeton, NJ: Princeton University Press.

ZWEITE, Armin. 2001. "Abstraction and authentic experience: Double strategies in the oeuvre of Sean Scully." In *Sean Scully: Paintings, pastels, watercolors, photographs 1990–2000,* 13–76. Düsseldorf: Richter Verlag. Exhibition catalog.

7 DANCING WITH GARDNER

WILLIAM ROTHMAN

In his so-called ethnographic films, Robert Gardner views each society he films, in all its otherness, as a reflection of our own. For we are other to ourselves. Far from being the dispassionate works some have taken them to be, films such as *Dead Birds, Rivers of Sand, Deep Hearts,* and *Forest of Bliss* are deeply felt meditations on the tenderness and cruelty, the longing for love and avoidance of love, we find when we look into our own hearts. He unburdens *his* heart by creating these sublime and beautiful cinematic poems that move us beyond words.

In *Dead Birds,* for example, the depth of Gardner's feeling is revealed, even as it is masked, by his voice-over narration—by the words he speaks, by the measured tones in which he voices them, by what he consigns to silence. When he registers the death of a child by invoking "all the work, and love, it takes to make a boy," it goes without saying that he is a father who has given such work and such love as well as a son who has received it and that, like all human beings, he was born into the world and is fated to die. It is the filmmaker's humanity, what he has in common with the "others" he films and with us, that gives him standing to speak about such matters. It also goes without saying how much work and how much love it takes to make such a film as *Dead Birds,* one that affirms that every human life is of immeasurable value and irreplaceable.

In *Deep Hearts,* Gardner all but forgoes narration, apart from his putting into his own words what he tells us is a Bororo's greatest fear: "to be devoured by another person's eyes or mouth, by the way they might look, or the words they might speak." From this fear follows the desirability, as a Bororo understands it, of having a "deep heart." When Gardner adds, "If their heart is deep, no one can see what it contains," he is speaking as an anthropologist, relaying to us what such "others" believe. But he is also speaking as a man who knows firsthand, as we all do, about such a belief or fantasy. When these beautiful men place themselves so flamboyantly on display, Gardner films them in close-up, inviting—or provoking—them to direct their solicitations to the camera. In these shots, the obliqueness of their gaze, as they present themselves, bespeaks a reluctance to disclose what is contained in their deep hearts, a reticence that is the other face of their theatricality. But Gardner does not try to put into words what is revealed to and by his camera. He does not try to speak for these men or for those whose favor they wish to win. Nor does he try to speak for himself as to the feelings aroused in him by their displays, which so vividly communicate—but not in words—what these men wish to make known. Gardner allows or calls on these faces-turned-masks, transfigured by the medium of film, to speak for themselves.

In *Rivers of Sand,* too, Gardner respects his subjects' ability to communicate what they wish to make known, in this case by delegating his role as narrator largely to an informant who addresses the camera directly and speaks with authority, as he cannot, about how it feels to be a woman in a society in which men routinely abuse their wives and treat them as slaves. When Gardner breaks his silence halfway through the film, it is to tell us that in this woman's society every day begins at night. This means, literally, that these people have so much work to do that they have to get up before dawn to start their working day but, beyond this, that even the satisfactions that gladden their hearts emerge from the suffering they endure and inflict. What Gardner goes on to say, in words a woman cannot speak, concerns the effects of this abuse on the men: their loss of self-esteem, their knowledge that they are compromising their physical and moral beauty.

The human need for love, which is the other face of the human avoidance of love, is a deep subject of all of Gardner's films. But his subject is no less the human need for beauty, our need to acknowledge and participate in the beauty—sometimes the cruel beauty—of creation. This is the other face of our avoidance of beauty, our ways of coarsening ourselves physically and morally.

Beyond its value as ethnography and as personal expression, a Gardner film aspires to be a thing of beauty physically and morally—that is, a work of art. A film like *Forest of Bliss,* as Stanley Cavell (1996) puts it, "acts to burst its form, as if its maker is challenging its origins, taking his work into its own exploration of the conditions of art and of life that make it possible, as if becoming answerable for, and to, the medium of film itself" (xxvii). In other words, Gardner's film is discovering its roots (its roots in the reality of its subjects and in the medium of film) but also breaking free from those roots, at once exploring and challenging the conditions of art (the arts of the people he films and his own art as film-maker) and of life (the lives he films and his own life). This is what Cavell means, I take it, when he speaks of *Forest of Bliss* as becoming answerable for and to the medium of film itself. Gardner's work strives to keep faith with the art of film. And it strives to vindicate or validate his faith in film, his faith in art. Cavell goes on:

> The absence of Western words among the film's eloquent tracks of sound is one sign of the film's respect for difference, for otherness, respect both for the other's mystery and for its own power to communicate what it wishes known. It is a version of that respect for his or her subject or material that every true artist manifests. (xxvii)

In *Forest of Bliss,* Gardner does not put into his own words his understanding of the lives he is filming as he did in *Dead Birds.* Nor do the people in the film address solicitations to the camera as in *Deep Hearts.* The people in *Forest of Bliss* communicate what they wish known but not by putting it into their words, either, as in *Rivers of Sand.* In *Forest of Bliss,* the camera's subjects communicate what they wish known simply by going about their lives as if no camera were present or, rather, as if a camera were already present, always present, in their lives. The absence of narration and of Western words in general marks Gardner's respect for the otherness of these people as they perform the rituals around which their lives revolve. It also marks his respect for the otherness of the shots and tracks of sound out of which the film is made, for their mysterious ability to communicate what *they* wish known, as it were, without anyone speaking of them or for them. Then again, it is film's ontological condition that the world re-created in its own image on film *is* the world, is *the* world, the one existing world transformed or transfigured by being "captured" by a camera and projected onto a screen. In *Forest of Bliss,* the world on film is at once the film's material and its subject. At one level, then, it is the art of film—film as a medium of artistic creation—that Gardner's art strives to respect. Without such respect for his art, for art itself, Gardner would not be a true artist, in Cavell's view.

It is no accident, then, that in the early 1950s, when Gardner was an even younger man than he is today, one of his first films, made immediately after *Blunden Harbour,* was a film called *Mark Tobey* (27 minutes, 1952), an "experimental portrait" (to borrow the description in the catalog for Documentary Educational Resources, which distributes the film) of the well-known painter "which tries to show in cinematic language how this man looked at the world" (http://www.der.org). *Mark Tobey* and its follow-up, *Mark Tobey Abroad* (27 minutes, 1973), approach Tobey's art with the same kind of anthropological interest, as we might put it, that *Blunden Harbour* takes in the dances and myths of the Kwakiutl. But, significantly, in creating all these early films, his interest in coming to know the way the people he films look at the world goes hand in hand with an interest in coming to know what he calls "cinematic language," film's singular powers of expression and its limits. Gardner comes to know the "cinematic language" in the only way it *can* be known: by finding something to say in this language and by saying it. In these earliest of his films, as in all his subsequent work, Gardner approaches the intersection of life and art, which is his abiding subject, as an anthropologist *and* as an artist. In the language of cinema, anthropology *is* art, art *is* anthropology, knowledge *is* creation. If anthropologists are not artists, they cannot be scientists, either.

It is, again, no accident but rather the happiest of inspirations that in recent years Gardner has created works—they are videos, not films—that focus on three artists he deeply respects—one a fellow filmmaker—in the act of artistic creation, returning to the rich vein he first mined at the outset of his career.

The earliest of these works, *Dancing with Miklós* (28 minutes, 1993), is the one I will primarily address in the remainder of this chapter. Before turning to it, let me say just a word about the others. When I sat down to write this chapter, I intended to devote equal time to each of these works. But once I started writing about *Dancing with Miklós,* I became so immersed in its subtleties that, when I finally surfaced, I had to resign myself to the fact that writing about the others would have to await another occasion. I promise myself that I will write about these works one day, though, for the simple reason that I have fallen in love with them, in particular, *Passenger: An Observation in Four Movements* (25 minutes, 1998; made in collaboration with Robert Fulton and Ryan Bradley) and its lighthearted companion piece, *Scully in Malaga* (7 minutes, 1998), a short film acknowledging the efforts of those responsible for installing the exhibition "Sean Scully 1987–1997" in Malaga.

Passenger is the title of a painting by Gardner's friend Sean Scully, the well-known American artist, done in his studio in Barcelona in the early summer of 1997. Gardner made what he calls "an observation in four movements" (the word "movements" registers the musical qualities that are, as Charles Warren notes in chapter 1 of this volume, so important to Gardner's work) the intention of which is, to borrow once more from the distributor's Web site, to "impart an experience of the engagement by Scully with the work in question, an engagement which is both physical and emotional"—and, I would add, spiritual. I would also add that *Passenger* "imparts an experience" not only of the painter's "engagement" with the work of art he is creating but of Gardner's "engagement" as well—his "engagement" with Scully's act of artistic creation and with his own as well (http://www.der.org). This description is fine as far as it goes, but it is too modest to convey the exhilarating impact of the video, which strikes me as nothing short of a masterpiece, one of the most inspired and inspiring works about artistic creation that I know.

Not far behind is *Good to Pull (Bon à tirer),* a short video—alternately amusing and chilling, sometimes both at once—about a collaboration between the artist Michael Mazur and his master printer, Robert Townsend, as they work on a suite of etchings drawn form the celebrated monotypes Mazur made for Dante's *Inferno.*

All of these works complement and illuminate Gardner's films about other cultures and confirm—not that this should have been in doubt—that his art manifests deep respect for its subject or material.

Celebrated for his extraordinarily fluid, ornate, and highly stylized camera work, Hungary's most respected director achieved international prominence in the late 1960s with such films as *The Round-Up* (1965), *The Red and the White* (1967), and other parables on the theme of tyranny and revolution, betrayal and resistance, and power and corruption. In the altered political context of postcommunist Hungary, Jancsó's films continued to explore these themes and to pursue his formal preoccupations. In 1991 and 1992, Jancsó taught at Harvard as a visiting artist, as so many major filmmakers have done. It was at this time that Gardner and his friend Michael Fitzgerald helped Jancsó finance his latest film project as an international coproduction. The result: the compelling political thriller known in English as *The Blue Danube Waltz,* for which Jancsó was honored as "Best Director" at the prestigious 1993 Montreal World Film Festival.

The *New York Times* Web site summarizes the film as follows: "When Hungary's newest prime minister is shot and killed at a reception, the resulting investigation is necessarily swift and comprehensive. This compelling political thriller uncovers two prime suspects: the woman who guns the leader down, and a man who was friends with both the prime minister and his murderer. Using video surveillance footage, as well as other more artful and symbolic imagery, the noted 'visualist' director Miklós Jancsó, who is known for his craft in getting his points across non-verbally, combines fantasy and reality in a highly ironic manner" (http://movies2.nytimes.com/movie/146545/Kek-Duna-Keringo/overview).

As a review in *Time-Out* puts it, "The political context may have changed, but paranoia and anxiety are still the order of the day as Jancsó's sinuous camera coils and uncoils its way around the characters, with video monitors within the unfolding action frequently offering different angles on the same material as we're watching it. Images, like truth, are definitely open to manipulation. The choreographic virtuosity of the director's lengthy takes is as impressive as ever, in a film which easily stands comparison with his acknowledged late '60s heyday" (http://www.timeout.com/film/newyork/reviews/68113/Blue_Danube_Waltz.html).

Gardner himself relates quite straightforwardly the circumstances of making *Dancing with Miklós:*

> When Michael Fitzgerald and I decided to help Miklós Jancsó make *The Blue Danube Waltz* neither of us even considered the possibility of not watching him do it. We both loved his work and we both, perhaps for our own reasons, wanted to know how he managed to make films of such immense visual power so quickly and so inexpensively. It was not long before I had succumbed to the by now banal idea of filming filmmaking... *Dancing With Miklós* is the outcome... It is, though admittedly lighthearted, a deeply felt tribute to a fellow filmmaker's grace. (quoted from the cover of the VHS cassette *Dancing with Miklos*)

Michael Fitzgerald is a shrewd but principled producer who has endeavored throughout his career to make admirable feature films on limited budgets. Thus, it is no mystery why he would want to know how Jancsó manages to "make films of such immense visual power so quickly and so inexpensively." But what was Gardner's reason? For some years he had been seriously contemplating directing a fiction film. Was he then, as a practical matter, hoping to learn a trick or two from this master craftsman?

Asserting independence from the Soviet montage tradition, Jancsó's sequence shots all but relegate editing to the dustbin of history. He plans his long takes in advance, down to the smallest detail, including in his design the camera's every movement as well as every gesture of every character. By contrast, Gardner's shots, even when relatively long in duration, are spontaneous, improvised, unrehearsed; they capture events as they are happening. It is in the editing room that Gardner's films achieve their structure. As we will see, Gardner is fascinated by the long takes that are Jancsó's stylistic signature—but not, I think, because he wants to learn from the master how to film them. Perhaps Gardner initially entertained some such idea. But in the course of making *Dancing with Miklós,* he finds himself confirmed in his own way of shooting, which is in a sense the polar opposite of Jancsó's.

Dancing with Miklós opens with a black screen. Light floods in as a group of soldiers open what we then recognize as the door to an abandoned factory inside which the camera is located.

The soldiers trot in lockstep all around this cavernous space, evidently looking for someone. Following their movement, the camera itself completes a circle when it frames the soldiers, now backlit silhouettes, as they exit empty handed. At the same moment the invisible camera completes its circling movement, a man with a video camera on his shoulder

suddenly enters the frame, his entrance effected at once by his own movement and by the movement of the camera (the invisible one, not the visible one). Presumably, he had been hiding, shooting the intrusion of the soldiers even as the invisible camera was shooting it.

This cameraman's entrance catches us by surprise. Evidently not caught by surprise, though, the invisible camera accommodates his sudden appearance without having to alter its trajectory. Apparently, it has already factored in this camera's presence.

It is at this point that Gardner breaks his silence, initiating a voice-over narration that will resume intermittently throughout the film. "In this oddly beautiful old abandoned factory, the Prime Minister of a country not at all unlike Hungary has just been assassinated, and the secret police begin their work..." As Gardner is speaking these words, the man with the video camera turns to point his camera at another man who has suddenly stepped into the frame.

Continuing to shoot him with his video camera, he follows this man, the invisible camera moving along with them, as Gardner's voice-over continues, "In the end, almost everyone in this film by Miklós Jancsó is assassinated."

With this line, Gardner's narration informs us—we already suspected it—that what we have been viewing, what we are viewing, was shot by Jancsó's camera, not his own. This announcement comes just in time for us to appreciate Jancsó's virtuosity in pulling off this complex sequence shot as, in a single long take, his camera segues seamlessly from following the cameraman and his subject, to a woman escaping from the building in a small white car, to the arrival of a police car, and back to the cameraman and the man he has been shooting, who is discussing the dire political situation with another man and who suddenly demands that the cameraman give him his videocassette. At this charged moment, a small frame-within-the-frame appears in the lower right-hand corner of the screen.

Within this frame-within-the-frame, we view what we recognize as the "same" moment but shot from a different perspective. While Gardner's invisible camera reframes to accommodate the movements of the people he is shooting, the image within the frame-within-the-frame expands to fill the entire screen. The world framed by Jancsó's camera is incorporated into or supplanted by the world framed by Gardner's, thus rendering visible the heretofore invisible camera, along with its operator and several members of the film crew. Among them is Jancsó. We are not told that this is who he is, but we can tell from the intensity of his absorption (emphasized by his being framed with his back to Gardner's invisible camera) that this is the director who is presiding over the world of his film and over the filming of that world.

Thus, in *Dancing with Miklós,* again not coincidentally, Jancsó's entrance—his first appearance and that of his camera as visible presences—coincides with the first appearance in the film—as an *invisible* presence—of *Gardner's* camera. (It is not until much later in the film that Gardner and his camera themselves are rendered visible.)

As several crew members laboriously move Jancsó's newly visible camera, which is tethered to the bulky apparatus of crane, dolly, and tracks, the director shifts his position to maintain his privileged view of the action (and his invisibility within his film). With the mobility his video camera allows him, Gardner, by contrast, can reframe effortlessly by pointing his camera or walking with it. And his way of shooting, unlike Jancsó's, allows him to capture revelations that were not—could not have been—planned in advance. There is a moment, for example, in which Gardner's camera frames only a portion of the dolly tracks—a part of the dolly itself, a young man helping to push—and Jancsó,

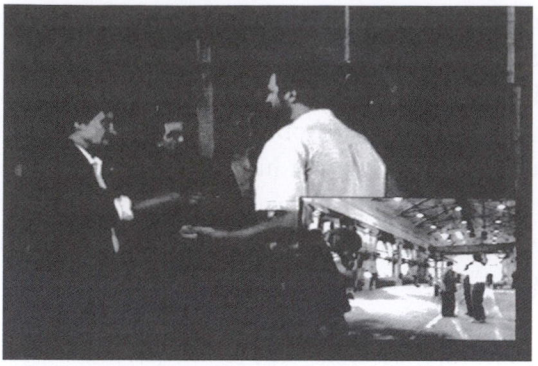

his hands on his hips, framed from behind and from the waist down. Shifting his weight from foot to foot and then taking measured little steps to follow the camera, Jancsó seems to be doing a little dance—in satisfaction? as an outlet for his tension?—in time with the movement of his bulky camera, which he seems to be envisioning as itself dancing. At this precise moment, the familiar strains of "The Blue Danube Waltz" begin—is it on the sound track of Jancsó's film or only Gardner's?—and a title card names the film we are viewing: "DANCING WITH MIKLÓS While he makes THE BLUE DANUBE WALTZ."

Jancsó's idiosyncratic practice is illustrated above all by the lengthy passage, late in *Dancing with Miklós,* in which Gardner films the Hungarian director blocking out and then presiding over the filming of one of the longest, most elaborate sequence shots in *The Blue Danube Waltz.* "Long takes, of course, require even longer rehearsals," Gardner points out in voice-over during this passage. "More importantly, they depend on a prodigious capacity to carry in the mind's eye the elaborate choreography of a scene often filmed not only with people but horses, helicopters, and a multitude of other elements that might go on for as long as ten minutes." When Gardner adds, a bit ruefully, "Sometimes"—presumably, this is one of those times—"it all seemed to me a game that only Hungarian chess masters should be playing," I hear him as acknowledging that Jancsó's way of filming is simply not for him.

To pull off such technically difficult long takes requires a large, close-knit team, an extended family of collaborators who share a common goal and work together so closely that it becomes second nature for them to communicate wordlessly with each other. Harvard doesn't work that way. Capitalist America doesn't work that way. No doubt, Gardner is also confessing his own as well as his society's limitation: he lacks the requisite "prodigious capacity" to carry elaborate choreography "in the mind's eye." Beyond this, I hear him as also saying—tactfully, as is his wont—that Jancsó's way of filming, which constructs such ingenious demonstrations of his own virtuosity, sometimes seems merely a game to Gardner, who is unwilling or unable to share that attitude. Be that as it may, Gardner's words are carefully chosen to suggest that there are times when Jancsó's way of filming seems otherwise to him—times when Jancsó seems to him a true artist, not a gamesman. Gardner refrains from saying how, at those times, Jancsó's art does seem to him. Not putting his appreciation of Jancsó's art into words but expressing it *cinematically* is Gardner's aspiration in the graceful finale that follows.

In effecting the transition to this finale, Gardner reprises the device he introduced in the opening sequence of using a frame-within-the-frame to distinguish the world captured by his camera from the world captured by Jancsó's. But this time, the frame appears in the lower left of the screen and contains the image captured by Jancsó's, not Gardner's, camera.

This frame-within-the-frame, too, expands to fill the entire screen. In effect undoing the opening sequence of *Dancing with Miklós,* the world framed by Gardner's camera becomes reincorporated into the world framed by Jancsó's. And at this moment, of course, Jancsó himself—who is vigilantly monitoring what his camera is filming—disappears from the frame. He now shares Gardner's condition of invisibility.

What Jancsó's camera is filming at this moment is a man being handcuffed, a prelude to his being led away (presumably to his execution). The aura of finality or fatality is heightened by the camera's movement in, which gives greater prominence to the wire grid in the background of the frame, and makes the prisoner loom large but faceless as he is led out of the frame to meet his fate.

At this very moment, the strains of "The Blue Danube Waltz" can once again be heard on the sound track, this time to chilling effect. The sense of foreboding is intensified when

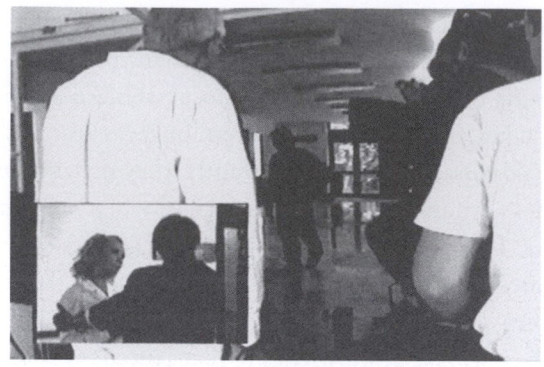

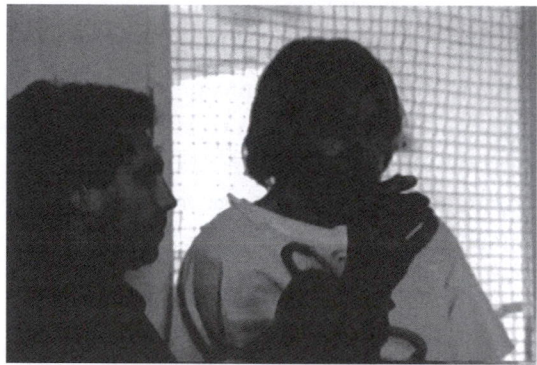

the camera continues moving in until it reveals the literal source of the music: a fiddler playing the tune on television. The camera keeps moving in until the image of the fiddler contained in the frame-within-the-frame of the television screen expands to fill the entire screen. Clearly, Jancsó's gesture here mirrors or is mirrored by Gardner's. Has Gardner's film appropriated Jancsó's spirit, or has it become possessed by it?

As he plays, the fiddler paces impatiently like a caged animal. At the same time, he gradually turns away from the camera, which continues moving in on him. By the time the camera

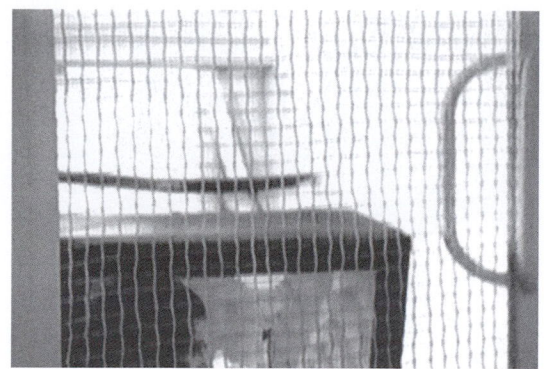

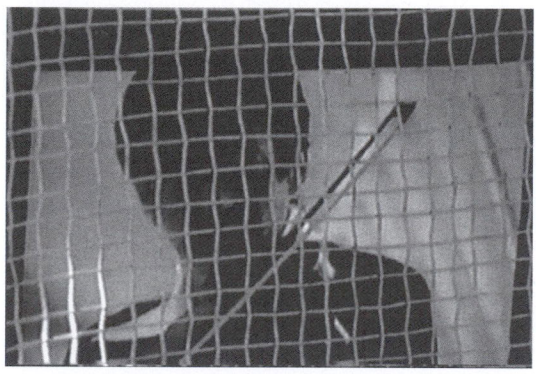

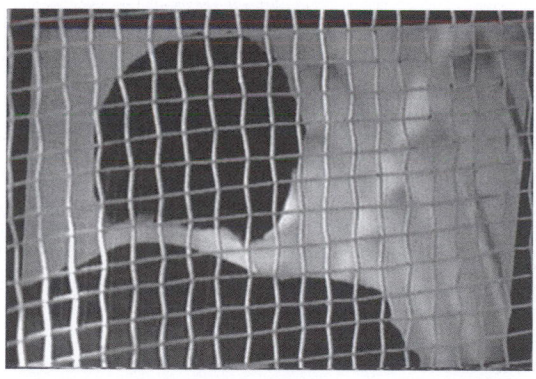

is near enough to frame him in close-up, his back is completely turned to it. The wire grid that separates his image from the camera enhances our sense that this music—and, by extension, Jancsó's film?—emanates from and addresses a condition of imprisonment, not freedom.

The Hungarian director's fatalism is highlighted but also transfigured by Gardner's exhilarating gesture of cutting at this moment to Jancsó, in what I take to be his living room, sitting in the gathering dusk with two of his colleagues. "The Blue Danube Waltz" continues from the previous sequence as if to suggest that these men are contemplating in

tranquillity the anything but tranquil scene that (I assume) they have just finished shooting. The song dissolves into another song, also heard earlier, that celebrates the Danube, Budapest's "blue waistcoat," and the attitude toward life—"So sweet, so sweet, with a little taste of salt"—of the denizens of this beautiful old city.

With this song continuing on the sound track, there follows a series of shots, taken in various locations, of Jancsó and crew members (in various stages of leave-taking, I assume)—including, remarkably, a shot (taken by Jancsó's camera?) of Gardner in the deserted factory that was the film's opening location, preparing to shoot and then shooting with his video camera.

The last thing Gardner shoots in this location is Jancsó's camera, aiming directly into its lens, so that what we see is a reflection of Gardner's own camera.

This series of shots culminates in an extended, breathtakingly beautiful helicopter shot following the Danube as it winds its way through Budapest. Is this Gardner's or Jancsó's shot? And are we inside or outside Jancsó's film? We cannot say.

The song, with its (quintessentially Hungarian?) admixture of sentimentality and cynicism, segues into "The Blue Danube Waltz." There is a cut—whether this is Gardner's or Jancsó's cut we again cannot say—to the singer (Tamás Cseh, a Jancsó regular) accompanying himself on the guitar and another man holding an umbrella over both of them. In this

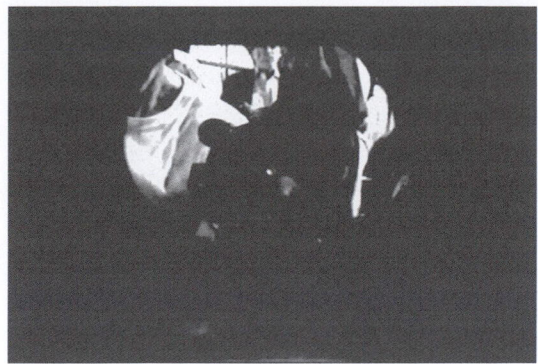

shot, the background swirls vertiginously behind them as if they—and the camera—were on a carousel.

We *are* back in Jancsó's film, it seems. Or are we? In the next shot, one of the few in the film taken by a stationary camera, "The Blue Danube Waltz" continues. Yet this shot takes us out of Jancsó's film and back into Gardner's. At one level, it seems to demystify Jancsó's shot by making perspicuous how it achieved its mysterious effect: the singer and his companion are on a platform in the middle of a circular track, turning slowly as the camera

circles around them. At another level, Gardner's shot acknowledges the mysterious power of Jancsó's cinema by summing up the Hungarian director's worldview in this haunting, metaphysically charged image or vision of circularity. (The circle of tracks strikingly resembles a clock face, as if in Jancsó's world time itself moves in circles, not straight lines.)

Asserting his prerogative as his film's author, Gardner resumes his voice-over, which was for so long dormant, by translating the last few words of the song, speaking them with feeling as if they were his own. "White steamer on the blue waves. A lady reading on the deck. She's reading a cheap novel, which is the story of my life."

The song completed, the singer and his companion stand motionless, and Jancsó's camera, too, stops moving. Astonishingly, there is a cut at this moment not back to the singer and his companion, as we might expect, but to Jancsó and Gardner, mimicking but reversing their pose. Jancsó is standing behind and slightly screen left of Gardner and holding an umbrella over both of them. Gardner, for his part, is not shooting with his video camera but simply holding it in his arms. Both men are looking at the invisible camera—whose camera?—with deadpan expressions as the final credits begin to roll.

Throughout *The Blue Danube Waltz,* Jancsó's restless camera performs an elaborately choreographed pas de deux with its visible subjects. In *Dancing with Miklós,* Gardner's camera performs an equally graceful duet with Jancsó's camera. Gardner is, indeed, "dancing with Miklós." But who is leading whom?

Dancing with Miklós is Gardner's film about Jancsó's filming of *The Blue Danube Waltz*. And yet, in a strange way, Jancsó's film also incorporates Gardner's filming into its own subject. In *The Blue Danube Waltz,* the camera possesses the mysterious power to anticipate the actions it films. In its man with the video camera, who keeps showing up to document what is happening, and in its ubiquitous television screens, the images of which represent an alternative perspective on reality, not only commenting on events but also seeming to hold sway over them, *The Blue Danube Waltz* seems to anticipate the presence of Gardner's camera as well.

Viewed from the Kafkaesque perspective of *The Blue Danube Waltz,* Gardner's camera takes on a sinister aspect. But viewed from the perspective achieved by Gardner's lighthearted yet deeply felt film, Jancsó's camera is characterized above all by what Gardner calls its *grace.* Ultimately, it is not Jancsó's craft, his cinematic technique, but his grace as an artist that Gardner's film celebrates. Jancsó's grace cannot be separated from the personal qualities that the Hungarian director possesses. Nor can it be separated from qualities possessed by the community that has stayed together so many years to collaborate on the creation of these deeply felt yet anything but lighthearted films or from qualities possessed by Hungarian society, which Jancsó's films reflect, celebrate, and, showing great courage, criticize—a culture, a world, different from Gardner's own.

In *Dancing with Miklós,* Gardner thus manifests his respect for Jancsó's difference, his otherness—his respect both for the other's mystery and for its own power to communicate what it wishes known. This is Gardner's version of the respect for his or her subject or material that, as Cavell asserts, marks the true artist. As exemplified by *The Blue Danube Waltz,* Jancsó's version of this respect requires that his films bear witness to his society's failure to respect difference or otherness, by its violent efforts to silence opposition, to deny people the power to communicate what they wish known.

The conditions of art and life that make Jancsó's films possible—indeed, necessary—are not the conditions of Gardner's art or his life. He has no fear that he might be imprisoned or shot for making his films. And yet Gardner's society—our society—has its own ways of failing to respect difference or otherness, its own ways of denying us the power to communicate what we wish known. What Gardner wishes his film to communicate about its subject or material—about Jancsó's act of artistic creation, about *The Blue Danube Waltz,* about film—is that, for all their differences, their cameras can dance together.

REFERENCE

CAVELL, Stanley. 1996. "Words of welcome." Foreword in *Beyond document,* ed. Charles Warren, Middletown, CT: Wesleyan University Press, xxvii.

8   GARDNER'S BLISS

DAVID MACDOUGALL

There is a serious gap between studying films as "texts" and studying how they are received by viewers, for within that gap is the largely unexplored territory of what the filmmaker intended by the film and how it came to fruition. Textual analysis and reception studies each have their limitations. The first tends to dehistoricize films, focusing on their internal construction and assuming wider understandings for what are often no more than the cultural and ideological responses of the critics. Reception studies, on the other hand, may provide insights into how different kinds of viewers interpret films, but they also tend to disconnect these from the actual process of filmmaking. Even when films are placed in an historical context, they are often interpreted within binary frameworks (idealist/materialist, artistic/scientific, romantic/classical, realist/visionary, and so on) that oversimplify their motives and the realities of the creative process. Assessments of nonfiction films, in particular, frequently measure them against a highly specific vision of historical or anthropological "truth," in which they must all too often be found wanting.

What we lack are more commentaries on the intellectual underpinnings and creative processes by which films are made. Ethnographic filmmakers, possibly even more than others, tend to write little about their work, perhaps believing that in the academic world this can result only in superficiality—a substitution of words for the products of their labors. They may even take a perverse pleasure in foiling this process. "Making a film," says Jean Rouch (1985), "is such a personal thing for me that the only implicit techniques are the very techniques of cinematography...It is also very difficult for me to talk about it and, above all, write about it" (32). Filmmaking also consumes more energy than is generally apparent to outsiders, often leaving little for writing. Moreover, it entails a fundamentally different attitude toward communicating with others. Rouch has made over a hundred films but produced only a handful of articles about film itself. Similar explanations could be given for the relative silence of other figures in ethnographic film, such as Robert Flaherty, John Marshall, Timothy Asch, and Ian Dunlop. It is not that filmmakers are unreflective, for they are often quite talkative about their work, but the ideas, descriptions, and reflections they express are ephemeral. This is the perspective most easily lost to history. What survives in writing is usually fragmented and anecdotal.

If we had them, more comprehensive, fine-grained accounts of the filmmaking process would allow us to compare our own ideas of films with an understanding of how the filmmaker's ideas and desires had been pursued in them, within the intellectual and artistic movements of their times. They would allow us to see how a film had progressed through the phases of planning, production, and editing and to witness the filmmaker's struggles to define issues, confront epistemological problems, and make his or her ideas and understandings manifest. Ideally, such an account would interrogate the filmmaker and the work at every stage of its production, although in most cases this is probably impractical. But until we have more full-length accounts by filmmakers, we will have to settle for less exhaustive testimony—diaries, production notes, interviews, and recorded conversations.

When Robert Gardner's *Forest of Bliss* received its first public screening at the Royal Anthropological Institute Film Festival in September 1985, it was introduced by Gardner's colleague and fellow filmmaker Timothy Asch. After the screening, Asch suggested to the audience that it was the film Gardner had always wanted to make and was, in effect, the crowning achievement of his filmmaking career. Since then, Gardner has made more films, but Asch was probably right in attaching such importance to this one. *Forest of Bliss* was many years in preparation and required several years more in the filming and editing. Unlike many films in which Gardner has been involved, it was not the result of a short-term collaboration such as *The Nuer* (1971), *Rivers of Sand* (1974), and *Altar of Fire* (1976), nor did it emerge from a group project, as had *Dead Birds* (1963); rather, it was a film Gardner had conceived and nurtured himself in a series of trips over several years to the city of Benares (now Varanasi). Although made with the close involvement of Ákos Östör, *Forest*

of Bliss really seemed to be a work close to Gardner's heart and the most mature expression of his creative thinking. More than that, it brought together two sometimes contradictory strands in his makeup as an artist—his desire to immerse himself in the physical existence of another society and his desire to explore its underlying symbolic systems and poetic resonances.

Two years after its release in 1985, *Forest of Bliss* became something of a cause célèbre through articles published in the pages of the *Society for Visual Anthropology Newsletter*. These included several incontinent attacks on the film and on Gardner himself (Moore 1988; Parry 1988; Ruby 1989), followed later by more temperate discussions (Kapur 1997; Loizos 1993; Ruby 1991, 2000). The attacks seemed to be fuelled by a kind of corporate outrage, as if Gardner had somehow let the side down or been guilty of insubordination. Several other articles appeared supporting the film (Chopra 1989; Östör 1989; Staal 1989), one of them as bracingly splenetic as those that had provoked it (Carpenter 1989).

Since then, much of the critical discussion of *Forest of Bliss* has revolved around the propriety of Gardner producing an interpretation of life (and death) in Benares that might reinforce the misconceptions of uninformed viewers. Gardner's subsequent reflections on the film, in a published conversation with Ákos Östör (Gardner and Östör 2001), was especially welcome in explaining his intentions and illuminating the film itself, although it will not do much to satisfy his detractors. Many of the critiques can in fact be read more as objections to Gardner's worldview than as any actual fear of harm being done. The film tends to divide its critics into those who have a view—of historical reality, of Benares, of India, or anthropology—that the film offends and those who, sometimes even in spite of this, see value in such a radically different kind of film being made. Nonfiction filmmaking is inevitably a perilous business, for it takes the stuff of real human lives and transforms it. There are some who see this as fundamentally immoral, yet it is also the process by which most of us observe the world around us and represent it to ourselves and others. One of the paradoxes of nonfiction film is that while we may deny it the possibility of objective truth (for it is always coded, always ideological), we somehow expect it to be "true" in its representations.

Gardner chose to remain aloof from the debate, perhaps thinking of the discussion of the film that he and Ákos Östör had recently recorded in 1987. In this conversation, the exchanges between the two are detailed and wide ranging, filled with speculations, fresh observations, doubts, and questions. To anyone curious about the filmmaking process, there is far more of interest in them than can be found in any number of critical essays and film reviews. Reading the edited transcript is like listening in on some very highly polished shoptalk.

During the course of the conversation, Gardner laments the fact that films over whose visual qualities the makers take endless care are so often shown in degraded copies. There is in fact a disjunction in public expectations about fiction and nonfiction films, when nonfiction is so rarely seen on anything but a small television screen. It is part of the popular mythology of nonfiction that it should be ugly and rough, that the camera eye should be imprecise, with no love or patience for the things it sees—even to the extent that fictionalized documentaries simulate a roughness that no nonfiction filmmaker would tolerate. All these things are, of course, anathema to Robert Gardner.

Partly because of the controversy surrounding it, *Forest of Bliss* has achieved a certain notoriety among ethnographic films. But the same was true of *Dead Birds* before it and several of Gardner's intervening films. There is more than controversy involved: the films announce themselves as deliberate and uncompromising works, demanding to be taken seriously. They are not simply films "about" something but the products of a distinctive and rigorous imagination.

I am one of those who has no problem in regarding *Forest of Bliss* as an ethnographic film, not because Gardner does (he is distrustful of the label) but because it seems to me to mark out new conceptual possibilities for visual anthropology. Ethnography on film—the description of particular sociocultural systems and settings—is open to a variety of strategies: illustrative, didactic, narrative, and associative. Gardner is one of the very few filmmakers who has attempted the last of these. I believe it is useful to see the film as a prototype: an experiment in a radical anthropological practice that explores the largely invisible interrelations of the visible world by visual (and, it must be added, auditory) means. Moreover, it seeks to do so in a fashion that resembles the way in which sensory awareness, cultural meaning, and metaphorical expression are combined in social experience and that film can evoke so eloquently. As Gardner remarks at one point, "We seem to comprehend the world in ways that the world itself provides for its comprehension, and metaphor is one of the tools at hand" (Gardner and Östör 2001, 65). *Forest of Bliss* provides an alternative way of thinking and feeling about the world, one that may strike some as familiar and others as utterly alien. It is a film that interprets reality by providing, to use Susan Sontag's phrase, a "reality in the second degree" (Sontag 1977, 52).

In 1957, Gardner wrote a statement about film and anthropology that can be taken as a prolegomenon for his later career in filmmaking. "At least two characteristics, fundamental to all people, help distinguish human beings from every other manifestation of nature. The first is the capacity for putting meaning into the reality apprehended by the senses...The second characteristic is a capacity for being responsive to the meaningfulness of each other's behavior, either of deed or of thought" (Gardner 1957, 344–45). *Forest of Bliss* is a challenge to filmmakers and film viewers to be more responsive to the meaning-potential of everyday life.

Gardner and Östör's discussion returns often to the ways in which objects in the film oscillate between the literal and the metaphorical and how they can be perceived as both. This is but one facet of the redoublement that lies at the heart of film itself or any representation. But it is especially pertinent to film as an indexical medium, in which one periodically has the sense of seeing through the images to the objects that occasioned them. Film, used with a sensitivity to this conundrum, offers a unique approach to the ways in which the mind and the senses integrate cultural experience. However one regards Gardner's particular Benares (and there are many others)—whether one would prefer a more "ethnographic"

Benares or a Benares more situated in contemporary Indian history and politics—Gardner's way of seeing social and cultural interconnections can still be productive for anthropology. But this way of seeing owes much to an older tradition.

In 1975, Jean Rouch (1995) wrote that it was to Robert Flaherty and Dziga Vertov "that we owe all of what we are trying to do today." He went on to quote Vertov, to the effect that "it is not sufficient to present fragments of reality on the screen, to represent life by its crumbs. These fragments must be elaborated upon so as to make an integrated whole which is, in turn, the thematic reality" (82–83). It is hard to think of *Forest of Bliss* without also thinking of Vertov's *Man with a Movie Camera* (1928) and the cluster of "city symphonies" made between 1926 and 1930 by Walter Ruttman, Alberto Cavalcanti, Mikhail Kaufman, Jean Vigo, and Robert Siodmak. Gardner's film belongs to this tradition in more ways than one. If ever a film were a "city symphony," *Forest of Bliss* is one, and if ever a film was the work of one man with a movie camera, this film certainly is. Gardner is not interested in Vertov's self-reflexive gestures, pointing toward the materiality of film, but he is interested in integrating fragments of experience into a thematic reality—a "film truth" that can never be the truth of other methods.

In *Forest of Bliss,* Gardner is committed to bringing us into a closer communion with wordless things and the networks of associations, by no means fixed, that may surround them. (Jyotsna Kapur is right in stressing the materiality rather than the otherworldliness of the film.) He is resolute in refusing, except for quoting a few lines from Yeats, to employ words or explanations or to translate speech in subtitles or in any other way to "linguify" the film (to borrow Lucien Taylor's expression). The published transcript of Gardner and Östör's explication of the film may thus serve as an antidote for those made uncomfortable by the lack of explanation in the film or what they see as a world made unnecessarily wordless. Gardner and Östör remark at several points that if speech in the film had been translated, we would not be much the wiser—it is the emotional tone of the various exchanges that is important. In eschewing verbal explanations, Gardner credits viewers with a good deal more intelligence and sensitivity to images and sounds than most other filmmakers would, and for an aficionado of words such as Gardner, this is significant. The film becomes a testament to seeing, but it is also intended as a challenge to our unthinking recourse to language as the first line of understanding. It is not that the film is so difficult, Gardner seems to say, only that we make it so.

Gardner and Östör's conversation about the film proceeds as a kind of gentle interrogation of Gardner by Östör. If there is sometimes a sense of each feeding off the other's views or of mutual congratulation, this is perhaps to be expected between colleagues and collaborators. And like the letters and diaries of writers and statesmen, the conversation was probably never meant to be wholly private: posterity was always in mind and publication always a possibility. It is not unexpected that these two would see the film through the logic of its creation. From their conversation, one begins to gain a sense of the knowledge and forethought about structural and anthropological issues that underlie the film but that the film itself wears lightly. One discovers that what some critics have seen as blind spots, such as political and ecological issues, were in fact matters of early debate and conscious choice. The filmmakers are aware of the limits of what a film can hope to achieve. At the same time, the film's meanings are never regarded as exhausted or exclusive of other views. The discussion is open-ended and a process of further discovery.

Early in the conversation (and in the film because they are working their way through it chronologically), Gardner and Östör refer to the scene of dogs fighting on the "far shore" of the Ganges. Gardner says that he had in mind an early warning to the audience that "the world is not the best of all possible places to be; to survive there is going to be an awful lot of anguish to deal with, and sometimes you don't quite make it" (Gardner and Östör 2001, 22). Thinking about the possible responses to the film, Östör remarks,

> I know that it disturbs people a great deal when they see this scene the first time. I remember on this occasion—and many others when we were filming such scenes—I was disturbed for reasons that I still have to puzzle out, and maybe in this conversation I will. While you were filming, I was really sensitive about the seemingly negative aspects of dogs, and you remember we had a lot of discussion and arguments about filming the filth and the corpses, all these matters that outrage the uninformed visitor. It's not that one wants to deny these things and play into the hands of the superficial apologists for a "modern" India. Benares is not a hell-hole of death and corruption, but if certain people

see any evidence for some of these things they will assume the basest motives for the images being included. (22–23)

Östör is modest about his role in the film, acknowledging that at times he could not visualize what it would look like, but he is also frank in his disagreement when this matters, both on points of ethnographic detail and in his assessment of Gardner's aesthetic choices. Sometimes he sounds less protective than Gardner of the viewer's sensibilities. This is the tone of one of their exchanges:

> *RG:* This is the first time that anyone actually sees cremation, a discernible body being consumed by discernible flames. This is the only time in the film that the audience is asked to see this way—passively, I would say, since there is nothing being asked of any-one except that they keep their eyes open. I was very concerned when I was doing this, and I remember this part as the hardest part of the film to edit. The rest of the film, by comparison, really almost edited itself. That's obviously not true, but it felt that way because it had a remarkable feeling of inevitability to it. But this part was very problem-atic, very difficult, and I wasn't sure what I should do. The whole Manikarnika episode in the film had to end in a way that resulted in some understanding and that also created some useful mystery. I worked a long time to get it to satisfy these two requirements.

ÁÖ: Well, I'm not sure. Here I find myself almost unequivocally on the other side, in the sense that it could have gone on much longer. The fire somehow makes it look more abstract. You weren't reticent about the earlier glimpses of corpses in the river and so forth, which have a far more recognizable and candid aspect. This body is somewhat screened by the fire.

RG: It has something to do with the obviousness of what is happening. I mean, when you set fire to something that's combustible, it's going to burn up. That's not only pretty obvious, it is completely unambiguous. But you are right about the possibility of ab-straction, the fire screening the body, and so forth. A lot depends on how the shot is made, what the camera does to the subject. I think I may not have been too resourceful here. (Gardner and Östör 2001, 106–7)

Interestingly, it is often Gardner rather than Östör who alludes to the need for fidelity to ethnographic detail, as when he includes in the film the healer, Mithai Lal, blowing three times on a conch shell, where many filmmakers would cut corners and show him blowing it only once (Gardner and Östör 2001, 50–51). The rhythms of actual life may here come into conflict with the rhythms of the film, but for Gardner the choice of which to observe is often a matter of respecting the dignity of a person or the forms of human invention, which may go deeper than we think. Later in the film a boat is being repaired, and rituals are being done for its "rebirth."

RG: When those hands are printed with yellow ochre on the pavement…I actually show all five times it happens. It would have been very easy to begin the shot with the third or fourth time it's done. It's a little like the three blowings of the conch at the be-ginning of the film. I think that five is an auspicious number on an occasion like this, so, ethnographically speaking, there may be a reason for shooting and editing the scene to include it all…Nonfiction films, especially those made for commercial release, will not usually give more consideration to the original shape of the behavior than to the editorial requirements of keeping the film moving. But my feeling on this is that if you ignore the internal rhythms of things, you stand to lose more than just authenticity. (Gardner and Östör 2001, 87–88)

It would be difficult to underestimate the importance of chance and circumstance in Gard-ner's thinking. Again and again, he refers to the filmmaker as the recipient rather than the bestower of gifts. The leitmotif of luck keeps surfacing, like the freshwater Ganges dolphin that makes an unexpected appearance—one so slight that Gardner did not see it until viewing the rushes. We are made aware, if we did not know already, how dependent the nonfiction filmmaker is on luck and, as a corollary, how often critics mistake luck for intention. And yet this is only half the story, for the filmmaker makes his own luck through patience and observation and a talent for anticipation. "I would guess," Gardner says, "that one of the ways an argument might be made that this kind of filmmaking has some art to it is to develop the idea of there being a sensitivity to the way things unfold in actuality. How much this is a talent and how much it is simply craft gained through long experience in observing life is hard to answer" (Gardner and Östör 2001, 36–37).

How then does luck becomes entangled in intention? Nonfiction filmmakers do not simply wait for actuality to happen to them, for, as Dai Vaughan (1999) has pointed out, "film is about something, whereas reality is not" (21). On the evidence of Gardner's observations, it is a matter of seizing the gifts that extend and deepen one's own vision and of respecting the world's enactments of itself. There was the moment when Gardner was filming the evening skyline and a monkey jumped into the frame, onto the roof of the tallest building. "How can such gifts of actuality be rejected?" he asks. To Gardner, "the monkey afforded a wonderfully surrealistic comment on the whole urban panorama... [as if] this world were being watched over by relatives of a lower order" (Gardner and Östör 2001, 113).

One sometimes has the experience while making nonfiction films that certain motifs recur uncannily in different combinations, as if they formed a thinly veiled network of underlying meanings—the sorts of meanings that in fiction seem consciously devised. These may become apparent immediately or emerge only long after the film is finished. At these times, the world seems metaphorically charged, as if there existed only a limited number of possible connections in human life. Are such experiences simply reflections of the

metaphors we live by and perhaps look for, or do they correspond to deeper resonances in the structures of society? Clearly, for Gardner, these are the taproots of his art.

Much of the talk between Gardner and Östör is about the convergence of elements that Gardner has chosen to focus on—water, wood, fire, boats, steps, marigolds, corpses, dogs, kites (as toys), kites (as birds), and so on. What astonishes Gardner as "luck" but what is objectively not really so astonishing is when some of these elements converge on their own, perhaps reinforcing the intimation of an underlying order that has attracted him to Hinduism in the first place. In a wholly constructed sequence, Gardner imagines a boy's kite pulling up the fire of the sun at dawn. He keeps on filming kites as ambiguous symbols of childhood, flight, the spirit, the body, and so on. "There was also," he says (with an air of innocence), "some obscure feeling that kites drifting off toward the far shore and sometimes falling into the river had a larger meaning" (Gardner and Östör 2001, 110). He keeps on filming kites, trying to film one falling into the water. One evening he is filming a boat drifting out to deposit a child's body in the river, and there happens a kind of magical event:

> Here, in the shot where the body is being dropped in the river, a kite falls in the background. So as the body is put in, the kite joins it. You know, the whole thing seems to get said in one quite simple symbolic passage that is, at the same time, powerfully actual. This was great luck, and someday we should ask ourselves what proportion of nonfiction film proceeds from luck. (110)

Hardly luck, one might suggest, but the other side of circumstance. For, as Gardner remarks at another point, "one of the few welcome accomplices of a nonfiction filmmaker is accident... I really think that putting oneself in the position to encounter accident is very much a part of succeeding in this genre" (60).

The conflict implicit in finding meaning in the randomness of life—when so much of the film rests on such a process—seems to be tested when such fortuitous situations as the kite scene fall, as it were, into Gardner's lap. In that particular scene, the relationship of elements is so subtle and the accidental quality of the events so evident that the problem is muted. But what if one filmed a body on a bamboo litter just as it passed by the bamboo worker's yard, as often happened? "No one would have believed it was really happening," says Gardner. Or, more to the point, "it would come off as something unquestionably contrived" (Gardner and Östör 2001, 58). There is a paradox, then, about asserting, at one and the same time, consequence and seeming inconsequence. Here, Östör goes to the heart of the matter more directly than Gardner when he refers to what is left *out* of a film: "It is symptomatic of the power to make things happen or make them not happen, and that says a lot about the very artificial crafting of these so-called real or actuality films. What is it that makes the 'realness' of one scene more or less acceptable than some other scene?" (58). I am not entirely convinced of the profundity of Gardner's reply: "I think part of the problem is that the very act of filming changes the state of realness in things."

Later the issue returns when, as the newborn boat is taken to the river, a body is taken to be ceremonially immersed. But once artifice has made its appearance, it cannot be conveniently suspended. "Here is a good case of actuality outdoing artifice," says Gardner. "Nevertheless, despite this sanction of reality, the inference might be drawn that the actuality is too contrived. I have not felt it was a mistake to use this comparison, only that it failed to be entirely convincing" (Gardner and Östör 2001, 87).

There is repeated speculation in the conversation about how many of the connections and associations intended in the film will come through to the audience. It is not a futile question, but nearly so without the benefit of reception studies (and these can rarely get at the subtleties involved). There are so many audiences; and each viewer will make a somewhat different set of conscious and intuitive connections, some intended and some not. One would really have to sound out many viewers at length to discover a consensus on even one point. Filmmakers are understandably reluctant to cross-examine their audiences, but there is also a certain vanity involved and a strong conviction as well. One makes the film for its own sake—less as a message than as a testament to what one has seen and what one cares about. Sometimes it is enough to know that the connections are there in the body of the work, available to those who may someday discover them.

Doubts about viewers' responses are aired early in the discussion in connection with the sounds of creaking oarlocks over several indistinct shots of boats in the mist. This sound will recur throughout the film, often evoking a boat that remains unseen. Gardner seems uncharacteristically tentative at this stage: "I don't think anybody just looking at this scene in the early morning mist would know what is gliding by, but the sound of the oars tells everyone water is involved... I have a feeling that at some level it is working" (Gardner and Östör 2001, 19). Not long after this, there is a shot of the holy fire at Manikarnika ghat. Östör says he associates the fire with steps, which are to become an important thematic element in the film. "I associate the steps with the fire," he says. "Well," Gardner replies, "maybe you can, but maybe nobody else can." What is curious here is that neither of them, here or elsewhere in the conversation, thinks in terms of a second or subsequent viewing of the film. It is always as though the film will be seen once and only once. Is this just hard realism, or is it a misapprehension among filmmakers? Or is it simply that they are impatient for the film to deliver everything of itself on the first viewing?

By the time the discussion is a little further advanced, Gardner sounds more confident. Perhaps it is because here the elements of the film are being assembled more bluntly. There are vultures wheeling overhead and a shot of an "unmistakable" corpse in the water. "Spliced together they're making the usual A + B = C," says Gardner, as though reciting a bit of Eisensteinian algebra. There's also a barge full of wood being rowed upriver. "It is not just for keeping people warm at night. I would hope all this is fairly clear from the editing" (Gardner and Östör 2001, 48).

A little later, Gardner again sounds a despairing note. The stairs above the ghat are a recurrent image in the film, and we have now moved inside the Mukti Bhavan, a charity-run

hospice for the dying, and are looking up a staircase. Gardner says that while he was shooting this, he was thinking of stairs in association with the transitions of life and death. But is there any point in all this?

> *RG:* The question I would like answered is when or even whether, with all the intentionality in the world putting as much metaphorical spin on the images as I or anyone else can manage, the audience is ever going to know that they are being asked to look at the stairs in this movie in a way they haven't thought to look at such things before. I think they will be willing to admit to a certain bombardment of their senses, but the question remains whether and how much they are focusing on the idea of stairs having more than just architectural significance. (Gardner and Östör 2001, 61–62)

The issue is never resolved in the conversation, but it is clarified at one point when Gardner concedes that the filmmaker's conscious linking of ideas and objects may never rise to the level of cognition in the viewer, and perhaps this is just as well. "We are being very precise about our associations. The average viewer won't be. He or she will just undergo, at best, some strong but quite inarticulate feelings" (65). This is the minimalist view, from which he can take some comfort, but it is not, of course, entirely true, nor is it expected to be. Even the "average" viewer (whoever that is) will understand some of the metaphors of this film at a cognitive level (the corpse-bearing litter as ladder, perhaps, or the kite as spirit).

The more important lesson here is that an *explication du texte* is not what any filmmaker is after. Despite a great deal of effort organizing a film, much of its power as a source of understanding necessarily works at the level of feelings and ambiguous possibilities. If one wants the viewers to live the film, it is counterproductive to encourage them constantly to decode it. Moreover, in Gardner's view, explanation can easily displace other modes of understanding. Given an explanation, viewers "will no longer need to pay quite the same kind of attention" (114). The problem one sometimes encounters with intellectuals who are unable to "see" a film is that they are too busy trying to think what they are supposed to be thinking about it. The consequence, of course, is that they are then likely to conclude that the film has "no" meaning or is "incomprehensible," as some critics did in this case.

In what Gardner regards as a highly pregnant sequence, a boy is seen trying to launch his kite in the air rising from the cremation ground, with a scale for weighing wood in the foreground. This is followed by a shot of an important Hindu shrine, with sparrows pecking at the offerings. Gardner observes, "I don't know whether the audience sees these connections. I would be content if they merely registered the facts: fires, scales, boys, kites, thermals. I'm confident they would then, at some level of their imagination, work out their meaning" (Gardner and Östör 2001, 83).

Gardner's obsession with metaphor becomes unsettling only when it seems to afflict him with the sort of interpretive tunnel vision that he would find excessive in others. He confesses to not knowing why he felt compelled to include shots of sand being loaded on the "far shore" and then unloaded in Benares. He seems to feel obliged to explain this as his response to the "ant-like" dreariness of human labor or to time itself (sand running through an hourglass). But people are not ants by choice. Gardner seems a little too inclined here to turn everything in the world metaphorically to his purpose, even the need of human beings to make a living or to dig sand for the cement to build their city. It is a detachment that sits uneasily with his more intimate moments of sympathy for human beings and their lot.

This sympathy expresses itself in a restraint that some may find hard to follow or mistake for coolness. Most nonfiction filmmakers have few misgivings about making films about other people—indeed, it is in filming them that they find an endless fascination. But for Gardner, this is presumptuous in the extreme. "The very idea of finding a way to reproduce some reality that can be called another person is, on its face, a total absurdity" (Gardner and Östör 2001, 99). His portrayals of individuals are therefore circumspect and, above all, respectful of what James Agee once called "the immeasurable weight in actual existence" of another human being (Agee and Evans 1960, 12). In his conversation with Östör, Gardner keeps circling around the problem of human dignity, never quite knowing how to find its center, except perhaps by indirection. Although there are three main "characters" in the film—the healer, the priest, and the Dom Raja—each maintains a mystery and autonomy that the film seems reluctant to break in on.

Gardner makes it clear that none of these persons is being developed "as a character in the familiar, narrative sense" (Gardner and Östör 2001, 49). The one to whom he seems closest in an oddly companionable way is the old healer Mithai Lal, perhaps the most mysterious

of the three. There is no clearly discernible core to this character, perhaps because so much of his stock in trade is mystification. And to Gardner, there are no obvious rules for respecting someone's dignity: one must assess each instance separately. Sometimes the result is counterintuitive. In the midst of a ritual, Mithai Lal gives a great belch. "I didn't really hesitate to include that when editing. Why hasn't it diminished his dignity? Could it have anything to do with the way it was shot? The way it was graphically delivered? That there is a context already provided within which to deal with this event?" (51). All the above, no doubt, but also because there has been no attempt to recruit Mithai Lal to a moral position within the classical structures of character narration. Within such a universe, there can be no real embarrassment. Perhaps that is the difference between filmmaking that strives to preserve good manners and Gardner's relative indifference to them. As he says at another point, it is amazing that fiction films that strain to achieve realism "never show anything as ordinary or as innocent as someone taking a pee" (41).

Fundamental to Gardner as a filmmaker is his desire to forge a closer relation with the physical world through the camera's almost prehensile vision. One is reminded of Barthes's notion of the *punctum* in photographs and his attention to the erotics of language. It could as easily be Gardner as Vertov, saying, "I am the 'cine-eye,' the mechanical eye; I am the machine that will show you the world as only the machine can see it. Henceforth I shall be liberated from human immobility" (cited in Rouch 1995, 82). For Gardner's camera is everywhere, climbing stairs, sweeping along laneways, stopping to glance at a child's broken kite on the ground, at a marigold, or at a pile of refuse. There is a sense of urgency to Gardner's filming, in both its movement and its moments of stillness, as if too little time remained to see the world with a clear eye. This way of seeing is strongly sensory, made all the more immediate by Gardner's refusal to allow us to see it through the screens of information or narrative. The subjectivity involved is explicitly his own, but it comes to us with a startling intimacy.

In Gardner and Östör's discussion, the erotics and haptics of filming tend to get covered over by the talk of meanings and connections. Occasionally, however, the conversation alludes to the more visceral aspects of bodily experience, including bodily functions. Gardner remembers the morning when he had to avoid stepping in piles of human excrement on the steps above the river and of finally resolving his feelings of aversion by including this in the film. About this, he remains a little ironic, referring to matter "of suspiciously human origin" as if less comfortable with naming than seeing. This diffidence surfaces unevenly throughout the discussion and the film. There are shots of a man defecating on the steps and another relieving himself in the gutter, both passed over fairly casually as matters of "innocence" and indifference.

About shots of human corpses, Gardner and Östör are forthright, and perhaps naturally so since this was bound to be an issue among viewers. I have already noted their discussion of the cremation sequence. Although explicit shots of corpses are rare in the film, Gardner and Östör discuss how they are likely to be received. Of one shot quite early in the film—of a water-whitened body being chewed by a dog—Gardner says he is "a little astonished when people don't know what it is." They are more offhand about another sequence, perhaps from having discussed it before—a body in the water, anus up, preceded by a shot of circling vultures. They choose not to point out the implications of this, that vultures begin consuming a body through its orifices.

Although the possibility of disgust (at violence to bodies and excretion) is given some attention, the possibility of visual pleasure is treated more tentatively. Much of Gardner's interest in filmmaking clearly lies in its potential for empathetic and corporeal involvement in the world, but this is more difficult to talk about than its literary aspects. He obviously takes pleasure in certain sensory qualities intrinsic to the film—its sounds, its moments of tranquility, the form and details of certain rituals. At one point, he speaks of the comparatively rare moments (ten, he estimates, during the whole time in Benares) when he sees something unfolding through the viewfinder with a kind of wonder—as, for example, when the Dom Raja is waking from his sleep. On those occasions "you're at the height of your power, at the height of your ecstasy as a filmmaker," he says. Gardner is more reticent about other empathies, such as the sensuality—perhaps in sheer relief from the dissolution of human bodies—of the healthy boatman rowing the wood barge upstream. This involves several extended sequences, but they are mentioned only briefly.

Forest of Bliss contains shots of a rather more formal pictorial composition, such as a huge rising sun and boats with sails at dawn and dusk, filmed with telephoto lenses from the "far shore." For me, these represent the only aesthetic slippages in the film—Gardner's occasional weakness for the conventionally beautiful image in place of the distinctive character of the rest of his filming. When speaking of these rather dreamy images, he has a tendency to invoke classical and literary parallels whence one reaches the final image of a rowboat in the mist, grainy like a pointillist painting, suggesting the crossing of the river Styx.

In contrast to his silence on some of these matters, Gardner regularly takes up questions of structure and rhetoric. He notes the arrival of the film at various crucial junctures: the end of the introductory section of 11 shots; the end of the "initial phase" of the film, with the return of Mithai Lal to his house; the point "two-thirds of the way into the film" when the wood barge docks; and so on. The idea of structuring the film around a single fictive day is raised early in the discussion as central to the film's conception. Thereafter, three forward structures are interwoven—the progress of the day from dawn to dawn, the movement of bodies from the inner parts of the city to the river, and the gradual convergence of symbolic objects. Gardner notes the way in which motifs that are "planted" at an earlier stage, such as the sound and sight of wood being cut and delivered or the making of the bamboo "ladders" and how these gradually reveal their fuller significance, resulting

in a sense of unfolding. One is reminded here of Flaherty's technique of presenting a series of details that gradually resolve themselves into a whole—with a sense, for the audience, of discovery.

At one point, Gardner and Östör discuss the general convergence over the entire length of the film of its chosen objects. Gardner has spoken earlier of the difficulty of approaching "complexity as complexity" since this almost invariably requires some sort of verbal exegesis (Gardner and Östör 2001, 45). It is also a potentially bewildering method for a filmmaker, who may end up simply filming unenlightening "grand confusion" (85). Instead, he has chosen to start with the detailed observation of "ordinary realities"—dogs, wood, kites, marigolds, and so on—trusting that their interrelationships can be gradually developed. And so we come to the sequence in which woodworkers are busy splitting pieces of wood and weighing them on a scale. The sequence brings together the stairs, the wood, the scales, the dogs, the boats, and the river. Here, as Östör observes, these elements become "incredibly charged." Gardner points to the two kinds of "layering" that can occur at such moments. In addition to the convergence of elements, forming a complex in which they are interrelated, each element can be layered "as to the significance or meaning of its content" (73). In other words, there can be an "optical" layering where we see the elements connected and a symbolic layering in which each element takes on multiple meanings from its associations in different contexts. We get an insight here into Gardner's strategy for creating a narrative of ideas and associations. The film gains much of its forward motion from a gathering comprehension of its larger structure.

The dynamics of this narrative also involve a gradual increase in the pace, scope, and directionality of the film as more and more bodies are brought toward the river: a "stream of death going down toward Manikarnika" (Gardner and Östör 2001, 91). At Manikarnika, the burning ghat, the film reaches its dramatic climax, after which Gardner acknowledges he faced a difficult transition. "The editing problem was to find a way to get out of this powerful place" (108). One of the rhetorical features of the film is its shifts of mood from intensity to relaxation and from "metaphorically loaded" to "realist" or observational modes of expression. These changes seem to propel the film forward, as though releasing and storing up energy, then springing forward in a new way. Östör comments that it is surprising to him that the film can encompass several radically different filmmaking styles. "It shows up the futility of legislating for film—saying what it should or has to do—because here an allegorical, even abstract, sequence is followed by real time without any conflict, the film form accommodating both" (34). Gardner confesses that it is hard for him to put himself in other people's heads but that, like any filmmaker, he tries to attune himself to a hypothetical viewer's sensibilities. After the audience has "had to work pretty hard," he tries to give them a respite, a chance to find their feet and reorient themselves. His remarks

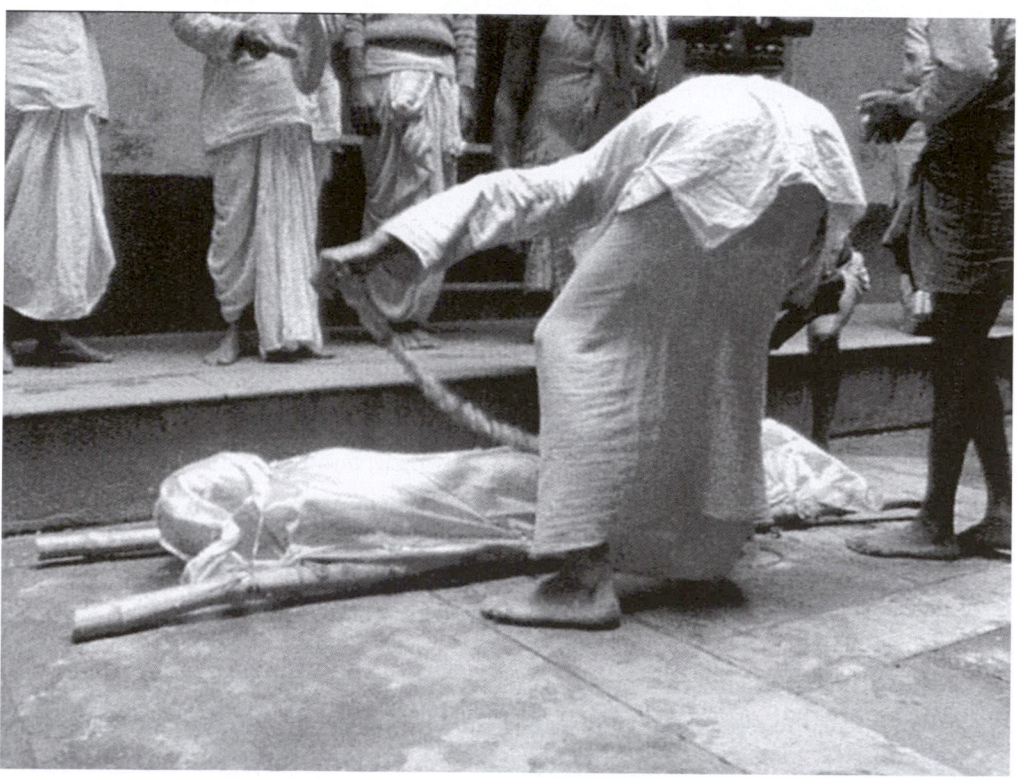

on placing the first marigold sequence give a sense of this method and also of the tension between the film's rhetorical and developmental requirements.

> Of course, the placement of this marigold passage here, after the Mithai Lal sequence, is to some extent arbitrary. I actually think it was done partly for the sake of the light in that I was trying to sustain the notion of a day passing; but I also put it here because I wanted another quiet passage before getting swept away by the din and clatter of Benares. (47)

There is the suggestion here of an analogy between musical and filmic construction, although music is ever explicitly mentioned as a model. However, *Forest of Bliss* would have to be one of the most musically constructed films of the 1980s, with its movements, recurring motifs, and fuguelike overlapping of actions. Gardner refers to preludes and rhythms and tempo and melody. Discussing the last shot before nightfall, he says, "I did feel that there should be a pause before the film went into its final sequences" (113), much as a composer might speak of a pause before the final return of the main theme. Possibly even more musical in feeling is the one instance of slow-motion cinematography—girls seen playing hopscotch—a characteristic Gardner touch.

Even if not in formal terms, the film could be judged musical for its uses of ambient music, ritualized speech and chanting, bells, and natural sounds. The sound of creaking

oarlocks is heard long before oars are actually seen, and this is the most important sound in the film, to which it keeps returning. Gardner notes that after a day of filming tree felling in the forest, all he wanted to use was the sound of it (Gardner and Östör 2001, 25). At four points at least, mention is made of the "enhancement" during editing of existing sounds, which Gardner regards as a way of correcting for the inadequacies of location recording. Mithai Lal's grunting as he goes up and down the steps refers not only to the effort and discomfort of an old man but also to the steps themselves, which will become prominent in the film. Later, the sound of a donkey's dead body being dragged down the steps is also enhanced, and entirely new sound is created for the tapping of a blind man's staff (68). Gardner often uses sound to evoke images that would be less expressive if actually seen or to create the sense of a larger world offscreen. Here, as always, he is as much concerned with the viewer's imaginative contribution to the film as with what the film itself can show.

In following the contours of the film, Gardner and Östör's discussion also reveals the contours of a particular set of assumptions about it. As it mediates between these and our own responses to the film, it constantly invites our rejoinders and interventions. It thus functions differently from most available writing on ethnographic film. It allows us to witness how memory and conversation bring to the surface ideas and intuitions crucial to a film's construction. In their conversation, Gardner and Östör seem to rediscover the film and, as they talk, come to understand it more deeply. In listening in on them, it may come as a revelation to some that films about social and cultural institutions can take paths so different from those of social and political science and depart so radically from the structures of expository prose.

NOTE

1.   An earlier draft of this chapter was published as "Gifts of Circumstance" in *Visual Anthropology Review* 17 (1, 2001): 68–85. Reprinted here with permission of the American Anthropological Association © 2007 American Anthropological Association.

REFERENCES

AGEE, James, and Walker Evans. 1960. *Let us now praise famous men,* 2nd ed. Boston: Houghton Mifflin.

CARPENTER, Edmund. 1989. "Assassins and cannibals, or I got me a small mind and I means to use it." *Society for Visual Anthropology Newsletter* 5 (1): 12–13.

CHOPRA, Radhika. 1989. "Robert Gardner's *Forest of Bliss*—A review." *Society for Visual Anthropology Newsletter* 5 (1): 2–3.

GARDNER, Robert. 1957. "Anthropology and film." *Daedalus* 86: 344–52.

GARDNER, Robert, and Ákos Östör. 2001. *Making* Forest of Bliss: *Intention, circumstance, and chance in nonfiction film.* Cambridge, MA: Harvard University Press.

KAPUR, Jyotsna. 1997. "The art of ethnographic film and the politics of protesting modernity: Robert Gardner's *Forest of Bliss.*" *Visual Anthropology* 9: 167–85.

Loizos, Peter. 1993. "Robert Gardner in Tahiti, or the rejection of realism." In *Innovation in ethnographic film: From innocence to self consciousness 1955–1989,* 139–68. Manchester: Manchester University Press.

Moore, Alexander. 1988. "The limitations of imagist documentary." *Society for Visual Anthropology Newsletter* 4 (2): 1–3.

Östör, Ákos. 1989. "Is that all that *Forest of Bliss* is about?" *Society for Visual Anthropology Newsletter* 5 (1): 4–9.

Parry, Jonathan. 1988. "Comment on Robert Gardner's '*Forest of Bliss.*'" *Society for Visual Anthropology Newsletter* 4 (2): 4–7.

Rouch, Jean. 1985. "The cinema of the future?" *Studies in Visual Communication* 11 (1): 30–35.

——. 1995. "The camera and man." In *Principles of Visual Anthropology,* 2nd ed., ed. Paul Hockings, 79–98. Berlin: Mouton de Gruyter.

Ruby, Jay. 1989. "The emperor and his clothes." *Society for Visual Anthropology Newsletter* 5 (1): 9–11.

——. 1991. "An anthropological critique of the films of Robert Gardner." *Journal of Film and Video* 43 (4): 3–17.

——. 2000. "Robert Gardner and anthropological cinema." In *Picturing culture: Explorations of film and anthropology,* 95–113. Chicago: University of Chicago Press.

Sontag, Susan. 1977. *On photography.* New York: Farrar, Straus and Giroux.

Staal, Frits. 1989. "Anthropologists against death." *Society for Visual Anthropology Newsletter* 5 (1): 2–3.

Vaughan, Dai. 1999. "The space between shots." In *For documentary: Twelve essays,* 9–28. Berkeley: University of California Press.

9 GARDENS OF WAR
MATERIALITY AND THE PHOTOGRAPHIC NARRATIVE

ELIZABETH EDWARDS

INTRODUCTION—THE HARVARD-PEABODY NEW GUINEA EXPEDITION

While Robert Gardner's lasting achievement has been broadly understood as being in film, there is a key body of still photography with which Gardner was closely involved and which deserves attention. In February 1961, the Harvard-Peabody New Guinea Expedition left the Dutch government post at Wamena, Dutch New Guinea (now Irian Jaya), and entered the Baliem Valley territory of the Dani (Gardner and Heider 1968, xi), where it spent five months, from April to August 1961. One of the major outcomes of the expedition was a book of photographic essays on Dani life titled *Gardens of War*, which Gardner produced in collaboration with Karl Heider. This volume presents 337 predominantly black-and-white images over 200 pages, divided into six sections, each prefaced by an essay and a set of captions. I intend to explore this volume because it is less frequently invoked than Gardner's film from the Expedition, *Dead Birds*,[1] yet it remains one of the few attempts to produce a large-scale photographic narrative of culture in book form. *Gardens of War* was published in New York by Random House in 1968.[2] Although it is on the shelves of almost every anthropology library in the world and many more besides, it has received scant critical attention. This chapter is an attempt therefore not only to redress the balance but also to bring an exceptionally rich and engaging body of photographic work more clearly into the visual anthropology mainstream by using it as a case study through which to explore the photo-essay book in anthropology.

Organized by Robert Gardner, the Harvard-Peabody New Guinea Expedition came into being through concerns about indigenous peoples of Netherlands New Guinea in the transfer of power from the Dutch to the newly emerged nation state of Indonesia.[3] The view was that urgent ethnographic research was required to establish the specific cultural identity of people of the interior in order to provide data to assess and act on the Dutch disquiet about them (Gardner and Heider 1968, xiii; Heider 2001, 62). In Harvard, this idea fell on fertile ground because Gardner had already been considering working in the region (Gardner and Heider 1968, xiii)—thus the Harvard-Peabody Expedition was born.

The expedition was composed of photographers, filmmakers, scientists, and writers. In many ways, it harked back to the scientific expeditions of the late nineteenth and early twentieth centuries in its interdisciplinary and methodologically multiplicitous nature. However, in its holistic vision, built of a number of lines of inquiry and inscription, the expedition was trying to do something very innovative in the contexts of 1950s and early 1960s anthropology, which was then premised largely on the individual vision of the field-work.[4] In addition to Gardner himself, as anthropologist and filmmaker, the participants consisted of Jan Th. Broekhuijse, who, as a Dutch colonial official, had well-established contacts in the region; Karl Heider, an anthropology graduate student at Harvard who went on to spend some two and a half years with the Dani in the period up to 1970; the *Life* magazine photographer Eliot Elisofon; Peter Matthiessen, a natural historian and, later, distinguished writer and novelist; and two recently graduated Harvard seniors, Michael Rockefeller, who became responsible for the photography and sound recording overall, and Samuel Putnam, who was about to begin medical school but had broad anthropological and linguistic interests (Gardner and Heider 1968, xiii–xv; Heider 2001, 62–63).

It was Gardner's particular wish "to make a study of a society still practicing what in anthropological annals is known as 'ritual warfare'" (Gardner and Heider 1968, xii) in order to explore the difference between "ordinary" and "ritual" warfare and the different cultural metaphysics of violence. "I wanted to see the violence of war through altogether different eyes" (xiii). Were there ways of conceptualizing conflict other than the cataclysmic twentieth-century experience of "the necessary evil"? The narrative of *Gardens of War* is inflected throughout with this interest for, in Gardner's estimation, the cultural demands of ritual warfare saturate all Dani social values, from children's games, as they develop the skills and values, to funerary ritual.

Gardens of War itself was originally to have been made by Michael Rockefeller, who had overall responsibility for the photography on the expedition but who had disappeared, presumed dead, on a subsequent trip to New Guinea in November 1961.[5] After a delay, the task was finally undertaken by Robert Gardner and Karl Heider, working with a young designer named Eric Martin as well as Random House designers.[6] They worked with the entire photographic output of the expedition, more than 18,000 photographs, sorting, selecting, and arranging the 337 images that appear in the volume. All members of the expedition are represented in the final selection, the largest number of photographs being by Heider and Rockefeller. However, the presentation in the book is of a collective vision in which "the identity of the individual photographer is almost obscured" (Mead 1968, vii).[7]

Rather than attempt a detailed analysis of all the images themselves, which cannot be adequately encompassed in a short chapter, my focus instead is the volume *Gardens of War* itself as an entity, as a performance of those images, and as a statement about Dani culture (see figure on next page). The volume was intended as serious ethnography but one that sought to project anthropological statements for a general audience rather than an exclusively academic one. As Gardner stated in his foreword to the book, "creating a careful and sensitive visual account of an unknown society was ample justification [for the expedition] in itself" (Gardner and Heider 1968, xi). However, the role of the book itself, as a material object, constructed through clearly articulated design values, becomes key in mediating the information presented. The poetics and politics of the process of publication are too often overlooked in writing about photography and anthropological representation, and key

issues, such as authority and narrative, are considered as solely abstract concepts. In contrast, here I am going to explore them as materially grounded in "the book." Before exploring this, however, I will also consider the photo-essay in anthropology as a mediating form because *Gardens of War* constitutes a series of linked photo-essays about Dani culture, which, as I will argue, are themselves materially mediated.

ANTHROPOLOGY, THE PHOTO-ESSAY, AND HUMANIST DISCOURSE

The values of engagement and translation have been key to the debates on the photo-essay and visual narrative in anthropology. Overall, a considerable amount of attention in the social sciences has been given to the role of documentary photographic practice and the relationship between image and word, evidence and meaning. In his much-quoted statement, Grady (1991) defines the photo-essay as "a statement about human affairs that purports to represent reality and is consciously and creatively crafted from non-fictional materials that are, at least in part, directly connected to the affairs thus represented" (27). Pauwels (1993) extends this, positioning images as forming "an integral part of the end product, exploring both the mimetic and expressive potential of the camera-image and offering an unmatched opportunity for integrating theory and observation" (200). Within this context, the photo-essay as a valid statement of anthropological or sociological endeavor and associated methodologies has been hotly debated. Are images descriptions or interpretations? What are the relations between scientific ideas, theories, and images? Between observer and observed? Between text and image? What are the ethics of working with the camera in the field? How is "voice" articulated through the visual? While detailed discussion of these issues is beyond the scope of this chapter and in any case have been discussed almost ad nauseam elsewhere (for informed comment, see Grady 1991; Harper 1987; Pauwels 1993; Ruby 2000; Simoni 1996), they are nonetheless ones that resonate throughout this discussion. As Grady's definition suggests, "the human" is a complex and intractable generality at the centre of the photo-essay, and it is perhaps the immediacy of photographs which accentuates the way in which "reality for people everywhere lies in the existence of human individuals in their social matrix" (Firth 1996, 9). But arguably, the way in which the photo-essay emerges from "the human" is, significantly and paradoxically, the root of anthropology's disquiet with the form. There is an unease not only with general concerns about the uncontrollability of the image in that there are too many meanings (Pinney 1992, 27) but also with popular and populist humanist agendas with which photo-essays had become associated, especially in the 1950s and 1960s.

Humanism has been a long-held value in relation to photography. Indeed, photography generally has been viewed intrinsically as a form of humanist endeavor. Its ability to translate a belief in the commonality of human experience in a way that transcends cultural economic, geographical, social, and ideological differences (Perivolaris 2003, 149) produces "a universal, transparent and comprehensible experience" for the viewer (Stallabrass 1997, 151). The potential lack of the discourse's engagement with the culturally specific and the ever-present tension between general and specific within the immediacy of the photographic image has presented anthropology with a problem here. Yet at the same time, the relativist assumptions underlying humanism accord with anthropology's own agendas. This is especially so in the course of the twentieth century, as anthropological ideas moved beyond their overtly "scientistic" foundations and concerned themselves with a "basic curiosity about the human condition with all its complexities of individual belief and action as affected by a network of social relationships, norms and obligations" (Firth 1996, 8). As Ruby (2000, 30) has suggested, academic humanism, along with, for instance, feminism, Marxism, and a range of reflexive methodologies of interpretative anthropology, has provided crucial positions for radical visual forms.

Nonetheless, as I have suggested, from anthropology's perspective there are some uneasy relations in all this. On the one hand, the photo-essay had developed as a humanist tool, linked strongly with both politically activist and progressivist social agendas

(Mitchell 1994, 281; Perivolaris 2003; Willumson 1992) in a way in which at that time anthropology, on the whole, was not. On the other, with populist consumption through the photographic magazines such as *Life* (which published a photo-essay of the expedition and the Dani in 1962 [Meiselas 2003, 59]),[8] it was associated with the way in which "the roots of the photo-essay in documentary journalism, newspapers, magazines, and the whole ensemble of visual-verbal interactions in mass-media connect it to popular forms of communication" (Mitchell 1994, 322). This was seen as problematic in the academy as the fluid interchange of image and text constituted a constant threat to the stability anthropological authority.

The photographs in *Gardens of War* draw many of their qualities from the classic values of documentary. Straight, equitable, and responsive, the images engage with the experience of others in a way that does not exoticize but rather explores difference within a sympathetic humanist framework. Humanistic photographic practice has, according to Hamilton (1997, 101), five central elements—historicity, "quotidienality," empathy, commonality, and universality, creating an inclusiveness. In many ways, these qualities also describe what would be recognized as effective and sympathetic anthropological photography.[9] These elements are clearly articulated in *Gardens of War*. For example, "empathy" is engendered by the pain on the face of the youth wounded in battle and the gentle hands supporting him (pp. 166–67, see figure below), whereas "quotidienality" is present in, for example, the photograph of a woman washing of sweet potatoes before cooking, watched by a young girl (who is, of course, learning to become a woman) (p. 50). Thus, while they

do not try to move readers in a social and political sense in the classic documentary humanist mode, the photographs might be termed an exercise in "ethnographic humanism." This is to say that the images and narrative engage the viewer with the specifics of Dani culture, but they also generate a common empathy with the subject matter. In this, they are images whose meanings surpass the local circumstances that provided their occasion (Stott 1973, 269) but without reducing to type or to the exotic.

The parameters of the photo-essay form in anthropology itself, methodologically, intellectually, and stylistically, had effectively been set by the *tour de force* of the social scientific photo-essay in Bateson and Mead's (1942) *Balinese Character* (1942). This volume constituted a major influence on the Baliem Valley Expedition's photography (Heider, personal communication, January 2005). Bateson and Mead's research on socialization in Bali[10] was conceived largely through a visual articulation that was fully integrated into research method—"we are attempting a new method of stating intangible relationships among different types of culturally standardized behavior by placing side by side mutually relevant photographs" (Bateson and Mead 1942, xii). Their project resulted in some 22,000 feet of film and 25,000 35mm photographs, 759 of which were published in *Balinese Character*. In this volume, Bateson and Mead used photographic sequences to demonstrate aspects of Balinese behavior. In these, the photographs are laid out rigidly, arranged in grids of between six and nine photographs to the page. Opposite each grid are detailed captions that guide the reader and clearly order the analytical narrative from image to image. As such, each opening forms a small photo-essay, exploring a form of behavior such as "Sibling Rivalry" or "Autocosmic Play." As Harper (2003) has argued, these photo-essays constitute an unfolding of events through a sequence of still images "rather similar to short movie clips" (243). Indeed, one can argue that it prefigures *Gardens of War* in the way in which filmic elements are used to construct the narrative, a point to which I will return.

Nonetheless, despite its scientistic approaches, *Balinese Character* is fully aware of its own subjectivity, and as such it can be seen also to embrace a broadly humanistic agenda: "we have to reorient the old values of many contrasting and contradictory systems into a new form which will use but transcend them all, draw on their respective strengths and allow for their respective weaknesses" (Bateson and Mead 1942, xvi). The project also anticipates *Gardens of War* in that it is not merely about a reified "custom" but "about" the people: as Mead puts it, "about the way in which they, as living persons, moving, standing, eating sleeping, dancing or going into a trance" (Bateson and Mead 1942, xii). For the intention in *Gardens of War* was to create an appeal to the viewer that was visual and intuitive as much as informational (Gardner, personal communication, December 2004), creating an expressive means to make a statement about cultural experience rather than merely didactic statements of the realist documentary mode. Berger and Mohr (1989) have described photographs as "the look of the world" in that they provide "the widest possible confirmation of the *thereness* of the world, and thus the look of the world continually proposes and confirms our relation to thereness, which nourishes our sense of 'being'" (87–88, original emphasis). Certainly, the volume was perceived as connecting in this way. One reviewer conceded that while *Gardens of War* might be "unduly subjective," nonetheless "cross-cultural interpretations however, must necessarily go beyond fact. The final test as to whether they should be regarded as merely subjective or truly insightful must be the degree of conviction they carry for the individual reader, viewer and listener" (Deddes 1971, 347).

In this light, the ambiguous and hybrid form of the photo-essay makes it necessary to consider briefly the broader representational paradigms outside anthropology from which *Gardens of War* emerged, for these values saturate both the photography itself and the discourses in which the book functioned. As I have already suggested, the humanist agenda, always working with that of the anthropological, underlay the expedition's approaches (Heider, personal communication, January 2005). As a comparison in collaborative photographic narrative, Margaret Mead, who wrote the preface for *Gardens of War,* alludes to *The Family of Man,* the exhibition that had opened at the Museum of Modern Art in New York in 1955. While her comment in this preface has the sense of a chance remark, it is an apposite one, for it positions the photography in a broader visual and cultural discourse that was profoundly influential, at least with an American public of liberal values, at whom *Gardens of War* was aimed. *The Family of Man* was perhaps the most popular photographic exhibition of all time, seen by 9 million viewers worldwide (Sandeen 1995, 4). It was born of what might be termed a post–World War II progressivist conservatism. Appearing liberal and inclusive on the surface, it acknowledged, indeed celebrated, the unity of mankind, universalist humanist values, and the commonality of human experience. As Edward Steichen (1955) stated in his introduction, "The Family of Man has been created in a passionate spirit of devoted love and faith in man" (v). Yet at the same time, there was an inherent conservatism, as it cohered a status quo, re-establishing Western, moralized traditional values through photographically articulated essences of the experience of birth, love, labor, suffering, belief, death, and so on—"the enduring elements of human behavior" (Sandeen 1995, 72).[11] In many ways, with the photo magazine such as *Life* (with which the exhibition was closely connected) and the British *Picture Post,* it set the agenda for mass consumption of humanist photography of the postwar period and inflected through photography more broadly.

To return to the photo-essay as exemplified through *Gardens of War,* the humanist foundation of the Expedition to Baliem Valley is articulated not simply through the photographic and, indeed, filmic values brought to the representation of the Dani but in the conceptualization of the expedition itself. As Heider (2001) has commented, "Gardner's vision was deliberately humanistic: a filmmaker, a novelist, a professional photographer, and an anthropologist formed the core of his group" (63). It had also been planned for a painter to join the expedition, although family commitments prevented him from doing so. There was a sense in which the humanist agenda emerged from the deep understandings of academic anthropology (Heider, personal communication, January 2005) in that it attempted to portray a Dani worldview. The scientific was articulated through the presence of trained anthropologists and the expedition's methodologies, especially the quality of their observation. Yet at the same time, from the beginning, a broadly expansive and expressive agenda was manifested through the configuration of skills, interests, and talents. This constituted a reflexive position that not only departed from the established modes of anthropology of the period but also worked against some of the didactic modes of classic documentary photography.

The Dani people themselves and their social experience are the focus for the narrative. Unlike some other photo-essays that have been produced within a broad ethnographic remit, from Berger and Mohr's (1976) *A Fortunate Man,* which focuses on a country doctor, to Doug Harper's (2001) use of specific families, such as the Fishers, as case studies in the industrialization of U.S. agriculture, there is no central character in *Gardens of War* around whom narrative is constructed. In this, it might be said to be closer to the homogenizing norms of ethnographic text of the period than of filmmaking, which often had a personalized narrative. Indeed, *Dead Birds* itself is strongly structured around two protagonists: Weyak, an adult man, and a young boy, Pua. The very nature of photography, the way in which it fragments space and time yet has fluid closures of meaning, allows photography to be both extractive and specific and to address general issues through the particular. As Berger and Mohr have argued, the fragmentary nature of the photograph is turned to its advantage in that expressiveness constitutes a long quotation from the real and contains the image's ambiguity within a greater extension of density and meaning. This relationship between fragment and whole, specific and general, is inherent to all representational practices and thus the way anthropological description functions; however, it is a key dynamic of the photo-essay as a form. One could argue, therefore, that *Gardens of War* is an example of the way in which the lack of the central specifics of "characters" in the photo-essay pushes the narrative into a more broadly humanistic realm, opening the possibility of symbolic resonances while simultaneously the immediacy of photography constantly restates the individual human experience. The images are also enhanced by their expressive qualities. The discontinuity, the relationship between the general and the specific, in the "instantaneous set of appearances, allow us to read across [photographs] and to find synchronic coherence" (Berger and Mohr 1989, 128).

Of course, in the photo-essay, captions provide a form of closure on the images. The actual style of captioning is significant in the creation of cohesion. Echoing Clifford's (1988) well-known arguments about generalizing and ethnographic authority, Scott (1999, 247) has explored the rhetoric of caption through two dichotomies: the clear "event" of the definite article and the generalizing indefinite article: from distanced third person to engaged first person. The interplay between these generalizing and specific forms of captions, represented in the discursive essays and then the descriptive captions in *Gardens of War,* embrace both general statement and specific observation of "ethnographic humanism." For instance, "From a crowd of mourning women, one waves helplessly toward the corpse" (p.100), or "Before the mist has lifted from the mountain wall, a boy takes two pigs for their day in a fallow garden (p. 45). In Gardner's essays, some people are named, and the ethnographic description is worked through them to engage the reader in individual experiences. This is especially so of descriptions emerging from direct observations or articulations of incidents rather than synthesis and extrapolation. For instance, in his account of the battle, Gardner gives almost a personalized catalog: "Siba was hit by an arrow in the thigh, Tekman Biok by a spear in the hip, and Yonokama by an arrow in the kneejoint" (Gardner and Heider 1968, 143). In this way, the book not only engages the reader in an identification with universals such as fear and suffering through a humanistic iconography of documentary but also suggests different, specifically Dani responses to them, engaging the reader in specificity of Dani experience.

GARDENS OF WAR AS PHOTO-ESSAY

The relationships between the humanistic and the anthropological are inflected through scope and ordering of the six photo-essays that make up the book: "Appearances," "Skills," "Nourishment," "Play," "Ghosts," and "Violence." The sections are consciously intended to move away from the simple functionalist categories, such as "subsistence" or "kinship," whose assumed privileged explanatory force dominated the structuring of description in the ethnographic monograph of the period. Rather, the categories, which emerged from the very broad sorting of images, were intended to extend the representation of Dani experience beyond that of scientific anthropology into a humanistic and more flexible structure (Gardner, personal communication, December 2004). "I . . . felt responsible to the realities of being Dani as we came to know them" (Gardner, personal communication, February 2005). In this, the classic anthropological concept of "the native point of view" resonates not merely methodologically but morally as well.

However, if the categories move away from the traditional categories of ethnographic description, the overall shaping of the narrative does not. The narrative created by the sections moves from generalized statements about "Appearances" of landscapes, settlement, and people through "Skills" and "Nourishment," "Play," and "Ghosts" to the final section, "Violence," which is concerned with the ritual warfare that had been the primary ethnographic concern of the expedition. With fighting comes death, and the final plate—in color—is of the funeral pyre of a young man killed in the fight. One is reminded of the classic ethnographic life cycle narrative ending with death and funerary ritual and similarly the equally classic sequence from concrete (e.g., food getting) to abstract (ghosts and death) (see figure on next page).[12] In this last section, the visual urgency of the fight, of moving figures spread out across the landscape in wide, light, open images, is followed by the sharp contrast the intensity of mourning in dark-filled frames. This moves toward a narrative and, indeed, visual climax as the story unfolds through visible action. Each image forms, as it has throughout the volume, a complex interplay of content and narrativity.

While the sections of the book operate in a mutually sustaining relationship, they function as discrete photo-essays, and these shift in narrative device, tone, and style through the volume. The presentation of images, which I will discuss further in relation to design, is not always simple linear narrative, represented through a sequence of photographs, but a montage of shapes, sizes, styles, and contents that preclude a clearly preferred reading. In the first three sections—"Appearance," "Skills," and "Nourishment"—activities are shown

not as complete sequences but rather as a configuration of images that give a sense of simultaneous actions glimpsed. Yet they stand for a cohesive whole as ditches are dug, gardens tended, and crops harvested. A clear narrative begins to emerge only in "Ghosts" and then "Violence," where the fragments cohere into the central and defining practice of Dani society—ritual warfare and its consequences. Echoing Berger and Mohr's concern with discontinuity, quotation and cohesion, it can be argued that the use of the series as an unfolding narrative at one level contradicts the aesthetic tenets of traditional photography in that it is premised not on the unique moment alone but on the juxtaposition of image in mutually sustaining tensions provided by the sequencing of image (Scott 1999, 13). But while individual photographs are often striking, the expressive power of the individual image, for example, mourning women (pp. 122–23), gains function and meaning only within the context of the whole, "a sequence of many sequences" (Stallabrass 1997, 146).

However, "intricacies of photographic containment and contextualisation" (Hughes and Noble 2003, 6) mean that, as I've suggested, photographs are rarely hermetically sealed. The photographs work in a way that might be summed up by Berger's (1989) comment that "in life, meaning is not instantaneous. Meaning is discovered in what connects, and cannot exist without development. Without a story, without an unfolding, there is no meaning. Facts, in themselves, do not constitute meaning...when we give meaning to an event, that meaning is a response, not only to the known, but also the unknown: meaning and mystery are inseparable" (89). Indeed one could argue that one of the functions and characteristics of the photo-essay is that it blurs the boundaries of image. Meaning is contained not only within the frame but also in its relations beyond the frame. This is demonstrated in *Gardens of War,* as I have noted, through the suggestion of multiple directions, filling spaces between frames, rather than simply a clear linear impulse.

So rather than the unfolding narrative eliding the fragmentation of photography, *Gardens of War* presents a set of vertical incisions, isolated vignettes of Dani experience, grouped around a theme. These actually use the fragment itself to full effect, creating a more "literary narrative" that is more "abstractly ethnographic" (Harper 1987, 6). Significantly, this juxtaposition of narrative and fragmentation, if we can term it that way, engages precisely with the temporal ambiguities of photographs. The fragmented simultaneity of the earlier sections, either as single images (see figure below) or short photo-essays within the sequence, such as "Saltmaking" (p. 53), contrast with the clearer linear narratives of the later ones. But even this latter temporality is not uncomplicated because within the photo-essay

[160]   [161]

the general narrative of battle is inserted sequences of personal experience, such as the wounded man and the surgeon (see figure above). Here filmic qualities and techniques applied to still photography come into play as the sequences of the photo-essay are paced through a series of long shots, cutaways, and close-ups. The juxtapositions of temporalities might be said to go to the heart of human experience, hence their efficacy within the broad "ethnographic humanist" agendas of the book.

Here we see the photo-essay as a multilayered construction. As a whole, it constitutes not merely a quotation from Dani culture in Berger and Mohr's (1989, 96) sense but an act of translation woven together by "the energy of countless judgements" (Berger and Mohr 1989, 93). *Gardens of War* might be said to anticipate not only Gardner's later film work, notably *Forest of Bliss,* which caused such a stir among anthropologists, but also the postmodern intersections of anthropology and documentary photographic practice that emerged in the late 1980s and 1990s (Edwards 1997, 58–60). Thus, arguably, *Gardens of War* might be seen as the work that moves a visualized anthropology not only toward a more popular form of consumption but also toward a more eclectic conceptualization of photographic value within the discipline.

This in part is due to the clear photographic values articulated through *Gardens of War.* These are expressed through the general treatment of the text. Mitchell (1994) has argued, "The text of the photo-essay typically discloses a certain reserve or modesty in its claims to 'speak for' or interpret images; like the photograph, it admits its inability to appropriate everything that was there to be taken and tries to let the photographs speak for themselves or 'look back' at the viewer" (289). In *Gardens of War,* there is a clear separation of image and text. They are different voices that are allowed their own space. There is also a clear separation of kinds of information. While image and text are fully integrated conceptually in terms of visual engagement and thus the apprehension of the narrative, they remain separate as two distinct forms of expression. As I have already suggested, within this, there are the two layers of "captioning"—a discursive ethnographic text and separate descriptive captions in sections. Yet text–image exchanges are to an extent resisted, they are made difficult by the construction of the volume, for there is no direct collaboration between image and text (Mitchell 1994, 292), only small, discretely placed numbers directing the reader back to the captions. The reader must turn backward and forward between image and caption. This arguably removes images from a solely ethnographic reading, again allowing a humanist agenda to emerge because it does not enforce a clear closure of meaning on the images themselves.[13] The narrative presented by *Gardens of War* remains ambiguous in its disciplinary statements: it is neither entirely an anthropological discourse nor solely a humanistic one. The intentional space for the reader inherent in visual appeal precludes a definite closure of meaning.

Faced with the ambiguities and subjectivities of *Gardens of War,* we have to ask, as Mitchell (1994, 289–89) has done more generally, whether photo-essay is actually the right term? Why not photo-novel or indeed photo-lyric? After all, Mead (1968, ix), in her introduction to the volume, speaks of the romanticism of both the subject matter itself and the viewers' responses to the unknown and distant. Mitchell's criteria for the photo-essay, which would appear to extend those of Grady, are drawn from the cultural idea of the essay itself. All apply to *Gardens of War* in that it is embedded in a reality and nonfictionality in its account despite the constructed narratives; it mediates personal experience of the expedition through the indexical trace and finally, mirroring the constraints of the photographic frame and fragment, conveys a sense of something beyond. "There is," as Mitchell (1994) has argued, "a root sense of the essay as a partial, incomplete 'attempt,' an effort to get as much of the truth about something into its brief compass as the limits of space and writerly ingenuity will allow" (289).

While photo-narratives might have a cohesiveness, they cannot have the full coherence of textual narrative (Scott 1999, 215) because of the unstable and mutable nature of the meaning of the image. This is especially so of *Gardens of War,* where different photographic styles, montaged together, point to the partial view. This is brought into high relief when it is compared to Bateson and Mead's *Balinese Character,* where the stylistic homogeneity of the images, combined with the direct juxtaposition of detailed descriptive text, demands a closure of meaning that denies or defies the partial. Yet *Gardens of War* as a production is very conscious of the values it is transmitting. It uses different styles, configurations, and textures to articulate and translate the complexity of Dani experience. It both uses the form of the photo-essay and at the same time refuses to be constrained by it, pointing to the complexity of the form. No wonder the photo-essay has been so hotly debated in anthropology.

DESIGN AND MEANING

Such photo-essays as *Gardens of War,* however, depend on more than simply the abstract idea of the juxtaposition of images. As will have become clear, many of the book's humanistic and narrative qualities are manifested through the material, that is, through the making of a socially salient object. In this case, we are concerned with a hardback book titled *Gardens of War*, which was made specifically to perform the complex narrative of the photographs of Dani by combining composition, sequence, and format. It is to this that I now wish to turn. All elements of a book's production, it could be argued, contribute to the way the images are perceived and interpreted—size, paper, typography, layout, binding, and dust jacket. Indeed, as Parr and Badger (2004, 7) argue, the most successful photo books give photographs an almost tactile quality, emphasizing the objectness of the book itself. Thus, it is through the mediation of the book that the concrete social encounter, represented in the expedition and their photographs, is further encoded and translated for the viewer/reader.

The materiality of the book—that is, the condition and implications of being a physical object—is often invisible in the way that that of photographs and, indeed, film is largely invisible (Edwards and Hart 2004).[14] This has certainly been the case in discussions of the photo-essay that too often have become an abstract concept divorced from the phenomenological experiences of looking at images and turning pages. Yet, as Miller (1998, 12) has argued, "things" are often most powerful when they are apparently marginal and unimportant. The book, as a solid material object, becomes the "physical stuff of texts—the surfaces on which they are inscribed, the materials used to do the inscribing and the aesthetic aspects of their creation and manipulation" (Danet 1997, 5–6). Thus, "institutional and interpretative assumptions and desires saturate design" as part of the book's production, circulation and consumption (Kratz 1994, 180) to the extent that its materiality precedes or dictates the meaning of the text. Even without text, "photographs are subject to, and diversified by, layout and framing" (Scott 1999, 265). Here the book itself, containing or comprising sequences of images, is the "storytelling artifact" that embeds the photographs and the narratives contained, communicated, and interacted with, within those contexts (Hughes and Noble 2003, 4).

The designer is consequently "at all times a mediator, an interpreter: through his imagination, his experience and his knowledge of the art, craft, and science of printing he converts the typescript into a book and expresses the author's words clearly and sympathetically to the reader" (Trevitt 1980, 34). *Gardens of War* has very clear and careful design values in its presentation in order to mediate that meaning.[15] As a book, it is intended to project anthropological values and the authority of disciplinary observation into a more general space and to let the humanistic concerns emerge through the treatment and design of the images, mediating and cohering the selection. The photo-essay or photo-story conceived of in a specific material form, that of the book, presents the reader with specific units of reading. Images are understood only in relation to other images on the page and their positioning on that page (Baetens 1995, 283). Consequently, layout, along with the quality of the printing and overall appearance of the production, becomes important, as design values consciously complement the subject matter and are an integral part of the communication of, here, Dani culture. Indeed, as Baetens (2005) has argued, in photographic books, "what dominates...is the materiality of the book, which influences and determines the form and content of the photographic images" (87). Such arrangements create a pace, an affective tone, and an embodied engagement with the material constructions of narrative. They set up ambiguities. They open a space for the reader in that there is an awareness that in order to see, one must turn the page, but one is precluded from ever seeing the whole despite the realist promise of photographs (Baetens 2005, 87).[16] In other words, the expressive qualities of the images are performed through the presentational rhetorics of book design.

I want first to consider the relationship between image and text and thus time as it is expressed through the structure of the book. Following the foreword by Margaret Mead and the introductory essay by Gardner, each of the six sections of the book is preceded by an ethnographic essay by Gardner and then a section of captions by Heider. The photographs then follow in a number of page configurations without captions. As I have already described, text and image are not directly juxtaposed but comprise discrete sections. Only small, discreet numbers beneath each image—or even within the image in some cases—assist the reading of the photographs, referring the reader back to the captions. Rather than being dictated by the demands of book production, this was intentional (Robert Gardner, personal communication, December 2004). Again this design decision opens a space for imaginative engagement. It was decided not to have captions with the photographs so as not to interrupt the flow of images, the visual narrative. Instead, blocks of information that embed but do not intervene between the photographs form a straightforward exchange of meaning between image and text as discrete units. The text must be read and formulated in mind and then the photographs read—this leaves space for imagination, "the excitement of my experience" (Gardner, personal communication, February 2005)—in that the caption cannot be used as an immediate closure of meaning on the photograph.[17] As Mitchell (1994) has argued, "This collaboration [between text and image] is also embedded in a complex field of heterogeneities that can never quite be accommodated to traditional dialectical forms of aesthetic unity" (316).

The forms of narrative and description are, however, clearly differentiated. Not only is there a physical division between text and image, but the discursive and descriptive functions of the text itself are also visually differentiated. Gardner's descriptive and expansive ethnographic essays, which set up a preferred reading of the images, are set in Times Roman, whereas Heider's captions, providing a forensic description of the images that enlarges on the preceding essay, are set in Helvetica.[18] While this is a common device to separate voices in a text, it nonetheless marks visually the relationship between the quiet authority of the essay and the clean accuracy of captions. The different typefaces encourage the act of reading and thus engagement with these different texts in different ways. Times Roman, with its small horizontal serifs, keeps the eye moving across the page of a descriptive discourse, whereas the clean sans-serif lines of Helvetica, arranged in columns, suggest a distanced anonymity of caption information.[19] But nonetheless, neither is particularly insistent; they maintain a crucial distance from the images themselves. In this, "they force us back onto the formal and material features of the images themselves" (Mitchell 1994,

293).[20] A formal presentation and expressive engagement of content, they bring us back to the aesthetics of the image to articulate an expressive incision into cultural experience. In this way, as we have seen, the photographs are able to mediate the space between general and specific, constituting both humanistic and ethnographic comment, independent of text.

Printing values play a large part in establishing the affective tone of the volume. These values, both the tonal ranges of the photographs and the paper texture, are also important in the articulation of the relationships between specific and general, humanistic and ethnographic. The text and images are printed on the same medium heavy matt-coated paper, while the color photographs, which are included in three of the sections, "Appearances," "Nourishment," and "Violence,"[21] are printed on a slightly crisper, gloss paper, sympathetic to color printing. The positioning of the latter is determined by the demands of book production, as the color had to be printed separately and brought together in the collation and binding of the volume.[22] The black-and-white photographs are printed in photogravure, a high-quality form of photomechanical reproduction.[23] With its rich tonal quality, photogravure was used in many publications of documentary photography at the period.[24] Overall, it has a dark, grainy quality, with rich middle tones. However, the paper quality lifts the highlights, giving a sense of light and, in some instances, a sense of space, for example, some of the images of play (pp. 76–77). Further, the sensuous black and whites, as opposed to the more subdued color, mediate the dichotomy between drama and realism inherent in photographs.

The relationship between the black and white and color also impacts on the perception and interpretation of the images. Although the black and white might suggest a sense of pastness, it is mitigated by the color section, which accentuates immediacy. However, the tonal and print qualities of the black-and-white images also operates to create the abstract and unified (Stallabrass 1997, 147). A graphic power emerges that accentuates the geometry of images moving them toward a purely formalist reading, for instance, the circles of women with their string bags of their backs (see figure on next page). In contrast, the printing values of the color photographs have a softer edge with emphasis on the red-brown tones, for example, the merging browns of skin and string bags, punctuated by the grays of a bandaged hand or smeared clay (pp. 58–59). With their more uniform formatting on the page (e.g., p. 55), the color photographs set up a tone of naturalism that suffuses the whole volume in a visual balancing between the two photographic forms.[25]

The book's dust wrapper is also an important element in the affective tone of the volume, identifying and establishing its rhetoric. Covering an oatmeal textured cloth binding, it comprises a single color photograph by Michael Rockefeller of the *edai* victory dance. Wrapped around the whole volume, figures rush out of the frame of the photograph, giving a sense of action and dynamism rather than ethnographic pastness.[26] This is accentuated by the red lettering of the subtitle and the bright white of the authors' names, which lift the neutral shades of the photograph. As Kratz (1994, 180) has argued, book covers depend on condensed visual signs to articulate an interpretation of the book's narrative objectives and

thus its broad cultural objectives. Here the cover is both extractive and synecdochical in its use of an image from the body of the book. The part represents the whole; it functions "to reveal to the reader what awaits in the interior of the volume" (Baetens 2005, 88), here perhaps signifying simultaneously the "difference," the specificity and dynamic of Dani culture.

I want finally to turn to the crucial issue of the placement of images on the page. While I have already discussed this in relation to narrative, the effect is created through the act of design. Beyond the basic and obvious demand of putting square/rectangular shapes (photographs) into another single square/rectangular shape (book page), *Gardens of War* departs from the grids of Bateson and Mead's *Balinese Character,* in which the homogeneity of presentation speaks to a contained and scientific intent. The formatting of the pages of the latter focuses attention in specific ways of reading the images and creates a scientific attitude to the visual experience offered (Cook 2004, 64). Becker (1981) has described *Balinese Character* as "forbiddingly scientific"; "the format becomes the means for creating, in a systematic way, the context Bateson and Mead thought necessary for understanding of individual bits of behavior" (13), constituting the kind of regularity of pattern and statement from which disciplinary discourse emerges.

The arrangement of images in *Gardens of War* is profoundly different from *Balinese Character,* reflecting both different methodological approaches and different conceptualizations of the interpretation of culture. As I have argued, in the co-equality of images and text articulated through the construction of the book, both are given their own independence while at the same time constituting a coherent whole. The photographs act as a series of discrete and separate glimpses of Dani culture that are built up into continuous experience through the small photo-essays that make up the book, for example, "Raising Pigs" (p. 52) or "Preparing a Funeral Meal" (pp. 110–11). Here the narrative unit, as I have suggested, is the page rather than a simple succession of images over turned pages. This articulation is addressed through design values. Choices of balance in size and format and positioning between the images, whether they are framed by white space or bled off into the gutter or off the page edge, are part of the building of the narrative and affective tone that guide the meanings of photographs.

As I have discussed, *Gardens of War* presents us not with a clear linear narrative, reliant on the re-temporalizing properties of sequence, but rather a sense of montage. I want to finish with a brief discussion of this quality because it is here we see intention fully articulated by design. There is a strong sense of the filmic in the book. The idea of filmic sequencing in photography first came to prominence in the Russian avant-garde of the 1920s, exploring sequencing within frames through montage and sequencing between frames as "the systematic analytic sequence" (Roberts 1998, 31). While 35mm formats and rapid wind-on cameras endow still photography with technical filmic analogies, what is clear from the sequencing and pacing of *Gardens of War* are the filmic values brought to the production of the photo-essay. The photo-essay, in general, has tended to adopt a straightforward temporalizing approach to sequencing, constructing a narrative through the sequence of turned pages and the juxtaposition of images in the page opening, one image following another in sequence. Within this, the integrity of individual photographs as discrete statements remains a possibility. The photographs in *Gardens of War,* as we have seen, constitute essays, but overall they do not tell "a story" in their own right, in a direct narrative sense. Rather, as I have suggested, they form a kind of montage, as Bazin (2005, 35–39, 50–51) has described it, building up possibilities, expressive modes, and meanings through juxtaposition as opposed to the continuum of reality.[27]

Martin has commented that, as designer, he clearly saw the task as "the creation of a 'filmic book'" (personal communication, February 2005). There are indeed sequences of almost pure filmic narrative in the book, for instance, that of "Play," which is arranged across the page like a series of film stills (see figure on next page). However, the filmic vision in *Gardens of War* is, at the same time, very much more complex. This is illustrated again in the opening pages 82 to 83, showing young boys playing a battle game. Here two images are placed above and below the second of the sequence; in this, they immediately begin to extend the narrative outward. The book therefore has the character not of traditional documentary film but of expressive, subjectively engaged and experimental filmmaking, challenging film's intrinsic narrative sequencing,[28] a characteristic that, as I have suggested, was increasingly to become Robert Gardner's hallmark.[29] The montage quality cuts through, forcing juxtapositions rather than a direct realist narrative, transforming many of the photographs.[30] The small sections of narrative are read within and across the page opening, montaged with expressive detail. For instance, pages 50 to 51, in the "Nourishment" sequence, make up a large bled-off image of a woman washing sweet potatoes with seven photographs in four different sizes, the two larger of which are descriptive, while the other four, despite didactic claims, suggest affective patterning of smoke and land (see second figure below). Here we see how design enables the values of montage—multivocality, simultaneity, multiple spatial and temporal experiences—communicated to the viewer through a sense of diverse realities (Pink 2001, 117–18).

Visual rhythm is also extremely important. Images are grouped but not necessarily sequenced as such. The eye can move in different directions. In this, one can argue that just as narrative in the photo-essay "follow[s] the contours of narrative in ethnographic film" (Harper 1987, 5), the design values of *Gardens of War* create a sequencing that assumes theatrical or cinematic characteristics (Baetens 1995, 284), the continuity of meaning being created by resonances between frames rather than within frames. As such, it is working against the fragmenting qualities of still photography.[31] "Photo sequences…make possible a documentary mode whereby juxtaposed photographs can be used to interrogate each other, to penetrate, as it were, each other's surfaces" (Scott 1999, 250). Precisely because the eye is not necessarily led through only one sequence, it can move legitimately in any direction across the page. This is accentuated by the consistencies of printed tone within the page (Scott 1999, 220), narrative interspersed and supplemented by affective tone that does not forward the narrative so much as broaden the perceptual possibilities and thus understanding. Repeated throughout the configuration of images, it becomes a form of rhetorical reinforcement (Mitchell 1994, 296). Format here is not about filtering out, as it was in *Balinese Character*, with the preferred scientific reading, constituted by arrangement and juxtaposition with text. Rather, the format design allows the content of the photographs space as the eye wanders over the page, making connections in no particular order. The smaller images are not simply about affective tone but also about articulating essential human experience. "Each pictures discloses a link to the next, a hint or germ of an antithetical image to follow" (Trachtenberg, quoted in Becker 1998, 5), yet they do not reveal the unfolding of events but, rather, small sets of visual incisions.

Scott (1999, 248) has argued that montage constructs unexpected continuities that allow the photographs to retain their indexical validity as documents while the discontinuities release the images into a more expressive realm, extending their range of meaning. The design of the formats, as I have suggested, accentuate this. Further, while the photographic style is quiet and unmanipulative, there are tensions between the documentary record, straight, frontal, middle distance, eye level, even flat light (Stott 1973, 270). Different styles and formats are put together. Direct images are placed next to more dramatizing/aestheticizing shots with odd angles, close-up or fragmenting views, or those with open light or, conversely, heavy contrast, for example, page 19 of "Appearances" (see figure on next page). These juxtapositions set an affective tone; in speaking to the partial again, it translates content onto a subjectively engaged level. For example, a descriptive narrative sequence of the stages of construction of a family house (p. 36)[32] runs down the right-hand side of the page and is anchored, bled off, into the gutter. The left-hand portion is headed by a half-size photograph of two men leveling the ground. Beneath it are eight smaller images that form a counterpoint of action and detail to the larger pictures, setting an affective tone of details of men working, details of materials, and straining bodies. Thus, the sequence not only speaks of real time (the construction of a house) but also presents a more impressionistic sense of being. The montage forms that more abstract form of storytelling that leaves room for the imagination (Bazin 2005, 36). Such a format is repeated, with variations in the grid arrangement, throughout the book. These

arrangements of images defy the desire for a simple linear narrative or forensic exposition alone but mediate the documentary and expressive translation of Dani culture. It is perhaps for this reason that a grudging notice in *Atlantic* magazine noted, "The pictures themselves range from the splendid to the incomprehensible" (Adams 1969, 103).

CONCLUSION

"Photographic monographs are always around, convenient and portable expressions of the photographer's work that have the potential for rediscovery and republication at any time, anywhere" (Parr and Badger 2004, 10). Perhaps it is time for a reassessment of anthropology's relation with the photographic book in particular and the publication of its images more generally (see Morton 2005). The way in which *Gardens of War* uses the narrative of the photo-essay to engage with the aesthetic and subjective prefigures later calls for a more expressive use of visuals in essay form (e.g., Becker 1984; Edwards 1997; Grady 1991). As such, it represents a profoundly important moment in the relationship between photography and anthropology. Its strong imagery, careful structure, and narrative pace make it unique. One can only wonder that it has received so little attention in either analysis or teaching in visual anthropology, for it raises many questions about the making and communicative power of the photo-essay. Further, in thinking of *Gardens of War* not simply as a series of images but also as a material performance of those images, I hope I have suggested a further set of questions we might ask about photographic narrative, extending it beyond the semiotic to include what is effectively a phenomenological element to our understanding. It challenges the dematerialization of the photo-essay, for, as I have argued, it can be understood only by considering the whole performance of the images, and as such it opens the way to think through the relationship between anthropological expression and photography.

NOTES

I should like to thank Robert Gardner, Karl Heider, and Eric Martin for generously sharing memories of the making of *Gardens of War*. Grateful thanks are also due to the following colleagues who have read, discussed, and guided so constructively at various stages of this chapter's development: Marcus Banks, Ilisa Barbash, Linda Eerme, Susan Meiselas, Chris Morton, Suzy Prior, Russell Roberts, and Lucien Taylor.

1. *Dead Birds* was a feature-length production, released in 1963. In addition to *Dead Birds* and *Gardens of War,* the expedition had numerous outcomes in anthropology and natural history, including more extended fieldwork by Karl Heider that resulted in two academic monographs (Heider 1970, 1979).

2. It is this American edition that is the focus of this chapter. A British edition was published a year later, in 1969, by André Deutsch, London.

3. Dutch or Netherlands New Guinea comprised the western half of the island of Papua. Now named Irian Jaya, it is part of the modern nation-state of Indonesia. The cultural and political tensions between Indonesian and indigenous peoples have resulted in a regime of suppression and violence for nearly 40 years. In 1960, Victor DeBruyn, head of the Bureau of Native Affairs in the government of Netherlands New Guinea, visited the United States. Netherlands New Guinea had been retained by the Dutch at the decolonization of the old Dutch East Indies because, they argued, the indigenous inhabitants were either Melanesians or Papuans, thus having little connection, culturally or racially, with greater Indonesia. On the other hand, Indonesia based its territorial claim in the maintenance of the integrity of the old Dutch Empire in Southeast Asia. The Dutch were interested in research on the ethnographic specificity of the region that would support their position (Heider 2001, 62).

4. While anthropology in the United Kingdom and the United States share the central disciplinary practice of fieldwork, the expedition tradition, especially in museum-based anthropology and archaeology, was not entirely extinct through the twentieth century as it was in British anthropology.

5. Rockefeller had visited Cambridge, Massachusetts, in the early autumn of 1961 to look over the photographs and had then asked to take the major responsibility for putting together a photographic book (Gardner and Heider 1968, xv).

6. Eric Martin was teaching in a program, "Light and Communication," which had a strong documentary/ethnographic bias, at the new Carpenter Centre for the Visual Arts (Martin, personal communication, February 2005). Martin went on to teach at the California Institute of the Arts.

7. There are two pages of precise photographic acknowledgments at the end of the volume so that individual photographic styles and interests can be isolated: the majority of images are by Heider (126) and Rockefeller (101), with Broekhuijse (29), Putman (29), Elisofen (22), Gardner (19), and Matthiessen (11) (Gardner and Heider 1968, 179–80).

8. The essay was published under the title "Dawn: Turn Back the Years" (September 28, 1962) and is reproduced in Meiselas (2003, 58–63). Similar photo-essays on the expedition and the Dani were published in *Stern, Panoramo,* and *Epoca* (Meiselas 2004, 59).

9. Hamilton also names a sixth element, "monochromaticity"—the scene is rendered in black-and-white representation. While this applies to *Gardens of War* to some extent in that a majority of the images shot were indeed in black and white, it does not appear to function with the same self-conscious stylistic/interpretative intention as it does in, for instance, the work of the French humanist photographers Henri Cartier-Bresson, Willy Ronis, or Robert Doisneau, who are Hamilton's focus (Hamilton 1997, 101).

10. Bateson and Mead worked in Bali from 1936 to 1938 and again briefly between January and March 1939 (Sullivan 1999, 1).

11. For an extended discussion of the exhibition *The Family of Man,* see Sandeen (1995). There is also, of course, Roland Barthes's well-known critique of the ahistorical, moralized sentimentality of *Family of Man* (Barthes 1972, 107–100). The exhibition was closely related to *Life* magazine and the humanist agendas of their photographers such as Margaret Bourke-White and others such as Henri Cartier-Bresson, Bert Hardy *(Picture Post),* or Pierre Verger. It also included a photograph by John Collier, one of the founders of visual anthropological method, and photographs by amateurs, presenting photography also as a democratic medium.

12. For instance, the last plate of Malinowski's *Argonauts of the Western Pàcific* (1922) shows a corpse wearing *kula* valuables, laid out and displayed to the camera *pietà*-like, the final social act (Edwards, quoted in Young 1998, 213).

13. Like the seminal photo-essay book, James Agee and Walker Evans's *Let Us Now Praise Famous Men* (1941).

14. The materiality of books usually becomes important only when they are deemed very rare, fine editions or are appreciated for the art of the printer or binder rather than for the text. Duncan (1983) has commented more generally that "the mass-production of books in modern times has both exaggerated and belittled their material significance. Their very ubiquity and diversity now seems to lend them, on one hand, a false, persistent autonomy disseevered from their communicative function and on the other, a cheap run-of-the-mill disposability" (91).

15. There is a massive literature of book design and typography that is beyond the scope of this chapter. My concern here is to bring the materiality of format into the analysis of the way in which Dani culture is represented.

16. This is, of course, also true of other time-based media from literature to video, but it is over overlooked in the analysis of the photo-essay.

17. For detailed consideration of the relationship between image and caption, see Berger and Mohr (1989), Hunter (1987), Scott (1999), and Stott (1973).

18. The text for volume was composed by Conzett & Huber, Zurich, Switzerland. The fact that this information appears prominently at the end of *Gardens of War,* "A note on production," further suggests the importance of the material qualities of the volume.

19. I am grateful to Linda Eerme, a historian of book design, for discussing this and other points with me.

20. Mitchell (1994, 292–93) suggests the possibility of placing such a division in relation to the aesthetics of Greenbergian modernism and the search the pure uncontaminated medium. Such a reading would not be anachronistic in the case of *Gardens of War,* but it cannot be substantiated.

21. A small color section acts as a frontispiece to "Appearances" and the final images of the color section bound with "Nourishment" actually relate to the following section "Play."

22. A sample of pages, in the possession of Robert Gardner, on a finer paper gives a very different affective tone to the images. The British edition of the book is printed on a marginally smoother coated paper which gives slightly different tonal registers to the photographs, especially the mid-grey tones.

23. The technology of mass-produced rotary gravure developed out of fine art photographic printing techniques of the nineteenth century.

24. For example, see Parr and Badger (2004), Trevitt (1980), and Wilson (1967). Photogravure was a more expensive process, and this is reflected in the selling price of *Gardens of War.*

25. The volume was printed by Amilcare Pizzi, S.p.A, Milan, Italy.

26. The dummy book, created by Eric Martin, suggests that the idea was originally for a small single image in the center of the cover. According to Kratz (1994, 185), the wrap-around cover image positions the book in a more popular domain. The cover image also appears, slightly cropped, within the book itself (pp. 60–61).

27. The word "photomontage" (from the French *montage*—fitting or assembling) originated after World War I and was put forward by Raoul Hausmann and colleagues, notably John Heartfield and George Grosz, to position their work not as "art" but within the assemblage of engineering (Ades 1986, 12). There are obviously earlier examples of photographic sequencing in pre- and proto-cinematic imaging, for example, the work of Muybridge in the 1870s and 1880s. But I am concerned here specifically with sequencing and rhythm that emerges from a clear cinematic aesthetic.

28. A constraint that experimental filmmakers have challenged almost from the beginning of the medium.

29. *Dead Birds* uses montage as an expressive engagement, especially in the battle scenes.

30. Tretyakov stated in 1936 that "if a photograph, under the influence of text [or indeed another photograph] expresses not simply the fact which it shows, but also the social tendency expressed by that fact, then it is already a photomontage" (quoted in Ades 1986, 17).

31. Many of the photographs work as individual images and have indeed been exhibited as such, for instance, Howard Becker's *Exploring Society Photographically,* one of the first exhibitions to explore the aesthetics of representation within the social sciences.

32. Constructed from three different actual events.

REFERENCES

ADAMS, Phoebe. 1969. "*Gardens of War.*" *Atlantic* 224: 103.

ADES, Dawn. 1986. *Photomontage.* Rev. ed. London: Thames and Hudson.

AGEE, James, and Walker Evans. 1941. *Let us now praise famous men.* Boston: Houghton Mifflin.

BAETENS, Jan. 1995. "John Berger and Jean Mohr: From photography to photo narrative." *History of Photography* 19 (4): 283–85.

——. 2005. "Motifs of extraction: Photographic images on book covers." *History of Photography* 29 (1): 81–9.

BARTHES, Roland. 1972. "The great family of man." In *Mythologies,* trans. Annette Levers, 100–102. London: Paladin.

BATESON, Gregory, and Margaret Mead. 1942. *Balinese character: A photographic analysis.* New York: New York Academy of Sciences.

BAZIN, André. [1967] 2005. *What is cinema ?* Vol. 1. Berkeley: University of California Press.

BECKER, Howard S. 1981. *Exploring society photographically,* Evanston, IL: Northwestern University Press.

——. 1984. *Art worlds.* Berkeley: University of California Press.

——. 1998. "Categories of comparisons: How we find meaning in photographs." *Visual Anthropology Review* 14 (2): 3–10.

BERGER, John, and Jean Mohr. 1976. *A fortunate man.* London: Writers' and Readers' Co-operative.

——. 1989. *Another way of telling.* Cambridge: Granta.

CLIFFORD, James. 1988. "On ethnographic authority." In *The predicament of culture,* 21–53. Cambridge, MA: Harvard University Press.

COOK, Simon. 2004. "Between book and cinema: Late Victorian new media." *Visual Studies* 19 (1): 60–71.

DANET, Brenda. 1997. "Books, letters, documents: The changing aesthetics of texts in late print culture." *Journal of Material Culture* 2 (1): 5–38.

DEDDES, William. 1971. "*Gardens of War* review." *American Anthropologist* 73: 346–47.

DUNCAN, Harry. 1983. *The doors of perception: Essays on book typography.* Austin, TX: W. Taylor Thomas.

EDWARDS, Elizabeth. 1997. "Beyond the boundary." In *Rethinking visual anthropology,* ed. M. Banks and H. Morphy, 53–80. London: Yale University Press.

EDWARDS, Elizabeth, and Janice Hart, eds. 2004. *Photographs objects histories: On the materiality of images.* London: Routledge.

FIRTH, Raymond. 1996. *Religion: A humanist interpretation.* London: Routledge.

GARDNER, Robert, and Karl Heider. 1968. *Gardens of war: Life and death in the New Guinea Stone Age.* New York: Random House.

GRADY, J. 1991. "The visual essay and sociology." *Visual Sociology* 6 (2): 23–38.

HAMILTON, Peter. 1997. "France and Frenchness in post-war humanist photography." In *Representations: Cultural representations and signifying practices,* ed. Stuart Hall, 75–150. London: Sage Publications/Open University Press.

HARPER, Doug. 1987. "The visual ethnographic narrative." *Visual Anthropology* 1: 1–19.

——. 2001. *Changing works: Visions of a lost agriculture.* Chicago: University of Chicago Press.

——. 2003. "Framing photographic ethnography." *Ethnography* 4 (2): 241–66.

HEIDER, Karl. 1970. *Dugam Dani: A Papuan culture in the highlands of western New Guinea.* Chicago: Aldine Press.

——. 1979. *Grand Valley Dani: Peaceful warriors.* New York: Holt, Rinehart and Winston.

——. 2001. "Robert Gardner: The early years." *Visual Anthropology Review* 17 (2): 61–70.

HUGHES, Alex, and Andrea Noble, eds. 2003. *Phototextualities: Intersections of photography and narrative.* Albuquerque: University of New Mexico Press.

HUNTER, Jefferson. 1987. *Word and image: The interaction of twentieth-century photographs and texts.* Cambridge MA: Harvard University Press.

KRATZ, C. A. 1994. "Telling/selling a book by its cover." *Cultural Anthropology* 9 (2): 179–200.

MALINOWSKI, Bronislaw. 1922. *Argonauts of the Western Pacific; an account of native enterprise and adventure in the archipelagoes of Melanesian New Guinea.* London: G. Routledge & Sons, Ltd.; New York: E. P. Dutton & Co.

MEAD, Margaret. 1968. "Introduction." In *Gardens of war: Life and death in the New Guinea Stone Age,* by R. Gardner and K. Heider, vii–x. New York: Random House.

MEISELAS, Susan. 2003. *Encounters with the Dani: Stories from the Baliem Valley.* New York: Steidl.

MILLER, Daniel, ed. 1998. *Material culture: Why some things matter.* London: UCL Press.

MITCHELL, W. J. T. 1994. *Picture theory.* Chicago: University of Chicago Press.

MORTON, Christopher. 2005. "The anthropologist as photographer: Reading the monograph and reading the archive." *Visual Anthropology* 18 (4): 389–405.

PARR, Martin, and Gerry Badger. 2004. *The photobook: A history.* Vol. 1. London: Phaidon.

PAUWELS, L. 1993. "Visual essay: Affinities and divergencies between the social scientific and the social documentary modes." *Visual Anthropology* 6: 199–210.

PERIVOLARIS, John D. 2003. "Humanism re-imagined: Spain as a photographic subject in W. Eugene Smith's *Spanish Village* (1951) and Cristina Garcia Rodero's *España oculta* (1989)." In *Phototextualities: Intersections of photography and narrative,* ed. Alex Hughes and Andrea Noble, 149–64. Albuquerque: University of New Mexico Press.

PINK, Sarah. 2001. *Doing visual ethnography.* London: Sage Publications.

PINNEY, Christopher. 1992. "The lexical spaces of eye-spy." in *Film as ethnography,* ed. P. Crawford and D. Turton, 26–49. Manchester: Manchester University Press.

ROBERTS, John. 1998. *The art of interruption: Realism, photography and the everyday.* Manchester: Manchester University Press.

RUBY, Jay. 2000. *Picturing culture.* Chicago: University of Chicago Press.

SANDEEN, Eric J. 1995. *Picturing an exhibition: The Family of Man and 1950s America.* Albuquerque: University of New Mexico Press.

Scott, Clive. 1999. *The spoken image: Photography and language.* London: Reaktion Books.

Simoni, Simonetta. 1996. "The visual essay: Redefining data, presentation and scientific truth." *Visual Sociology* 11 (2): 75–82.

Stallabrass, Julian. 1997. "Sebestiao Salgado and fine art photojournalism." *New Left Review* 223: 131–60.

Steichen, Edward. 1955. *The family of man.* New York: Museum of Modern Art.

Stott, William. 1973. *Documentary expression in thirties America.* New York: Oxford University Press.

Sullivan, Gerry. 1992. *Margaret Mead, Gregory Bateson, and Highland Bali: Fieldwork photographs of Bayang Gedé 1936–1939.* Chicago: University of Chicago Press.

Trevitt, John. 1980. *Book design.* Cambridge: Cambridge University Press.

Willumson, Glenn. 1992. *W. Eugene Smith and the photographic essay.* Cambridge: Cambridge University Press.

Wilson, Adrian. 1967. *The design of books.* London: Studio Vista.

Young, Michael. 1988. *Malinowski's Kiriwina: Fieldwork photographs 1915–1918.* Chicago: University of Chicago Press.

10 INTERACTIVE MEDIA AND THE CONSTRUCTION(S) OF MEMORY IN NONFICTION FILM
THE CASE OF *DEAD BIRDS*

RODERICK COOVER

TRAILER

Dead Birds, a 1964 film made by Robert Gardner about the Dani of New Guinea and their practice of ritual warfare, ends famously, universalizing,

> Soon both men and birds will surrender to the night…They will rest for the life and death of days to come for each both awaits but with a difference that men, having foreknowledge of their doom, bring a special passion for their life…they will not simply wait for death, nor will they bear it lightly when it comes. Instead they will try with measured violence to fashion fate themselves. They kill to save their souls and perhaps to ease the burden of what birds will never know and what they, as men, who have forever killed each other, cannot forget.

The specter of violence stands with stubborn resistance at memory's door. And, anthropological film, too, must always grapple with a challenge it cannot forget, that its quest to capture and remember is simultaneously its participation in a process of erasure and death, otherwise known as our globalizing modernity.

SIDEBAR 1: ESSAY MENU

- TRAILER
- MENU 1: Tests and Commentaries
- DESCRIPTION: An Art Of Memory
- MENU 2: About the DVD
- COMMENTARY
- METACOMMENTARY 1: E-mail from Ilisa Barbash
- ANALYSIS: Cruel Theaters of History
- METACOMMENTARY 2: E-mail from Karl Heider
- METACOMMENTARY 3: E-mail from Robert Gardner
- CREDITS

With original materials and metatexts, the exemplary film *Dead Birds* is now in a new form, released as a DVD. In this work, Robert Gardner looks forward by looking back. It is as if the questions asked years before remain unsolved; they linger in the world between the frames: in the splices and outtakes, journal notes, roundtable discussions, commentaries, and metacommentaries of this rerelease. These provide a view into a filmmaker's ongoing concerns and evolving views about the goals of anthropological filmmaking and its capacity to speak to issues of our times.

DESCRIPTION: AN ART OF MEMORY

David MacDougall (1994, 260–69), in his essay "Films of Memory," describes the wide-ranging genres of nonfiction *films of memory* and the synesthesia of signs by which filmmakers construct impressions of the past in a cinematic present. These include films that use objects and testimonies as *signs of survival* (images of objects that have a physical link to the past as well as, presumably, eyewitness accounts), *signs of resemblance* (evocation through analogy), and *signs of absence* (by which versions of the past are shown to have limits and deceptions, often through ironic juxtapositions like those, presumably, found in the films of Marcel Ophuls or, as MacDougall [262–66] cites, *The Trials of Alger Hiss*). The signs of memory include the iconic, symbolic, and enactive, and the genres cited include histories, ethnographies, abstractions, reconstructions, and visual essays. Add to a filmmaker's repertoire of tools in the representation of memory an invention not yet known at the time of writing that essay, the DVD commentary. Layered on an existing film—often with its original sound playing lightly in the background—the new text(s) speaks to an older film. Reissues of older films with DVD commentaries incorporate several presents some of which would already have been in the original. In *Dead Birds,* these include (1) the moment of the making of the film and the raw stock recorded at that moment that is then processed back in Boston, (2) the editing and recording of the original narration and sound effects later that year, (3) the reedited release print that was widely distributed and is featured here, and (4) the DVD commentary recorded about 40 years later. Add to these several other presents embedded in the interactive world of the DVD: (1) a slide show developed during postproduction, reedited and represented with journal notes from the past; (2) outtakes of the answer print with its original narration that were cut after the filmmaker screened the work to preliminary audiences in the United States and New Guinea; (3) a section of a roundtable discussion about the film recorded in 1973 almost 10 years after *Dead Birds* was released but 30 years before the DVD; and (4) differing commentaries made at various moments in which diverse speakers discuss outtakes and other materials not included in the famous release print. In this way, the DVD offers a dialogical construction of memories that layer on and intersect with each other through the spoken thoughts, images, and sounds. Meanwhile, there remain other ways DVD structure is not explored, such as through uses of hyperlinked digital data, voice recordings, response pages, and peer-to-peer linked research data. Many of these elements would expand the ways past works are represented. As a step toward the realization of George Marcus's (1998) notion of multisite ethnography, such tools offer multiple perspectives and reveal interesting questions about the layering of times and evolving views of the communities studied and the ethnographers who forged connections with these communities and produced works about them. The benefit of such elements may be more significant in new works, as they can be integrated in the design of projects from the moment of preproduction forward.

As an example of the use of DVD technology, *Dead Birds* is not unusual in its structure. The two-DVD set follows conventions commonplace in the short history of DVD. However, as *Dead Birds* illustrates, the model offers a unique and multilayered recontextualization that returns viewers not only to the original text—that is the film itself—but also to the layered presentation of the intellectual motivations for making such a film and the state of anthropology at the time. The layering of commentaries provided in Gardner's DVD provides insight into these artistic and ethnographic choice-making processes. A viewer sees how these choices impact research and postproduction as well as the onsite ethnography and filmmaking. Gardner's choices are shown to grow from philosophical and humanistic goals, including, first and foremost, a desire to understand something about violence in his own culture though a study of the violent acts of another.

An example of temporal layering in *Dead Birds* can be found in a segment of *Screening Room* that is included in this DVD. *Screening Room* was a television show that Gardner hosted in the 1970s in which he would invite documentary filmmakers to screen and discuss their works or other exemplary works of ethnography. In 1973, Gardner presented *Dead Birds*. The screening was followed by a short discussion between filmmaker Gardner,

MENU 2: ABOUT THE DVD

The film *Dead Birds* was the result of the Harvard-Peabody Expedition, which Robert Gardner led to Papua New Guinea in the spring of 1961. The expedition included Karl Heider, Jan Broekhuijse, Peter Matthiessen, and Michael Rockefeller. It was funded by the National Science Foundation, the government of Netherland New Guinea, and the Rockefeller family. The film was cut shortly after Gardner's return to Harvard. The answer print was screened at several locations, reedited into a shorter version, and released in 1964. The DVD was published by the Film Study Center at Harvard University 40 years later in 2004 and layers together materials recorded throughout that 40-year period—materials that the viewer pieces together to better understand the project, the times, and the maker.

- **Disc One** of the DVD contains the original film with three voice tracks: the original narration by Robert Gardner, a French voice-over read by Jean Rouch, and a recently recorded commentary in which Gardner discusses the film with filmmaker Ross McElwee.
- **Disc Two** features outtakes cut from the original answer print and samples of a black-and-white version, both with original sound and a recently recorded commentary about the clips in dialogue with Lucien Taylor. In addition, there is a collection of silent outtakes, provided with little explanation, and a brief set of Gardner's journal notes, which are read by the filmmaker and supported by a digital slide show.

poet Octavio Paz, and historian William Alfred. In this discussion of his own film, which at the time of this screening was already 10 years old, Gardner reflects on the issues that originally drew him to want to make a film about the ritual warfare of the Dani. The dialogue provides one slim view of how Gardner uses film to explore the place of violence in the cultural imaginary while also considering what roles anthropology should play given our own cultural predicaments; it offers a glimpse into the life of a filmmaker that gains value in relation to the other materials of the DVD. These same issues are revisited 30 years later in Gardner's metacommentaries to his film and in the outtakes of *Dead Birds* that are also included. Thus, through this common DVD structure, moments of history and of reflection are juxtaposed one by the other: an excerpt from *Screening Room* (1973) is used to offer a timely viewpoint following the broadcast video screening of a work shot on film, and both the original film and the later conversation from the television show are recontextualized through their inclusion on a DVD. From *Screening Room:*

> *Robert Gardner:* The film [*Dead Birds*] can be said to be about the consequences of mortality, or at least the consequences of men knowing they must die.

> *Octavio Paz:* In this case they know they are mortal…the important thing is that with this knowledge we make symbols, metaphors, and with these metaphors we make civilizations…Culture starts with the knowledge of death.

> *RG:* Do you think that our culture doesn't handle this very well?…We hide death.

> *William Alfred:* Yes, and in the past 20 years there has been a cult of anger…in this society [of *Dead Birds*] it manifests itself in warfare, but in our society we have this notion that if you could really let the anger go, you would be able to purify the society; so in a sense, the ideas that are in modern society are very like that [of *Dead Birds*].

> *RG:* At times I used to feel when I saw the picture or even when I was making it that perhaps it was a parable that would teach us something about how to cope with the violence within us or the problem of death…But there are vast differences between our way of handling our violence and their way of handling it.

> *WA:* Yes, there are vast differences, but I was thinking that we have a tendency, because of primitivism since the 18th Century, to celebrate certain primitive things which certainly, when you look at this film, can give you pause.

> *OP:* Well you know that anthropology is a very peculiar science, because the moment that we can see a film as your film, this society is disappearing. Even the fact that you are using the cinema as a way to know them, in this moment they are disappearing. The…object of anthropology is corroded by anthropology itself.

COMMENTARY

> Gardner's vision was deliberately humanistic: a filmmaker, a novelist, a professional photographer, and an anthropologist formed the core of his group. (Heider 2001–2002, 63)

Moving between modes of inquiry—between literary, philosophical, aesthetic, and anthropological methods—is a characteristic of Gardner's education and filmmaking. The filmmaker references and quotes writers such as Philip Larkin, W. B. Yeats, and Octavio Paz, and his short films have concerned the works of artists such as Joan Miró, Alexander Calder, and Mark Tobey (Cooper 1995, 26). Gardner's interweaving of the humanities, arts, and social sciences is indicative of a view that experience cannot be embodied by a single mode of representation, producing what Ilisa Barbash (2001) calls Gardner's "aesthesodic cine-eye." Gardner draws on a range of verbal and visual artistic tools to build a synesthesia of tropic connections that are tied to cultural objects, humanities activities and the dramas that hold together individuals and their communities.

Gardner builds a lyrical and metaphorically rich world by returning continually to common visual elements in the cultural landscape, such as the birds, the river, and the watchtowers. The use of bird feathers in ritual, trips to the river, and the manning of watchtowers are all practical aspects of Dani daily life. At the same time, all these are shown to have

greater meaning in the cultural imaginary. The birds are interconnected with the narrative of life and death. The watchtower is an ominous reminder of a life of warfare. The river becomes a site of danger and death. These evocative and tropic dimensions are constructed for the viewer through repetition and frequent recontextualization so that the symbolic elements of culture take on multiple meanings. The film viewer experiences the spontaneous and intellectual process of isolating essential characteristics—that is, the characteristics of the elements that gain meaning *in relation to* other aspects of the culture (or film).

These tropic connections are built through both images and sound. Perhaps his technique, expanded greatly in later films such as *Forest of Bliss,* is a result of working with the non–sync sound recordings that were collected by Karl Heider, often with the two working separately. Gardner's editing provides a layering of audio references to the images that connect them to other aspects of the culture and landscape. His highly interconnected and referential use of sounds and images brings viewers into what Barbash (2001) describes as a "pre-linguistic mode" (379). The result of such filming and editing is the construction of worlds in which "a viewer feels propelled, caught up in the interconnectedness of it all, transfixed by the propinquity of the sacred and the profane" (379).

To create these aesthesodic cine-worlds, Gardner must find means to identify and characterize audiovisual signifiers and show how these gain meaning in a cultural realm when seen from one perspective or another in ways not always captured by simple verbal explanation. Gardner tends toward the abstract, and for this reason the filmmaker claims he first conceived of many of his film images in black and white. The uses of black and white provides for a greater emphasis on the form and movement of an object and helps establish connections between visual elements—objects, animals, gestures, expressions, and so on— that have some aspects of form or movement in common. Gardner was so convinced of this need for a black-and-white view of the Dani that, at the time of editing, he produced an entire black-and-white version of the film. In dialogue with Taylor over a brief sample in the DVD of the beginning minutes[1] of this rarely screened black-and-white version of the film, Gardner explains as follows:

> *Robert Gardner (commenting over* Dead Birds' *opening image of a bird in flight):* You know this scene in color because it is the beginning of the movie. Seeing the bird in black and white does sum . . . up for me all of the virtues of black and white, because for me that bird is much more a bird in black and white than it was in color—that flight was much more flight. To see it in some more lifelike way in color did not enliven the bird; it burdened the bird with data that was irrelevant to its birdness, and so taking it away . . . was the answer to arriving at its quintessential view of flight.

> *Lucien Taylor:* [. . .] it is the symbolism of the bird . . . that we are now free to attend to more than we would be if we were attending to the variegated shades of green in the background. But it is not just the symbolism, it is also the physical material experience of sight and of movement . . . of watching this bird move across this treescape,

this landscape, that is actually heightened and accentuated in black and white. ... The physical sensation goes hand in hand with the symbolism.

Why, one wonders, is not more of the black-and-white version included? I can only speculate that this might reflect one of the significant limits of analog and digital video technologies, including DVD. They cannot represent the subtleties of gray and the characteristics of reflected light and shadow as well as film, and they lack essential characteristics of a work shot on film, projected through film, and watched as an indirect (reflected) rather than direct image. The potential of abstraction in black and white has much to do with the human ability to detect and discern the elements of an environment through movements of shadows, depth of shadows, curvature and perspective as indicated by shadows and so forth. As film is itself reflected, the gradations of gray are almost like shadows of shadows—they provide an element of mystery in the image that awakens the mind to the nature of that essential gap between a thing and its likeness. Finding ways to bridge this gap is especially important in developing images of other times (and memory images). This bridging helps a viewer to understand the audiovisual realm of other cultures, where the meanings of objects and actions are discerned by differing characteristics and read in relation to the culturally specific webs of significations—webs that are built through collective memory. While the ambiguity of black-and-white provides an effective tool in the construction of likenesses and difference,[2] the flattening of the image in video and DVD limits some of the signifying potential of the object.

If the DVD provides insight into Gardner's lyricism, creative vision, and philosophical interests, it also reveals how choices in the edit room limit and expand these. What emerges is a view of a filmmaker's struggle to strike a balance between maintaining the linear threads of narratives that Gardner draws out and the dialogical representation of the impact of Dani symbolic structures on daily life.

Back at Harvard, in the summer of 1961, Gardner began piecing together his film. He worked without the aid of a Steenbeck or Moviola, instead running work-print clips through projectors lined up side by side—a remarkable way to construct a film that offers such precision in its rhythms, juxtapositions, and multilayered motifs. The result was a little-viewed answer print that was much longer than the final version and of which only select (but spectacular) outtakes are included on this DVD.

The first answer print may not have been a complete success, or at least there are varying opinions about the little-viewed print from which the outtakes on the DVD are extracted.

METACOMMENTARY 1: E-MAIL FROM ILISA BARBASH, MARCH 28, 2005

"Aesthesodic," I used just because it points to the multi-sensory synaesthetic quality he (Gardner) aspires to, and often achieves, in his films—and how antithetical this is in most of what passes as ethnographic cinema—and the "odos," or way, as something leading directionally to that end.

Gardner recalls what was perhaps the first showing, when he screened the answer print to a group of friends including Lillian Hellman and Peter Matthiessen, who had written a book based on visits with the Dani (Matthiessen 1962). The result of that scotch-filled night was both admiration and the suggestion that Gardner trim the film to make it more compelling as a narrative, after which, Gardner explains, he then recut the film to produce a shorter version that focuses more tightly on its two primary subjects, a warrior named Weyak and a boy named Pua.

The comments Gardner received from that screening must have had a significant impact on his decision to reedit the film; not mentioned are the other screenings of the answer print during this interesting period, such as the showing in New Guinea described by Karl Heider (2001–2002) in his essay "Robert Gardner: The Early Years." Heider recalls a more chronological, multinarrative, and symbol-oriented cut:

> [After filming] Gardner took his footage back to the Film Study Center at Harvard and spent the next month editing. I stayed on alone in the Grand Valley, concentrating on my own research. Then, in July 1962, Gardner returned to Netherlands New Guinea with the first cut of *Dead Birds*. A grand screening took place at the Governor's palace in Hollandia, attended by the top officials of the Dutch colonial government. I think they had mixed feelings about the film. They appreciated its power, but were perhaps unhappy that it showed warfare in an area that had just been pacified. The first cut was long—perhaps an hour longer than the final eighty minute version now in distribution. It was a more complete account of the events during the five months in 1961 as they happened. For example, a funeral of a young warrior that is only represented now by a few shots under the opening titles was covered at length. As I remember it—I have not seen it for decades now—the most important difference was Gardner's extensive treatment of the central symbols of life and death, the birds. That still exists in the final release print, but in this first cut it was developed at greater length and the narrative was much more explicit about it. I thought that was a more effective and satisfying film, but Gardner was finally talked into cutting it drastically.

Noting the effectiveness by which Gardner understood the symbolic world of the Dani, Heider voices his regret that some these images were cut. Heider is recognizing the emergence of an audiovisual realm—a cultural imaginary built through the visual and audio referents that surrounds and by far exceeds the narrator's story and the film's explicit concern with the primary characters:

> One purpose of bringing the first cut back to New Guinea was to give me a chance to correct any real problems, since by then I had been living with the Dani for 15 months. I had many small comments, but then—as now—it seemed very true to Dani life. My one major concern was the symbolism, especially the birds-as-death motif that Gardner so stressed...As soon as I returned to the Grand Valley I turned to the symbols. By then, of course, I knew a great deal more Dani, and was getting a much better grasp of the

general themes of the culture. Using clues that Gardner had intuitively picked up on gone on to incorporate in the film, I asked people about the birds and snakes and life and death and quickly came to the conclusion that I had simply missed what Gardner had worked out. The symbolism was indeed there in Dani thinking and, if anything, was underrepresented in the film. (69)

This quality is built through the intertwining of referents[3] that continually point to worlds beyond the frame and place simple actions in the context of a larger theater—so appropriate for the study of ritual and performative acts, in this case of a sometimes horrific and violent nature.

ANALYSIS: CRUEL THEATERS OF HISTORY

Gardner claims that his interest in Dani warfare is a result of broader questions about the nature of violence and how humans confront the image of their own mortality. His search for an understanding of ritual violence and how it mirrors back the play of symbols in the collective imagination has a parallel with ethnographic filmmaker Jean Rouch, who by no coincidence reads the French narration to the film. Gardner's lyrical and character-oriented filmmaking techniques have antecedents in works such as *Nanook of the North* (Flaherty) and *Song of Ceylon* (Wright) (Cooper 1995). His goal to make anthropological films that speak to issues of our times and own culture also has clear roots in the works of John Grierson (Cooper 1995) and develops also through his collaboration with John Marshall. But *Dead Birds* holds a particular affinity with the issues and filmmaking style that Jean Rouch explores in his groundbreaking documentary *Les Maîtres fous* (1957). Both works show their respective filmmaker's deep interest in the nature of violence and in the lessons that the practices of their respective subjects might provide the Western world. Indeed, both approach their subjects with a remarkable optimism; through the violent acts they record, they articulate universal questions and aspirations. Consider Rouch's dramatic flourish to *Les Maîtres fous*:

> When comparing these smiles [of his subjects, who yesterday were possessed by the Hauka] with the contortions of yesterday, one really wonders whether these men of Africa have found a panacea for mental disorders, one wonders if they have found a way to absolve our inimical society.

Gardner interviewed Rouch on *Screening Room*. In that interview, one of the first to be released on DVD by Gardner's own production house, Studio 7 Arts, Rouch discusses ways that the Hauka used ritual performance to put into symbolic play the objects of colonial violence or strangeness that they witnessed in their daily life. Their dialogue is about *Les Maîtres fous*, but the conversation could be as much about his *Dead Birds*:

> *Robert Gardner:* [*Les Maîtres fous*] is a film which seems to speak to a larger issue than the immediate imagery that it is showing…it has a kind of extensive metaphorical qual-ity helping us as viewers of this film to understand what is going on in the minds of all

people. It isn't just the story of Ghanaians or just the story of West Africans, it seems to me it is the story of oppressed people, and most people are oppressed all over the world.

Jean Rouch: And then they have to find a way out.

RG: They invent a theater to deal with this.

This notion of theater in *Dead Birds* may be more akin to René Girard's (1979) descriptions of sacrificial violence than Rouch's *Les Maîtres fous*. In Rouch's film, the violence seems cathartic and remarkably efficient in relieving the anxiety of immigrant life in the colonial metropolis of Accra. Among the Dani, however, violence extends into daily and domestic life through further acts of aggression, the construction of heroic models, the magic given to war-related symbolic objects, and even through the war play among the children. Viewers see that the death of a warrior leads to women having their fingers severed and

METACOMMENTARY 2: E-MAIL FROM KARL HEIDER, MARCH 23, 2005

. . . Gardner's view was from the intensive five months we all spent with the Dani when their traditional warfare was going full strength. I was there then but stayed on after pacification for a total of nearly three years mainly in the early '60s, but with additional visits in '68, '70, '88, and '95.

I was impressed by the various limits on the violence of war—mainly through unspoken norms—e.g., during battles no shooting arrows in volleys (like Olivier's Henry V), no fletched arrows (making them relatively inaccurate), contained raids and ambushes—all this for what I call the ritual phase of war. Then, every decade or so a brief uncontained spurt of secular warfare breaks out, rearranges alliances, and things settle back into the paced ritual phase. This on the basis of long-term observations and also comparisons with other New Guinea highland groups. Mervyn Meggitt, working on the east side of the island, wrote about prudes and lechers—seeing the strained and violent relations between men and women as being either disgust- or rape-oriented. By these standards the Dani were neither—relations between men and women were very easy, friendly, even at times loving. (We see some of this in *Dead Birds*).

Later, when war was ended—I predicted to the Dutch that since war was obviously so rooted in Dani culture and psyche, without it things would go seriously awry. That didn't happen. Even the finger chopping of little girls was easily discarded—I accounted for that as a holdover from a different time and incongruous in the context of the obvious fondness Dani adults have for children. But when the missionaries suggested that the Dani change, they for the first years resisted changing anything except finger chopping, which they immediately gave up—I imagined with even some relief that they were not obliged to continue that discordant trait.

And killing pigs—well, you have to get them dead somehow. Elsewhere in the highlands people club their pigs to death. On the whole an arrow to the heart is relatively less violent. But is it sacrifice?

that the pathos surrounding the death of a young boy by the river is matched with a violent scene of animal slaughter during the ritual funeral rites. Such images provide an ominous warning about how violence can manifest itself in other aspects of society; grim images of women's short and stublike fingers contrast with those of the agile, long-fingered males; a young girl with undamaged hands also knows a future that awaits her.

The desire to witness violence that runs through horror and adventure genres, news programs, and cartoons like *Roadrunner* may offer means by which to grasp through image and play what would be unbearable to experience in fact. Another kind of attraction to the representation of violence can be found in the Nazi filming of genocide or U.S. military home-movie images shot at Abu Ghraib prison during the second Iraq War. Films like *Dead Birds,* historical films such as Alain Resnais's (1955) holocaust documentary *Night and Fog,* contemporary mainstream dramas such as *Hotel Rwanda* (George 2004)—which was released a few years after the Rwandan war and during yet another genocide, this time in Ethiopia—or vanguard media arts projects such as Norman Cowie's (2001–2002) *Scenes from the Endless War* all offer approaches to using the medium to understand violence. Not unlike Rouch's interest in recording the Hauka, Gardner's motives are explained in idealistic and humanistic terms: a belief that a film about the violent practices of the Dani might offer some clues to understanding violence in Western culture. This notion is reiterated several times through the DVD's commentaries and supplemental materials. At one instance, Ross McElwee even notes how the questions being asked in the original film aren't so different from those being asked 40 years after its production in relation to the U.S. aggression in Iraq and media representations of that warring violence. Just as anthropology is charged with being inescapably implicated in the cultural forces of colonial and postcolonial cultural homogenization, one wonders if cinematic investigations into violence might not also reinforce film's cultural role as a (perhaps ritualized) forum for the expression of violence; or, inversely, does a critical use of film (or now of DVD) give us insight into Western ritual behavior of which film is itself (perhaps inevitably) a part?

The answer may lie in how film reveals as much about itself as its subject. The repeating present of a replayed moment is a continual reminder of loss—a nostalgic recognition of time passing. Notions of time, memory, and loss are built into the form of film itself; each frame is dead and past in the very moment of its being recognized, yet it is forever also relivable. Film exposes (among others, presumably) a shock of experiencing time as something measured by machine, not nature. This witnessing of time—and, with it, mortality—from outside oneself is a feature that complements ritualized spectacles of violence; the self-reflexivity of the DVD helps draw the critical analyses of content and form together. Gardner's ethnographic investigation to understand something about "what they, as men, who have forever killed each other, cannot forget" is a cinematic one, and Gardner's very first and central question to Jean Rouch in his *Screening Room* interview of 1980 could as well be turned on himself, when he asks, "Do you consider yourself an anthropologist or a filmmaker?" For Gardner, as perhaps for Rouch, the question cannot be answered because their practices of film and anthropology cannot be separated. The layering of a

DVD gives additional perspective on these questions not only by allowing takes, cuts, and commentaries to be viewed through the lens of differing arguments but also by allowing a discourse built through diverse temporal perspectives (the commentaries recorded and constructed at differing moments) to intersect with one about the relation between form(s) and content(s). And the "texts" of this discourse are made up equally of language, image, and sound or, indeed, also of edits, links, and menus.

One view of how Gardner reveals his evolution as ethnographer-filmmaker is provided on the DVD through a sample of field notes—the ethnographer's staple—that were apparently compiled and edited shortly after filming to accompany a slide presentation about the project (or vice versa). The brief sample offers a view into the daily difficulties of working within an unfamiliar culture. Reflecting on the changing conditions of New Guinea, Gardner wonders out loud what will become of the Dani under Indonesian rule; this is about as close as the filmmaker gets to confronting questions of colonialization and postcolonial conditions, and his return visit has not yet resulted in a film. But not all important stories make good films—a practical reality for the anthropological filmmaker or filmmaking anthropologist is that the tool must match the task. For now, the gift for the rest of us from that return visit is Susan Meiselas's (2003) book *Encounters with the Dani*. Made with Gardner's participation, the book charts the cultural transformation that occurs through the Dani encounters of the past century with Dutch colonial expeditions, missionaries, survivors of a plane crash in the Grand Valley and the team that came to rescue them, the Dutch administration, and the Indonesia government, following its invasion of New Guinea, in 1962. Meiselas's book is constructed through fragments gleaned from these encounters. Her scrapbook-like approach emphasizes how twentieth-century Dani history was shaped by fragmented encounters with significantly different kinds of foreign visitors each with their own intentions, biases, methods, and worldviews. What also emerges in Meiselas's book is a picture of various forms of violene, both overt and insidious, that are enacted upon the Dani and refracted in various ways.

However, one can't do it all, and that is no less true of a DVD than any other work. What is gained—and of which *Dead Birds* is an example—is a fascinating insight into a process. The DVD layering reveals intentions, choice making, and self-reflection as well as

METACOMMENTARY 3: E-MAIL FROM ROBERT GARDNER, APRIL 29, 2005

This re-visiting, which is ongoing, has been disturbing in its relentless calling up of repressed memory...

At the bottom of all representation I think there lies a struggle with "absence," with death, if you will. I would venture further—in an effort to address your references to "violence"—and say that violence is a particularly rich arena in which to "practice," come to grips with, death and dying.

the varied voices of others, in this case, of fellow filmmakers and anthropologists that have been collected over time. Through the combination of notes, photos, outtakes, and recollections of moments that couldn't/wouldn't be filmed—when it just wasn't permissible, was too dark, or was not thought essential at the time or when simply there was no more film in the magazine—the viewer constructs at least two imaginaries, not one. There is the world of the Dani and another: that of Robert Gardner at work in the field or in his studio, edit room, screening room, or lecture hall.

Through the rescreening of *Dead Birds* and the resulting conversations about it, a past is made meaningful again, whether in the context of evaluating the role of anthropology in the face of ever-increasing globalization, of investigating why we still fight wars, or in reimagining uses for film and other new tools by which we might express what lies beyond words in the imagined worlds we construct and in which we live. In piecing together the fragments of a work scattered among the dialogues of a career of numerous important films, countless courses and students, and fascinating conversations bridging the arts, humanities, and social sciences, the viewer also learns of memory's own processes of selection and an individual's changing perspective on experiences past in the contexts of conditions present.

From the commentary to *Dead Birds:*

> *Robert Gardner:* As soon as I heard that there was the opportunity to go to a place where ritual warfare was being practiced I said "Yes!" [...] The reason that I was so excited by the idea was because I naively thought... if I could begin to understand what this meant to them... I would chip away at least at our own concerns and our own preoccupations of killing each other. My whole notion was that anthropology was meant to be a way of curing the world of its ills, this being the biggest piece of naiveté of all...

> *Ross McElwee:* Well, another word for naiveté is idealism. It seems as if you did have an idealist premise for making this film that was firmly situated in the time in which it was made... You did really focus on one small group of people that had for me broader implications for where the world was at that time and continued to be for 25–30 years, and, with a slight shift, still is. Why do we make war?

> *RG:* To show how unsuccessful I was things have just gotten worse since I made this film.

> *RM:* We don't blame you Bob, it's not your fault.

CREDITS

Thanks to Ilisa Barbash, Robert Gardner, Kark Heider, Susan Meiselas, Ákos Östör, and Lucien Taylor for their input and for the materials they supplied.

NOTES

1. The black-and-white samples in the DVD include the first 4 minutes and 20 seconds or so and the final 145 seconds. These may be too short to know whether Gardner achieved this pure vision; one wonders if in making a black-and-white version he should not have edited it differently to make a film that would maximize the essential and abstracting aspects of vision.

2. An interesting introduction into the use of black-and-white imagery and its relation to memory is presented in Berger and Mohr (1982). Images used as quotes function together in the construction of story, in part because black and white forefronts abstract qualities and enables a construction of memory through the likenesses of these qualities.

3. For more on the construction of referential systems in films by Robert Gardner, see Coover (2001).

REFERENCES

BARBASH, Ilisa. 2001. "Out of words: The aesthesodic cine-eye of Robert Gardner." *Visual Anthropology* 14 (4): 369–413.

BERGER, John, and Jean Mohr. 1982. *Another way of telling.* New York: Pantheon.

COOPER, Thomas W. 1995. *Natural rhythms: The indigenous world of Robert Gardner.* New York: Anthology Film Archives.

COOVER, Roderick. 2001. "Worldmaking, metaphors, and montage in the representation of cultures: Cross-cultural filmmaking and the poetics of Robert Gardner's *Forest Of Bliss.*" *Visual Anthropology* 14 (4): 415–33.

COWIE, Norman. 2001–2002. *Scenes from the endless war* (film, 32 minutes).

GARDNER, Robert. [1985] 2001. *Forest of bliss* (DVD [film]). Cambridge, MA: Harvard University Film Study Center.

——. [1964] 2004. *Dead birds* (DVD [film]). Cambridge, MA: Harvard University Film Study Center.

——. [1980] 2004. *Screening room with Robert Gardner: Jean Rouch* (DVD). Cambridge, MA: Studio 7 Arts.

GEORGE, Terry. 2004. *Hotel Rwanda* (film, 121 minutes).

GIRARD, René. 1979. *Violence and the sacred.* Baltimore: Johns Hopkins University Press.

HEIDER, Karl. 2001–2002. "Robert Gardner: The early years." *Visual Anthropology Review,* 17 (2): 61–70.

MARCUS, George. 1998. *Ethnography through thick and thin.* Princeton, NJ: Princeton University Press.

MACDOUGALL, David. 1994. "Films of memory." In *Visualizing theory,* ed. Lucien Taylor, 260–69. New York: Routledge.

MATTHIESSEN, Peter. 1962. *Under the mountain wall: A chronicle of two seasons in the Stone Age.* New York: Viking.

MEISELAS, Susan. 2003. *Encounters with the Dani.* New York: International Center of Photography.

RESNAIS, Alain. 1955. *Night and fog* (film, 31 minutes).

PART THREE: REMINISCENCES

11   ANECDOTE OF A SEASON

STANLEY CAVELL

On various occasions over the years, I have expressed in some detail my admiration for the films—and the writing about films—of Robert Gardner, and I hope there will be future such occasions. At this moment, my mood seems drawn toward a wish to capture some realization of the fact that Robert Gardner and I have known each other going on four complete decades and—I feel I can speak for both of us in this—each taken some heart from our continuously intersecting, however differently manifested, loves of the arts, of course, most particularly, of the newest of the great arts. As teachers, and inspired by the talent of the young that Harvard University attracts, we seemed to have arrived separately at the idea of a curriculum in film studies driven by the making of film and including reflection on film's possibilities and necessities that would welcome philosophy (as well, say, as anthropology) among its interlocutors. It was not hard to see that Harvard's Carpenter Center for the Visual Arts and Robert Gardner's presence there attracted gifted and articulate younger filmmakers, together with visiting masters of the medium, and with the talent of the Harvard faculty continuing across the street and down the street, how could the value of such an experimental curriculum—unique, as far as I was aware, among the ideas for programs in film study in the universities I knew—not become generally obvious and catch fire, not merely transforming the study of film but affecting the idea of university study as such?

I think of the joint undergraduate seminar motivated along such lines that Gardner and I offered jointly in the mid-1960s, making super-8 cameras available to something like a dozen students, together with a list of readings, and hoping to let shooting and weekly conversations thrive in each other's company. As in other domains, it turned out, however fascinating the experience and individually fruitful, that love does not live by love alone but requires friends and strangers and institutions and recognition and ratification to know and to sustain itself and to make the sort of difference in the world that it deserves to make and that the world needs to have.

While the future we envisioned did not by magic realize itself, many eventual crossroads have been negotiated since then, countless conversations held, further films imagined and captured, books made about them, courses constructed, in and beyond and because of the Carpenter Center for Visual Arts, a major archive formed, friendships lost and found and furthered. Is there some way for such eventualities to measure the consequence and effect, for example, of that one distant seminar Gardner and I put together? Is the measure important?

But here the experience of film teaches something about what teaching and learning can be. More specifically, the experience of documentary impressions or the documentary element in any of film's impressions of the world and of ourselves and others in it tells us perpetually about human existence that we do not know ahead of time the significance of what we do and say and of what happens to us. One could say it teaches the irreducible role of patience in teaching and learning.

I have wished to understand Wittgenstein's *Philosophical Investigations* as a book of instruction, and I have found myself at odds with what I believe is or was an undisputed reading of the marvelous moment in that text that I call its scene of instruction: "If I have exhausted the justifications I have reached bedrock, and my spade is turned. Then I am inclined to say: 'This is simply what I do.'" The prominent reading of this passage understands the teacher here as threatening the pupil with rejection, exclusion, whereas it reads to me (at least equally) as, on the contrary, a description of waiting, leaning on one's spade, acknowledging human limitation. If we say of the former (threatening) reading that it is strong, we might wish of the latter (waiting, showing patience) that it is weak. But it must be an active waiting, an interested patience, not an easy matter to describe, however easy to sense, if you have the sense for it. In his conversation with Ákos Östör about the making of *Forest of Bliss,* Gardner calls this species of waiting anticipation and regards it as a capacity indispensable for the documentary filmmaker "to keep that critical, anticipatory instant ahead of what's happening" (Gardner and Östör 2001, 37).

I do not know whether Gardner realized that he was anticipated in this emphasis by Thoreau, who in *Walden* speaks of his desire, or resolve, to "anticipate, not the sunrise and dawn merely, but if possible Nature herself." Contrariwise, something Thoreau may not have realized is a matter that Gardner seems to have divined in describing the start of his film *Forest of Bliss* as "the sun rising…being pulled up by that boy who's flying a kite," namely, that the idea of anticipation, of grasping something beforehand, is particularly bound up with the idea of grasping a thread (or string?), as for weaving. In my introductory remarks to *Making Forest of Bliss,* I also adduce Heidegger's reading of the opening words of Hölderlin's *Ister Hymn*—"Now come, fire"—as calling on the sun to rise because having been called by the sun, assuming that Heidegger (even though he knew that his indispensable Nietzsche was memorizing Emerson while still in high school) did not know of the anticipation in Thoreau.

Something I have learned or, I guess remembered, more recently is that Wallace Stevens, another reader of Emerson's, thought of the work of poetry as that of coming early, anticipating. In a late essay of his, "A Collect of Philosophy," Stevens says, "According to the traditional views of sensory perception, we do not see the world immediately but only as the result of a process of seeing and after the completion of that process, that is to say, we never see the world except the moment after" (1989, 190). Yet Stevens counteracts the suggestion that we may therefore never see the world as it is in the short poem he places at the end of his *Collected Poems,* a poem to which he gives as its title "Not Ideas about the Thing but the Thing Itself," which concludes, "It was like / A new knowledge of reality." The approach to reality, to a world, as Kant put the idea, outside of me (to which skepticism scandalously denies the human mind access) is here understood by Stevens as requiring that we come to it early and earlier. Each of the opening two (of the six three-line) stanzas of the poem invokes the idea of a new or renewed knowledge of reality by way of an anticipation, something coming early, coming before. I quote these two stanzas:

> At the earliest ending of winter,
> In March, a scrawny cry from outside
> Seemed like a sound in his mind.
>
> He knew that he heard it,
> A bird's cry, at daylight or before,
> In the early March wind.

But am I confusing my claim that teaching has unanticipatable effects, calling for a species of patience, with the idea that there is an indispensable teaching that is a product of a capacity for anticipation? I want both, of course, and I find an implication to be that one ambition of teaching is to make yourself anticipatable, opening your thoughts sufficiently, vulnerably, to allow your interlocutor to get ahead of you, so that revealing what you are not, perhaps cannot be, certain of becomes as useful as telling your confidence.

There is another implication. A university that, along with its expected departments of the humanities and the social sciences, also welcomes the practice of filmmakers, artists in film, such as Robert Gardner, is an environment, or promises to provide it, in which such crosscurrents of effect are part of the air one breathes. To the extent that my talents have allowed, Robert Gardner and film at Harvard University have meant this for me.

REFERENCES

GARDNER, Robert, and Ákos Östör. 2001. *Making* Forest of Bliss: *Intention, circumstance, and chance in nonfiction film.* Cambridge, MA: Harvard University Press.
STEVENS, Wallace. 1989. *Opus posthumous.* New York: Knopf.

12 THE ETHNOGRAPHER'S (VISUAL) KNOWLEDGE
FIELDWORK WITH CAMERA AND NOTEBOOK IN VISHNUPUR, 1982 AND 1983

ÁKOS ÖSTÖR

What do ethnographers know? Can one "do" anthropology with camera and tape recorder? Is there visual knowledge? Is there a genre of ethnographic film? What has cinema to do with anthropology? In the 1970s and 1980s, Robert Gardner and I addressed these and other questions in discussions, seminars, and film production. Eventually, we made four films together, motivated by a desire to bring film and anthropology together in the most felicitous ways possible, without discounting the potential of either. We did not set out to invent or even define a genre, but we had a few ideas we wanted to put into practice.

In this chapter, I try to capture the spirit of those years when we worked most closely together. I came to film from anthropology, and our collaboration had a major impact on my life and work. In the process, film has become anthropology for me in ways beyond a mere subdiscipline, without any imposed conditions and preconceived requirements.

I came to know Robert Gardner soon after arriving at Harvard University in 1974 to take up an appointment in the anthropology department. *Dead Birds* premiered then at the Carpenter Center for Visual Arts, and we began a lifelong dialogue about film, art, anthropology, and life. By the time I moved to the Department of Visual and Environmental Studies, in 1982, we were ready to make films together. The first season of filming took place in 1982 with Allen Moore, himself a product of the Harvard film study program. Allen came out of that unique and remarkable group of filmmakers around Boston and Cambridge who worked in association with the Film Study Center founded by Bob Gardner in 1957. Bob was also directing the Carpenter Center then, and both centers were open to people with ideas and commitment to film. Official appointment to Harvard was not a prerequisite: photography, film, painting, sculpture, and inventive, compelling work of all kinds found a home there. In 1983, I went back to India for further filming, this time with Bob. The planned feature-length film became a trilogy of shorter films that premiered in 1985 at the Festival of India in Washington, D.C. In 1984, we went to Benares to film *Forest of Bliss,* which was released in 1986. Two years later, I went to Wesleyan University to lecture and research in both the anthropology department and the Film Studies Program, an appointment institutionally more congenial than Harvard could offer.

This chapter is based on notes I wrote after leaving Harvard and used in talks at different venues. I offer the remarks here as an indication of the work we did at the Film Study

Center in the 1980s. To put it in rather abstract terms, I was struggling then to formulate a relationship between film and anthropology, and the "Pleasing God" trilogy became a testing ground and a journeyman product. More immediately, the films were an attempt to apprehend visually and aurally the world of Bengali sacred ritual.

My anthropological work in Bengal—writing in the late 1980s now—already spans some 20 or so years, and its products come increasingly in the form of films as well as monographs. Both forms yield critical knowledge and understanding, both rely on fieldwork and cultural constructs, and both utilize observations, narratives, images, symbols, and categories. Ethnographic and filming practices must deal with relationships between the observer and what is being observed, subject and object, inside and outside, particular and general, unique and universal. These dichotomies are not paradigmatic, nor are they mere contrasts: depending on what is done with them, they denote dialectical relations from which increasingly complex world constructions can be derived, that as will be clear from the examples here, reveal mediated oppositions rather than mere isolated contrasts.

Making films and monographs has come to mean to me working with concepts and creating narratives both ethnographic and anthropological, indigenous as well as theoretical, comparing symbols and categories. These concepts are as good as those of any other discipline: we don't have to look to philosophy, literature, or history to justify our conceptual usage. At the same time, we should heed anthropological discourse in all its dimensions: the concepts we use can make sense at both local and global levels.

Films and books encounter an objective world separate from the observer (India, Bengal, Bishnupur, as well as America). But my apprehension of the world is not through its externality and autonomy but through images and concepts, which are not a separate reality. My studies are not directly of an objective world but of things constructed by human beings. Hence, I film and write about images, concepts, and symbols through images, concepts, and symbols. Anthropology (written or filmed) is different from fiction (the novel), the feature film, art, poetry, and the natural or physical sciences, but it can be criticized, accepted, refuted, changed, revised, verified, or reinterpreted as an account or image of the world. In the interpretive mode of anthropology, we work in the field; we construct, objectify, and invent cultures, both our own and those of the people around us.

My first case study exploring these complex issues comes from a Bengali bazaar, specifically the Chowk bazaar of Bishnupur (Östör 1984). While I worked in that town, about 100 miles northwest of Calcutta, I did not study the town, nor did I write a local history. But the "local knowledge" I gained did provide access to place and time in more restricted as well as wider senses. Festival and ritual, administration and politics, kinship and caste, bazaar and commodity markets, the world system and the like can, I found, be apprehended through the same, patient ethnographic approach that yields puja, rajniti, bajar, and jati. The local participates in the global (and vice versa), and the representations of the observer enter into reciprocal relations with those of the local people. But the local cannot be read out of the general, and all our constructions and linking have to be established. What can the ethnographer tell and show us? What kind of knowledge and how constituted? By whom and for whom?

The Chowk (or rectangular) bazaar has a distinctive appearance with its shops and platforms, covered and open-air trading areas, storehouses, and temples. Piles of agricultural produce alternate with aluminum pots, hand-loom and factory-produced cloth, tea stalls, and sweetshops. The Chowk is linked to smaller bazaars in the town and bigger ones beyond and to other arenas of activity, such as local and regional administration, political parties, courts, production, and transportation. It occupies a distinctive locality in the center of town, surrounded by residential neighborhoods (paras), temples, open spaces and ponds, bus stations, government offices, and workshops.

The people of the bazaar enter into many relationships with each other. One of the many terms attached to people describes what they do: arotdar and mahajan (major or big merchants), paikari and kuchari (smaller traders), chasi (cultivators), silpi (artisans), khoddar (customers), and agents, drivers, and carriers. The ways of trading are also linked to kinds of people and relations among people. Bazaar practices are in turn linked to kinds of produce. Items and terms of trade are organized around concepts such as cahida/sarabaraha (glossed in English as demand and supply), amdani/raptani (import and export), beca/kena (buying and selling), adan/pradan (an exchange relation), mul dhon (capital or stock with aspects of credit, a time-based concept), bebosay (business practice), and cakri (salaried job). Each of these terms refers to other ones in the context of bazaar practice, and each implies a time lag between the different components of the action to which it refers. For example, cakri in the bazaar refers to government service and as such designates the relations between government, administration, and bazaar. Thus, a person with government service may regulate the supply of controlled materials (kerosene, oil, and sugar in ration shops) and procure rice quotas through mills and farms.

The terms I described so far are also practices in which persons are engaged. The persons and practices themselves can be observed in the daily life of the bazaar. Equally real are the indigenous systems of concepts that link these and other terms in complex sets of category, person, and practice, such as baki, rhin, and len-den, all terms that refer to owing, giving, and taking in some kind of credit–debt relation that persists over time between kinds of persons.

Time itself is not ruled by one of its senses, the clock-based, linear, and measurable time that dominates working life in industrial societies. Duration, cycle, and season are other aspects the observer may group with "time in the bazaar." Lines of produce come and go, rise and fall in demand and production, and coincide with festivals, seasons, and family rituals. Price (dor, dam, mul) is equally complex: a set of concepts and relations that expresses the worth and value of goods and practices at a time or over time (Östör 1993).

Relationships and practices obtain among persons as traders (arotdar) and cultivators (casi). The arotdar collects, stores, and transports produce from a number of cultivators in the villages around Bishnupur and supplies other big traders in Calcutta and elsewhere. He also supplies smaller traders (paikari) in the Chowk and other bazaars of the town. There are many aspects to these relationships that I will not detail here, but they involve the other concepts and practices I have already mentioned. On the surface, these relationships are dual and reciprocal, but they are not isolated and cannot be aggregated to yield a system. They are mediated relations branching off in many directions to produce more dual exchanges. Thus, the bazaar system is underlain by a structure of threefold relations where the third term is the mediating aspect that allows the emergence of another exchange relationship in a different direction. There may be only two persons, one of whom is the superior mediator, while each one may turn the exchange into yet another relationship: the arotdar to another big trader elsewhere, the paikar to the customer (khoddar) engaged in household consumption.

Beyond the bazaar, in relation to the government, merchants have to deal with officials who mediate the trade in controlled goods. These structural relations may involve two, three, or more persons, but in all cases a triad is involved: even in a dyadic relationship, one of the categories is the mediator. The mediating category represents an ability to initiate and carry through exchanges in different directions and on different levels of enveloping hierarchies. This structure of mediation is an anthropological construct but it is built up after the living reality of the bazaar, and the concomitant values are also indigenous categories having to do with respect, ability, and power. These relationships obtain among people, not things. People call on each other with the superior mediators being able to manipulate time, stocks, credit, and other relationships to involve more people in their activities. Such an ability or power (karma khamata, karma sakti) commands respect (sanman). Ability and power have to do with directing other people's actions within the system of categories and practices in the bazaar, potentially reaching into other domains of relationships as well.

The categories I discussed point to an indigenous system of knowledge, linking meaning, practice, and value. This is what traders mean when they talk about bajarer bhab (the thought or idea of the bazaar). The bazaar as system of thought is the qualitative aspect of business, ability, power, and more, a system of meanings and values linking persons and practices. The whole complex is designated by terms related to bhab: the buddhi (intelligence), biddha (knowledge), and gun (quality) of the bazaar. The translations are imprecise, but the implications for an order of knowledge are clear: persons of the bazaar know some things the process and structure of which can be ascertained in context as value, quality, and meaning (Östör 1984).

I have made numerous references to the people of the bazaar as persons engaged in forms of trading. But persons are also relatives, caste brothers, devotees, and more. The domain of "kinship-marriage-caste" enters the bazaar in terms of the blood (rakta) or marriage (kutum) relationships (samparka) among relatives (attiya). The system extends to everyone in the bazaar since everyone participates in "kinship by relationship" (samparke attiya). The person is made in marriage through the contribution of mother and father, constituting descent lines and overlapping marriage cycles. What Marcel Mauss termed the "moral person" is completed through a series of life cycle rituals over time: the bazaar person carries all these identities, including the constructs acquired in the life of the bazaar, but need not call on them at any given time. The people of the bazaar are persons in many ways: in terms of caste, kinship, marriage, and the bazaar itself. Among themselves, they are brothers and sisters, uncles and aunts, and nephews and nieces to each other. They are also moral persons in terms of ultimate realities: karma (reaping the consequences of past actions), purus artha (the ends of human life: dharma, sacred law; artha, means; kama, desire; moksa, liberation), tin gun (three qualities: sattva, truth; raja, energy; tama, inertia), and janmantar (the cycle of births and deaths ending in liberation of the atma, soul/self. The different aspects and levels I described (in hopelessly abbreviated form and with rather rough English equivalents) are integrated (sometimes in harmony, sometimes in tension or even conflict) in the lives of individual persons through the cultural forms in which these aspects and levels participate. The bazaar itself, life cycle rituals, family, and other institutions of everyday life (sangsar) are such forms in each of which principles and practices come together, collectively and individually, in distinctive configurations.

It may come as no surprise that the people of the bazaar gather, at the end of the Bengali year, to celebrate the divine, sacred power of Shiva, the Great Lord (Mahadeb), and his consort Kamakkha Devi (an aspect of the goddess Durga). The weeklong ritual cycle, the Gajan of Shiva, is the climax of the bazaar year, Shiva himself being Mahakala ("great") time itself, while Kali is another aspect of the goddess, his consort. The men of the bazaar become bhaktas (devotees and sons of Shiva) and renounce everyday life, living like ascetics for the duration of the festival. While women participate in the various temple rituals of the gajan, only men become bhaktas. They fast, sleep at the temple, and worship Shiva. They celebrate the power and energy generated by the union of Shiva and the goddess, who are brought together in the cycle of rituals. They participate in the creation of that power (sakti) and are regenerated as a result. They are able to face the tasks of the coming year with renewed power and ability to act. Thus, we come back, in a full circle, to karma khamata and karma sakti, the ability to influence others' actions within the system of categories and practices in the bazaar (Östör 1980, 2004).

It is clear from my account that the observer, ethnographic practice, indigenous systems of categories and practices are closely intertwined at every step of the analysis and interpretation. Giving a seemingly straightforward description of the bazaar is to implicate a social science and a local knowledge. From the very beginning, I introduced patterns (locality, domain of action, person) and categories (bazaar, ritual, government, kinship). I moved back and forth between anthropological and indigenous concepts. Observation (as thought and action) was dialectically related to the ideas and activities of people, a step toward the constructing different levels and forms of culture: family, neighborhood, town, region, and nation.

My second case study is drawn from the "Pleasing God" trilogy set in Bishnupur. The films look at Hindu belief and ritual with an eye to exploring how people experience, practice, and, in part, explicate their beliefs and rituals. *Loving Krishna, Sons of Shiva*, and *Serpent Mother* deal with, in different ways, directly or indirectly, the same matters I have discussed previously. Bazaars and traders make an appearance in all three films, raising questions of medium, substance, form, and interpretation in visual ethnography. Here I write about something that is to be seen: only the first of our difficulties. Films deal with visual images and sounds, a different medium with unique properties and abilities that concern, most of all, motion in space and time. At its best, film is a way of visual and aural thinking, one that is capable of offering an interpretation. The linking of images, in various forms of editing, evokes mood and feeling, expresses experience, and yields abstract thought. Saying this, we immediately implicate an aesthetic. Image, form, and composition on the one hand and the intuitive apprehension of a totality on the other are shared by all the visual arts, including film. Aesthetic experience itself can be comprehended cognitively and thus made to yield critical knowledge.

Bazaar, itihasa, and puja are given form and interpreted in our films, though in ways fundamentally different from written ethnographies. In filming, as in writing, we deal with issues of representation, analysis, or interpretation and the relation between general and particular. But the forms and contexts are very different. One of the most intriguing and problematic aspects of film is what Kracauer called its ability to render nature whole, to represent something realistically. The tendency toward realism, achievable as if directly, with only slight mediation, and to be objective and scientific at the same time, is both an illusion and a temptation anthropologists have handled, on the whole, rather badly. Anthropological debates surrounding ethnographic film (in the 1970s and 1980s) are still premised on a film showing and telling an ethnography like it is, without too much interference by the artistic aspects of filmmaking, the more mediated world of aesthetics, which is supposedly the imposition and whim of the filmmaker.

In film studies, critics have called attention to the dual tendency of cinema from the beginning: one toward realism the other toward abstract expression. Film, as far as anthropologists are concerned, has its own contrast between scientific objectivity and subjective interpretation. For those who praise the former, the latter presents an unending source of trouble: aesthetics is equated with "embellishment" and takes away from ethnographic validity. Refusing to manipulate lens, focal length, composition, color, tone, and camera movement, the champions of objectivity would move film closer to the scientific enterprise of anthropology. Approved strategies may involve long takes, minimal editing, and a limited set of camera angles. But film is not a mirror of nature or a record of reality. It is a made, mediated artifact, a representation of reality but not a direct record, rather an interpretation of reality through the manipulation of camera, lens, light, motion, and composition. Significant changes are wrought when separate bits of film, the shots or takes, as they come out of the camera, are joined together in editing.

The "Pleasing God" trilogy, made by Bob Gardner, Allen Moore, and myself, does not fall easily into the conventional categories of the nonfiction cinema. It is a documentary, ethnographic film independent of any written work but one that combines film aesthetics with the concepts and methods of anthropology. Our aim was to represent indigenous ideas and practices through the use of visual symbols and images. We combined concrete particulars with abstract ideas to suggest a central interpretation behind appearances and surfaces. The first film, *Loving Krishna* (Moore and Östör 1985), is about the worship of Krishna and the meaning of devotion. It introduces the town of Vishnupur, where all three films were made. The urban and rural character of the town is explored in view of the close relation between the royal past, everyday life, work in traditional arts and crafts, bazaar exchange, and sacred rituals and festivals. Public and private devotional life is shown by detailed visual narratives of the Chariot Journey of Krishna, celebrated by the whole town with pomp and circumstance, and the Birthday Festival of Krishna commemorated on a much smaller scale in intimate family worship. Throughout the film, interviews and narration emphasize the continuing relevance of history, the links between worship and work, the meaning of symbolism in the rituals, and the significance of Krishna's teachings for contemporary life.

The second film, *Sons of Shiva* (Gardner and Östör 1985), is a sustained attempt to film a four-day festival, the annual worship of Shiva. Here the activities of the devotees are shown from beginning to end, with close attention to the gradually intensifying action culminating in a variety of ascetic and self-denying practices. The film follows devotees from the moment of taking the Sacred Thread through individual devotional practices to a climax in formal temple and group rituals. Devotees are seen in informal activities as well: preparing food, singing religious songs, and listening to the recital of Bauls, a mendicant devotional order.

The third film, *Serpent Mother* (Moore and Östör 1985), explores devotion to the goddess of snakes and the importance of divine female power in the lives of the towns-people. The worship of this goddess is usually ascribed to the lower orders of Bengali society just as Krishna is usually associated with the upper castes. Yet devotees insist on the unity of all devotional practices, and the film attempts to capture this internal meaning of ritual. The film concentrates on the Jhapan Festival, the great annual celebration of snakes. It follows the preparations for the festival, the participation of traditional arts and crafts in the worship of the goddess, devotional singing, as well as an exposition of ritual action. A contrast is drawn between daily devotional practices and the excitement of the great snake festival where adepts play with dozens of poisonous snakes for the glory of the goddess. Throughout the film, the difficult and complex symbolism of the ritual is explained by participants and an anthropological commentary making accessible what might seem, at first glance, even in other parts of India let alone outside, inexplicable and exotic behavior.

The three films are not directly about the bazaar social relations, so in terms of substance they do not match my example of the written ethnography. Nevertheless, the formal, structural, and interpretive issues are similar, so a comparison between the written and the visual can be made. The films exhibit a certain style (having to do with the way they were shot and the decisions about light, tone, aperture, and camera movement as well as cinematic and photographic appearance) and a certain form (the shape and appearance of each film as a separate and complete whole). They carry conviction: being mediated, two-dimensional images and sounds, the films are about Bengali rituals that took place in Vishnupur in 1982 and 1983 and not on a back lot in Hollywood. They are authentic documentary or ethnographic films, but they were subject to their makers' intentions and to the circumstances, the subjectivities, and the collective, public lives of their participants.

Furthermore, the films have a structure (the particular relationships between the parts and the whole) in the sense of both film structure and the cultural structure of ritual.

The "Pleasing God" films are made or unmade in editing: they are given form, rhythm, and flow by their makers. Provided that the filming has been informed by anthropological considerations of the kind that (more usually) result in books, the particular shots joined in the editing process are also efficacious and veracious in an ethnographic sense. Joining different shots together also creates film structure but only if the relation between parts and whole is a guiding principle throughout the process. Structure is related to form: the separate parts change when they are joined together, giving an entirely different shape to the film than the assemblage of disparate bits with which the editing started. Considerations of form have also to do with the pace, flow, and rhythm of the film—cinematic demands on ethnography that govern the relations between sequences that are lighter or darker in appearance, slower or faster in motion, more or less verbal, or narrated or subtitled in translation. The point of view, angle, continuity, and direction of the shots are aspects not only of form but also of intention and style and ultimately of the cultural meaning that the film is attempting to convey. In this way, we come back to the ethnography that informs the filming so that film may contribute its unique possibilities of interpretation to anthropology.

Editing determines the balance of sound and image, the continuity of place and time. Editing creates the metaphors for a film by the manner in which it places visual and aural elements in a sequence. Thus vessels of invocation, images of the gods, and gestures of ritualist and artisan are filmic and ethnographic elements that become metaphors of devotion and worship, given their recurrent use in the film. Needless to say, such placing is at the same time a structural feature of the film.

There may be problems on all the previously mentioned accounts: the visual narrative may not be clear enough, the metaphors may not be meaningful or may not be symbolic on any level (or, on the contrary, may be symbolic on too many levels), and the editing may wittingly or unwittingly invoke exoticism and sensationalism. Rituals and bazaars present special difficulties to anthropologist and filmmaker alike. Ritual (as bazaar) is a cultural form with its own structure, which ethnography represents in terms of cultural categories, interpretation, multichannel communication, and analyses of various kinds. Film can represent ritual but in terms of cinematic style, structure, and form. Clearly, anthropology and film differ from ritual as kinds of cultural form, yet in either case we try to gain access to forms through forms, to concepts through concepts, to symbols through symbols, and to images through images.

Film can do better than ethnography in representing some aspects of ritual; the converse is true about other aspects. Yet both narrate, interpret, analyze, and evoke in different ways, to varying degrees. They are complementary to the extent that both strive to comprehend the same reality whole, but they cannot do the same things equally well, not even in their different ways. Missing from the films is the explication of the system, structure, and cultural principles I gave in the first half of this chapter: the articulation of bazaar, caste/kin, and ritual domains. The films do, however, show the effect or implication of these analyses and principles in a different manner by projecting the appearance as well as the form and meaning of bazaar and ritual.

Missing from the written ethnography is the motion and sound, the multichannel flow of life that film can represent and evoke as well. Surface, appearance, light, tone, and mood are rendered uniquely in film. We are given a sense of being there: as if in an instant a whole complex reality were conjured up in front of our eyes. Most important is the simultaneity of sound, movement, color, and object, the myriad details surrounding human action and habitat that film can render whole, together, at the same time. These are all aesthetic considerations, but they do not exclude critical knowledge. *Loving Krishna* and the other films may provide an intuitive grasp of a totality, a ritual, an exegesis, or a way of life. But the extreme particularity and concreteness offered by visual images exceeds the amount of detail in any written work. The information is presented simultaneously along many channels that cannot be decoded all at once but can be studied on repeated viewing or frame-by-frame analysis. Such detail remains in the background and need not be explicated in the main narrative but is nevertheless built into a film through ethnographic intention. Although images are specific to one particular festival of Krishna, an individual shot and series of shots combined in editing can be made to yield abstraction and represent ethnographic meaning.

In the case of the Vishnupur films and books, ethnographic films and monographs converge in the endeavor to interpret cultural forms: bazaars and rituals have their own form and structure, and there are styles and intentions among their practitioners. Films and ethnographies also have form and structure, they succeed or fail in convincing, and their makers endow them with style and intention. How these similarities are realized and how the made works are built up after the realities of ritual and bazaar in Vishnupur make all the difference.

The bazaar appears in all the three films, especially in a long sequence near the beginning of *Loving Krishna*. The films present festivals and rituals in everyday life; hence, bazaar activities are shown in many scenes either as a part of representing the town and its history or as a part of the many contexts in which rituals occur. The different items and systems of trade, the localities, and the people of the bazaar are shown directly or indirectly as an integral part of ritual performance. The key elements here are the links between different domains of thought and action: ritual, economy, history, locality, and the people and objects that participate in these domains. The first 12 minutes of *Loving Krishna* is a visual and synchronic sound account of the town. Within this narrative is placed an assemblage of shots about the bazaar, including a brief morning worship of the goddess Sitala. The sequence of shots moves from the outside, open bazaar to the covered inside portion surrounded by shops and stalls. The look of the bazaar, the interaction of different kinds of traders and customers, and the range of goods and implements are woven together in brief sequences with the daily worship. In what may pass as a visual essay on the bazaar, itself a fraction of the entire film, not only appearances but also synchronous sounds are presented. The result is a full and rich narrative, shown with great economy, one that cannot be matched by a written account, even at the cost of using more words. The simultaneous verbal and audiovisual sequences complement each other and still allow for the possibility of an anthropological commentary and/or subtitles. The sequence of worship shows not only the ritual itself but also the contexts of the bazaar, the interaction between priest and merchant, and the roles of ritualist and worshipper, while the rest of bazaar life goes on as usual.

The implication is that economic exchange and religion are not separated by hard boundaries, that the same person can act in many ways in the same place, and that the items and actions of ritual and everyday life complement each other. All these aspects of the bazaar are discussed at great length in chapter 2 of *Culture and Power* (Östör 1984). While that chapter deals with much more than the five minutes of film, it also takes 90 pages. Later in the film, an assemblage of about four minutes shows the relationship between handicrafts, rituals, and artisans. Brief sequences follow the processes of weaving, conch shell carving, drum making, and bell-metal utensil casting. The resultant objects are used in the festivals celebrating and serving the gods, the central concern of the film. The other two films include similar sequences, especially the making of divine images, in the course of showing the Shiva and Manasha festivals.

Most of the activities of the bazaar I described in the first half of this chapter are represented in parts of the three films. The films flow along several channels of communication at once, including verbal and written. But writing for film is very different from ethnographic writing, a fact most apparent when the narration or synchronous speech (with translation spoken or subtitled) is read from a page. In these films, the ethnographic writing complements rather than dominates the image. Hence, a lot of information about the system of trade, the concepts and categories of business, is missing from the film. It is not inherently impossible to deal with the structure of the bazaar on film since scientific films in other disciplines, for example, take their central concerns to be explanation and information and use diagrams, charts, animation, and other aids to those ends. In many of these cases, images serve to illustrate and report. The result is another kind of film, issuing from a different set of aesthetic and ethnographic decisions. The sequences of ritual and bazaar activity are built into *Loving Krishna* for their own sake and for the contribution they make to the rest of the film; hence, the relation and balance between the scenes of the town, the bazaar, and the Krishna festivals are crucial. The ways these sequences were shot already foreshadow the film as a whole and can be taken in only a number of limited directions. It would be equally difficult to make either a completely scientific or a poetic film out of this footage.

This does not mean that the Bengal trilogy cannot deal with abstractions, concepts, and cultural values. It can, and it does. The apposite comparison here is with my monographs about rituals and festivals. The films convey critical knowledge about ritual: the concepts of puja (offering and worship), lila (the divine play of the gods), and sakti (sacred female power) are equal in complexity (if not more so) to karma khamata, bhab, and bebosay, which I have already discussed. Indeed, often the same terms of value and category come up in my interpretations of the bazaar as well as ritual. But the films deal with abstractions indirectly (except for the few instances of direct narration in an anthropological voice). Similarly, a film about the bazaar would have to devise a visual solution to the problems raised by concepts of business, mediation, and power.

Even then, the film would not be the equal of the monograph in sheer information and explanation. Scientific films also embody aesthetic choices and decisions and have to present a balance of sounds, words, images, and graphics within the frame of the whole work. Even the most evocative film about bazaar or ritual will have conveyed knowledge and information in the rhythm and succession of its images. Where a film resorts to narration (by an outsider or a participant), it tries to create a flow and a balance between word and image to give shape to the film. In dealing with the abstract notions of sacrifice, devotion, and sacred power, the films use the events and experience of participants to capture a mood and establish an understanding for the viewer, combining critical knowledge with a sense of being there, emotion, and affect. As such, the films are neither more nor less knowledgeable than the monographs, nor are they a sleight of hand to replace immediate experience, but they utilize elements of both in terms of a film structure and aesthetic.

It may be of some consequence today to affirm the possibility and value of knowledge obtained from anthropological films and monographs. Films and ethnographies, among other things, are kinds of knowledge, and the processes involved in their making yield kinds of understanding. Forms and methods differ, but in the end the results converge: a dialectic of indigenous and outside categories—partial, though infinitely extensible to deeper, more compelling truths. Some distance is always kept between anthropologist/ filmmaker and the contexts within which he or she works. This is true even for those indigenous to Bengal or India.

Filmed and written anthropology differ, yet they are equally mediated—neither being capable of apprehending and recording aspects of reality directly. Both are artifacts, made up and given an interpretation by a person—a process in which many people are involved. The made aspect is neither completely subjective and internal nor objective and external— rather, it draws on a dialectical encounter between person, experience, category, method, discipline, and aesthetic. Films and books create knowledge, although neither general, direct, separate, nor absolute. The knowledge gained is more particular, indirect, context based, and relative. It is constituted dialectically in the process of work, between outsider and insider, local people and filmmaker/anthropologist. It is built up after reality through comparison and the reciprocal processes of field research and writing, filming, and editing. It is mediated through persons and cultures, particularities and generalities, anthropological/ filmmaking traditions, and indigenous cultural domains.

So much for my ruminations of some 15 years ago. Looking back, I see perhaps that I was excessively preoccupied with legitimating film through anthropology. In my writing, at least, I was trying to transform monographs into films proving the latter equal to written work in the quest for understanding. In making films, I already began to think of ethnography in visual terms. Today I see the matter in less dichotomous terms. I went on making films, always in collaboration with others, conceiving new projects in cinematic terms inseparable from anthropological knowledge. I came to think more and more in filmic terms from the initial idea to the finished product, more accurately, to have thought and worked film through anthropology and anthropology through film as a single integrated movement. It means not writing a separate ethnography or engaging in the kind of research translatable into both cinematic and monographic form. In the past 15 years, a lot of new work has been published about film and anthropology. Only a few of these have approached Gardner's work with the same disciplinary scope and intellectual rigor as they apply to other filmmakers. No doubt, scholars will rise to the challenge of studying the remarkable body of films to which he is still adding new products. Gardner's contribution is beyond question and his work still controversial. Yet new generations of students are growing up with Pua, Weyak, Omali Inda, the Dom Raja, Ragul Pandit, and Mithai Lal. They become conversant with film aesthetics and a more pluralistic anthropology and will tread the paths Bob has pioneered. For myself, I feel amply rewarded in having learned the craft of filmmaking from a master whose unique vision both challenges and moves us: difficult, uncompromising, solitary, and utterly entrancing.

FILMOGRAPHY

"Pleasing God," A film trilogy produced by Robert Gardner and Ákos Östör for the Film Study Center, Harvard University:

Loving Krishna. 1985. Allen Moore and Ákos Östör (16mm, color, 40 minutes).

Serpent Mother. 1985. Allen Moore and Ákos Östör (16mm, color, 27 minutes).

Sons of Shiva. 1985. Robert Gardner and Ákos Östör (16mm, color, 27 minutes).

Forest of Bliss. 1985. Robert Gardner. Produced by Robert Gardner and Ákos Östör for the Film Study Center, Harvard University (16mm, color, 90 minutes).

REFERENCES

Östör, Ákos. 1980. *The play of gods: Locality, ideology, time and structure in the festivals of a Bengali town.* Chicago: University of Chicago Press. Revised, illustrated, and expanded in 2004, New Delhi: Chronicle Books, DC Publishers.

——. 1984. *Culture and power: Legend, ritual, bazaar and rebellion in a Bengali society.* Beverly Hills, CA: Sage Publications.

——. 1993. *Vessels of time: An essay on temporal change and social transformation.* Delhi: Oxford University Press.

——. 1994. "*Forest of Bliss:* Film and anthropology." *East-West Film Journal* 8 (2): 70–104.

——. 2007. "Robert Gardner's Ambivalent anthropological filmmaking." In *Memories of the origins of anthropological film*, ed. Beale Engelbrecht. Frankfurt: Peter Lang.

13 THE ROCK OF GIBRALTAR

DUŠAN MAKAVEJEV

Bob reminds me of Gibraltar Rock.

A fragment of nature with personality.

Powerful and silent, and you never know his next move.

1971

Somebody called Gardner left the message in my Cannes hotel.

Wants to talk to me. No details.

I moved through the Cannes crowds to find out about this guy.

My quest ended with a description of a mysterious man, an adventurous scientist with a camera.

He travels to distant places without phones or even radio, and disappears.

A German ex-priest who got married with the Pope's permission and became a leftist filmmaker described Gardner as someone admired by Guarani.

The next day either I was leaving or Gardner had already left.

You'll never hear from him again, I was told.

Jungle Jim, Flash Gordon, Mandrake and Prince Valiant rolled in one.

My adolescent memories brought to mind images of B. Traven, Jack London, Jules Verne.

Back home people were losing their sense of humor. The era of Strictly Controlled Trains was turning into Twilight Zone and The Day When The Earth Stood Still.

At a reception in Belgrade an unknown man hands me a phone number of the British Embassy. Give this number to your wife. If something happens to you she should call us immediately. At another corner of the room somebody whispers to Bojana an equally cryptic message and gives her the US Embassy's phone number.

It was time for me to disappear from my own city.

First stop Munich, in winter under the heavy fog. Next stop, the tiny hotel "Odessa" that's across the street from Montparnasse Cemetery.

September 1974, Colorado

In the middle of nowhere the road ends in the ghost town of Telluride, framed by long-abandoned gold mines at 10,000 feet, populated by a few dozen people.

The three-day film festival is about to happen, opened by Bill Pence, James Card and Tom Luddy.

Francis Ford, Gloria Swanson and Leni Riefenstahl are all expected.

Skies are painfully clear and blue. The air is freezing under the blazing sun.

Led by Philip Lopate, a few of us take off our clothes and jump into a small heated pool to warm up.

By the small creek two guys are approaching. I recognize Vlada Petric and the Mayor of Carmel, CA, Clint Eastwood.

They spot us and stop by. I am looking up from the pool. Marlboro Man fills the glorious skies above. Clint is looking straight at me.

He smiles at me and says, "Hi! You don't know me, but I know you."

I open my mouth in awe, about to say something stupid, and he interrupts me, "My name is Robert Gardner. I've been looking for you for several years now."

Near us, Vlada Petric jumps in the pool and splashes Bob's face. Vlada breathlessly asks everyone in the pool, "Why don't we get Leni (then aged 72) to direct a re-make of *Die Blaue Licht* [The Blue Light] here?"

Bob Gardner is smiling, wiping his face.

He asks, "would you be interested in visiting us in New England?"

1977

Three Septembers later, I am teaching a filmmaking class in Sever Hall at the big H. Chris Gerolmo, Tina Rathborne, Matt Duda, Dan Algrant—brilliant, inspiring kids. Squirrels peep at us through the open window.

Across the street in Corbusier's concrete monstrosity, Bob navigates a spaceship called the Carpenter Center for Visual Arts while in the basement Vlada runs the new "in" place, the Harvard Film Archive.

1996/1997

The first pocket-size digital cameras are on the market.

With support from three sides everybody in my class gets a camera.

Bob Gardner is one of the angels for the project:

SLEEPING WITH A CAMERA UNDER THE PILLOW.

The improved title of the project was

WITH MEDVEDKIN TRAIN IN THE POCKET.

2005

The Adventurous Scientist With a Camera who made us aware and curious of things different and strange still puzzles me.

With some paradoxical sense of distant warmth and closeness I wonder how Bob could possibly tolerate Vlada Petric and myself at the same time? My guess was that as Wild Slavs we played the role of some kind of lunatic Alter Egos.

I know that he always wanted to get Harvard into the experience of how the earth moves.

Moving images were the perfect cover.

(If in doubt call Stanley Cavell to the witness stand).

14 BOB GARDNER AND ME

SEAN SCULLY

I went to Harvard in 1972 on a modest fellowship given by Frank Knox, who was the erstwhile running mate of Alfred Landon for the presidential election. He was a powerful man who in the best American tradition of philanthropy gave money so that disadvantaged urchins like myself could come over to America and then contrive ways not to return to Europe and end up as American citizens. So I came to Harvard.

In 1972, I had a giant studio in Hunt Hall, where I worked on my acrylic, brightly colored grid paintings, anticipating eagerly the very occasional visits from the "high and mighty" at the Carpenter Center for Visual Arts. That meant the director and the professors.

I was, in fact, graciously invited to a professors' meeting (as a courtesy to a foreign person of no fixed title). And this was where I famously fell asleep to be woken by an American voice at the very end of the session. It must have been Robert Gardner himself. Everybody else in the room appeared to have a soothing middle European accent, at once reassuring and vague, steeped in history and its soft, cultured weight. So even if they said "I like coffee," it sounded special. And perhaps it was. But Robert Gardner was the tall, ruggedly handsome, laconically striding lone American in the room. He was the one who could and did "cut to the chase," as they like to say at the races.

The next time I saw Robert Gardner—the mythic director of the program who took no salary because he was idealistic and didn't need it and whose grannie or great aunt or whatever Isabella Stewart had her own museum—was when the celestial committee of four came to visit my studio to see what the boy from London was up to. Rudolf Arnheim (the famous art historian) asked me if I ever drew circles instead of straight lines. Eduard Sekler (the famous architectural historian) said I was painting in straight lines and he liked it because it was architectural. Toshi Katayama (the less famous graphic designer, soon to be director) said we had to distinguish between painting and decoration, and I thanked him for the assignment. And then finally, like a breath of fresh air and as noble as Mount Rushmore, was Bob Gardner, who simply said, "Sean, you're painting up a storm." What kind of a storm it was he didn't seem to mind. But I definitely got the idea that he liked storms.

Since I was now a registered human in the family of "Visual Harvard," I was invited to a party at Gardner's house in Brookline. In best London student tradition, I decided to turn up with an acceptable $5 bottle of wine to help out with the expenses—to share the load, so to speak. When I arrived at the house, there were people in black suits parking cars, and I started to lose my nerve regarding the bottle of wine. In London, I had been more in the business of parking other people's cars after I'd stolen them. But I persisted with the bottle up to the point that the front door began to move in on itself. Then I dropped it in the bush that was conveniently located under my left hand. This allowed my right hand to greet the opener of the door guiltlessly as I entered.

Then I was in a beautiful house. And Bob Gardner's collection of extraordinary masks and shields began to unfold itself, along with the paintings of Mark Tobey. It was a wonderful party. I told someone I was a garbage and refuse collector because she was getting on my nerves, but other than that it was great.

And I saw that Bob Gardner carried himself with an aristocratic ease that I found very attractive. He was impressive as a presence. After that, I didn't see Bob for a long time. He called me up one Sunday morning about 10 years ago when I was in New York. Then we were more like equals. And since then we have been friends.

We made films together. He made some of me. He showed me others that were tough and challenging. We made one together that included my parents and a small bird that was filmed by Bob's dear friend Robert Fulton. All those characters are now gone. I can't be sure about the small bird. But if it's still around, it's drawing its bird pension. My parents were near the end of their journey, and what I have of them now is what Bob gave me on film—thereby demonstrating the power of film to stop time. Bob Fulton gave me his Swiss Army knife in a tender moment, between men, in a bar in Barcelona. But then Bob Fulton died in his plane in an outdoor storm. So what we have in our seven-minute film are three stories overlapping and ignoring each other as stories do as they go about their own business. We have the story of my exhibition in Palacio Episcopal in Malaga, the story of the little bird being saved, and the story of my parents dancing with me in my exhibition for the first and last time. So now when I want to visit them, I always have to do it when they're dancing. Bob Gardner has left my parents dancing forever in their son's exhibition.

After that, we became even deeper friends, and Bob gave me an African fertility figure made of wood about two feet high. She is beautiful and, like Bob's films, tough. Robert Gardner makes a film of what is, where he shows something. He doesn't try to make it better than it is. He doesn't try to convert us, to make us like it. He shows what is there, and yet his works are not neutral. They are rough, tough, and frontal films. She has a huge wooden punani. I stood her on the top of my library in my intimate drawing room in Manhattan. Every time I look up, the very first thing I see is her wooden punani, so maybe I'm going to put her somewhere else where I get a more balanced view. And then we'll enter into a constructive relationship. I put her in my drawing room because Bob gave her to me and because I believe in the power of these things.

15   58 HIGHLAND STREET

SUSAN HOWE

Writing as a nonfiction filmmaker, Robert Gardner says in *The Impulse to Preserve* that the chance nature of reality draws his attention to one thing instead of another and compels him through some mysterious urgency to follow and preserve what he sees. He could be describing my experience as a poet compelled to use documentary material in almost everything I write. With the help of lightweight, synchronous sound and film equipment, he follows the dictates of circumstance and chance through foreign cultures and countries in search of the mysterious thing he hopes he will arrive at via short takes, shifting camera angles, multiple viewpoints, and sound mixes. I, too, am a hunter-gatherer. I do my telepathic foraging in the hushed enclosed stacks of libraries. Armed with call numbers, I find my way among scriptural exegeses, totemic ancestors, ethical homiletics, outdated war manuals, antiquarian researches, prophets, and poets. In a state of readiness, I follow the principle that ghosts wrapped in appreciative obituaries or dedications presented at vanished community field meetings, in a capricious moment of accidental recognition, can be grasped by a quick-eyed searcher according to some mysterious law of association.

Even if Gardner has said that "the life of a nonfiction filmmaker is really a search for ways to be there *before* something happens," watching *Dead Birds, Forest of Bliss,* and *The Nuer,* I experience each one as *last* chapters in process of becoming history. These films made during the latter half of the twentieth century illustrate his deep sense of the uncanny force of the past. His interpretive consciousness is moral in terms of historical sense and the needs and conscience of viewers. Countering minimalist severity with a fascination for emotional extremities of ecstatic experience, Gardner retains the conscious control of an artist.

Today, February 28, 2007, is the fortieth anniversary of my father's death. In 1967, our family was living in Cambridge in the house Robert Gardner lives in now. Space of time grows shorter as we grow older. 58 Highland Street contains the nature of past experience during the 1950s lived through only once in youth. Some abstract surviving portion survives in the final poem of a series I gathered together under the title "118 Westerly Terrace." That's the street Wallace Stevens lived on in Hartford for most of his writing life. In 1948, when he was 69, he wrote to the Irish poet Thomas McGreevy: "What you say in one of your letters about your westwardness as a result of living near the Shannon Estuary interested me. The house in which I was born and lived in as a boy faced the west and wherever I have lived if the house faced any other way I have always been pulling it round on an axis to get it straight." The numbers in Stevens' Hartford street address running "like sparks in burnt-up paper" create an opening through his poems into mine.

> I know you saw the child
>
> waving signal at stairhead
>
> Last night the door stood
>
> open—windows were port-
>
> holes letters either traced
>
> or lost—historical fact the
>
> fire on hearth or steam in
>
> a kettle year and year out

Like a poem—or a house—a nonfiction film is a spontaneous space closed in on itself.

FIGURES

CONTRIBUTORS

Ilisa Barbash is Associate Curator of Visual Anthropology at the Peabody Museum, Harvard University. In 1998, she founded the Graduate Program in Transcultural and Ethnographic Filmmaking, at the University of Colorado, Boulder, which she directed until moving to Harvard in 2002. Her film works (co-directed with Lucien Taylor) include *Made in U.S.A.* (1990), a film about sweatshops and child labor in the Los Angeles garment industry, and *In and Out of Africa* (1992), a video about authenticity, taste, and racial politics in the transnational African art market. She is also the co-author of *Cross-Cultural Filmmaking* (1997).

Marcus Banks is Professor in Social and Cultural Anthropology at the University of Oxford. His publications include *Rethinking Visual Anthropology* (co-editor, 1997), *Visual Methods in Social Research* (2001), *Organizing Jainism in India and England* (1992), and *Ethnicity: anthropological constructions* (1996).

Stanley Cavell's books include *Must We Mean What We Say?* (1969) and *The Claim of Reason* (1979), and most recently *Cities of Words* (2004), *Philosophy the Day After Tomorrow* (2005), and *Cavell on Film* (2005). He is Walter M. Cabot Professor of Aesthetics and the General Theory of Value, emeritus, Harvard University.

Roderick Coover is Assistant Professor in the Department of Film and Media Arts at Temple University. His documentary and experimental films and videos, and new media works, include *Cultures in Webs* (2003) and *The Language of Wine: An Anthropology of Work, Wine, and the Senses* (2005). He is also the author of numerous articles on ethnographic image-making and hypermedia.

Elizabeth Edwards is Professor and Senior Research Fellow at the University of the Arts London. Previously Curator of Photographs at the Pitt Rivers Museum, and lecturer in Visual Anthropology at the University of Oxford, her most recent monograph was *Raw Histories: Photographs, Anthropology and Museums* (2001) and she is editor of *Anthropology and Photography* (1992), *Photographs Objects Histories* (2004), and *Sensible Objects: Colonialism, Museums, and Material Culture* (2006). She has worked extensively on the history of photography in anthropology.

Anna Grimshaw is Associate Professor at the Graduate Institute of the Liberal Arts at Emory University. Her publications include *Visualizing Anthropology* (2004), *The Ethnographer's*

Eye: Ways of Seeing in Modern Anthropology (2001), *The C.L.R. James Reader* (1992), and *Servants of the Buddha* (1992).

Karl Heider is Carolina Distinguished Professor of Anthropology at the University of South Carolina. He has done three years of fieldwork with the New Guinea Dani, and another three years with the Minangkabau of West Sumatra. His many publications include *Seeing Anthropology* (1997, 2001, 2004, 2007), *Grand Valley Dani* (1979, 1991, 1997), *Indonesian Cinema* (1991), *Landscapes of Emotion* (1991), *Ethnographic Film* (1977, 2006), and, with Robert Gardner, *Gardens of War* (1968). He has also directed three films, *Tikal* (1974), *Dani Sweet Potatoes* (1974), *Dani Houses* (1974).

Paul Henley is Professor of Visual Anthropology and has been Director of the Granada Centre for Visual Anthropology at the University of Manchester since its foundation in 1987. He has made ethnographic documentaries both in Latin America and Europe, and has published extensively both on visual anthropology and on his specialist ethnographic region, Amazonia. He shares with Edmund Leach the distinction of having been twice awarded the prestigious Curl Essay Prize of the Royal Anthropological Institute.

Susan Howe's most recent books are *The Midnight* (2003) and *Kidnapped* (2002). Two CDs in collaboration with the musician/composer David Grubbs, *Thiefth* and *Souls of the Labadie Tract*, were released on the Blue Chopsticks label in 2005 and 2007. Her critical study *My Emily Dickinson* (1986) was re-issued by New Directions in 2007 along with a new collection of poems, *Souls of The Labadie Tract*. She held the Samuel P. Capen Chair in Poetry and the Humanities at the State University New York at Buffalo until her retirement in 2007.

David MacDougall is a leading ethnographic filmmaker and writer on cinema. His first film *To Live with Herds* won the Grand Prix "Venezia Genti" at the Venice Film Festival in 1972. Since then he has made prize-winning films in Australia, Africa, Europe and India. He recently completed five films on the Doon School, an elite boys' boarding school in northern India, and a contrasting film on a shelter for homeless children in Delhi. He is the author of *Transcultural Cinema* (1998) and *The Corporeal Image: Film, Ethnography, and the Senses* (2006). He lives in Australia and conducts research at the Australian National University.

Dušan Makavejev is a Serbian filmmaker, renowned for his pioneering films of Yugoslav cinema in the late 1960s and early 1970s. His films include *Man is not a bird* (1965), *Love Affair* (1967), *Innocence Unprotected* (1968), *Mysteries of the Organism* (1971), *Sweet Movie* (1975), and *Gorilla Bathes at Noon* (1993).

Ákos Östör is Professor of Anthropology and Film Studies at Wesleyan University. Educated in Hungary, Australia, and the USA, he has carried out fieldwork or documentary filming in India (West Bengal and Varanasi), Sudan, and Tanzania. His ethnographic films include *Loving Krishna* (with Allen Moore, 1982), *Sons of Shiva* (with Robert Gardner,

1985), *Serpent Mother* (with Allen Moore, 1985), *Seed and Earth* (with Lina Fruzetti, Alfred Guzzetti, and Ned Johnston, 1994), *Khalfan and Zanzibar* (with Lina Fruzetti and Alfred Guzzetti, 1999), and *Fishers of Dar* (with Lina Fruzetti and Stephen Ross, 2002). His books include *The Play of the Gods: locality, ideology, structure, and time in the festivals of a Bengali town* (1980), *Puja in Society* (1982), *Culture and Power: legend, ritual, bazaar, and rebellion in a Bengali society* (1984), *Concepts of Person* (co-editor, 1992), *Vessels of Time* (1993), *Kinship and Ritual in Bengal* (with Lina Fruzetti, 1994), and *Making Forest of Bliss* (with Robert Gardner, 2001).

William Rothman received his PhD in philosophy from Harvard University and is the author of several renowned books, including the landmark study *Hitchcock—The Murderous Gaze, The "I" of the Camera, Documentary Film Classics*, and *A Philosophical Perspective on Film*. He is editor of the highly regarded "Studies in Film" series published by Cambridge University Press, and Professor of Motion Pictures and Director of the Graduate Program in Film Studies at the University of Miami.

Born in Dublin, Ireland, in 1945, **Sean Scully** is an internationally renowned artist whose paintings often consist of panels of thickly textured surfaces and contrasting colors. His work is variously influenced by Minimalism, Abstract Expressionism, and Conceptual Art, and is in the collections of the Museum of Modern Art, The Tate Modern, the Guggenheim Museum (New York), the Irish Museum of Modern Art, and the Smithsonian American Art Museum.

Lucien Taylor is an anthropologist and filmmaker. Recent works include "Sheep Rushes" (with Ilisa Barbash) an eight-channel video installation that probes the ambivalence of the American pastoral. Earlier films and videos include *Made in U.S.A.* (1990) and *In and Out of Africa* (1992) (both co-directed with Barbash). His books include *Visualizing Theory* (ed., 1994), *Cross-Cultural Filmmaking* (with Barbash, 1997). He edited David MacDougall's first collection of essays, *Transcultural Cinema* (1998), and teaches Anthropology and Visual & Environmental Studies at Harvard University.

Charles Warren writes frequently on nonfiction film. He is the editor of *Beyond Document: Essays on Nonfiction Film* (1996), and, with Maryel Locke, *Jean-Luc Godard's Hail Mary: Women and the Sacred in Film* (1993), and author of *T.S. Eliot on Shakespeare* (1987). He teaches film studies at Boston University and in the Harvard Extension School.

INDEX